HADLEY FREEMAN grew up in New York City and London. She has been a staff writer at the *Guardian* since 2000 and has contributed to many other publications, including *Vogue* (US and UK). This her fourth book. She lives in London with her partner and their three children.

Praise for *House of Glass*:

'This is a startlingly original book, remarkable and gripping'
EDMUND DE WAAL

'A magnificently vivid re-creation of her Jewish family's experience of twentieth-century Europe, Hadley Freeman's book is also an acute examination of the roots, tropes, and persistence of anti-Semitism, which makes it an urgently necessary book for us to read right now'
SALMAN RUSHDIE

'This is an utterly engrossing book: one that manages to be an intimate family history and a meticulously researched account of a shocking period of world history at the same time. It may be an overused term of approbation, but it truly is unputdownable'
NIGELLA LAWSON

'*House of Glass* opens the door on to the past, and its light spills sharply across the present'
Sunday Times

'By the end, I was completely wrapped up in the sharply contrasting characters of the Glass family, and the parts their different temperaments – trusting or sceptical, outspoken or conciliatory, ambitious or carefree – played in determining their fates . . . wonderfully lively book'

CRAIG BROWN, *Mail on Sunday*

'Wonderful . . . half a sweeping tale of family history, half a history of what it means to be Jewish in Europe in the last hundred years, it is moving and at times devastating . . . the book is impossible to sum up in a neat review . . . there are so many bits that make your heart leap and plummet . . . it's paced so beautifully almost like a thriller . . . an extraordinary feat of work; it teams with research but it wears it so lightly'

PANDORA SYKES, *The High Low Podcast*

'This deeply moving book is so beautifully written – like hearing a fascinating conversation about the past, then being warmly welcomed into the very heart of it. This is a stunning memoir, and a thrilling detective story. I completely lost myself in its many worlds'

MARINA HYDE

'With high drama, heart-breaking tragedy, thwarted love and walk-on parts for Pablo Picasso, Marc Chagall and Christian Dior, Freeman's memoir *House of Glass* would feel too neat if it were a novel. It certainly reads like one, and if I were a film director I'd be snapping up the rights . . .'

Jewish Chronicle

'Filled with vibrant characters, rich in historical detail, this excavation also bears the traces of its author's passion at the injustices of a terrible history, which now again can seem too close for comfort'   *Observer*

'Beautifully written . . . breathtakingly compelling'
Evening Standard

'Captivating . . . Past and present exist in a state of constant interaction, and this finely honed and engaging account draws the threads between then and now'
PHILIPPE SANDS, *Guardian*

'Freeman brings her ancestors exquisitely to life in this scrupulously told history, through which Europe's own black story of collaboration and the horrors of anti-Semitism runs like aw live electric wire'   *Metro*

'Freeman provides a moving and frightening picture of the ways ordinary fates are mangled by the machinery of politics, war and hate. It should be read by anybody who believes history is an abstraction'   *The Times*

'Freeman is a meticulous, dogged researcher, deftly pulling the strands of these many stories into a narrative and going on to trace the family members' post-war lives . . . An intelligent and lively book that could not be more timely'
Literary Review

'An achingly poignant history of her Jewish family and the traumas it faced in the 20th century'   *Independent*

'I shed many tears reading this book, such are its stories and its heart . . . A magnificent tale of survival, *House of Glass* is about identity and belonging, about how quickly life can fall apart, but also how it can be rebuilt. It shows we have much to learn from those who came before us, if only we care to look'   Fiona Sturges, *i Newspaper*

By the same author:

Be Awesome

Life Moves Pretty Fast

HOUSE
OF
GLASS

The story and secrets of a
twentieth-century Jewish family

HADLEY FREEMAN

4th ESTATE • *London*

4th Estate
An imprint of HarperCollins*Publishers*
1 London Bridge Street
London SE1 9GF
www.4thEstate.co.uk

HarperCollins*Publishers*
1st Floor, Watermarque Building, Ringsend Road, Dublin 4, Ireland

First published in Great Britain in 2020 by 4th Estate
This 4th Estate paperback edition published in 2021

2

A catalogue record for this book is available from the British Library

ISBN 978-0-00-832266-3

Images on p. 404 © Natasha de Betak and p. 416 © Billy Farrell/BFA.com
Image on p. 344 believed to be by Pablo Picasso and image on p. 377
believed to be by René Gruau.

Broken Glass by Arthur Miller. Copyright © Arthur Miller and Inge Morath,
1994, used by permssion of The Wylie Agency (UK) Limited.

Printed and bound in Great Britain by
CPI Group (UK) Ltd, Croydon, CRO 4YY

MIX
Paper from
responsible sources
FSC
www.fsc.org
FSC™ C007454

This book is produced from independently certified FSC paper
to ensure responsible forest management

Find out more about HarperCollins and the environment at
www.harpercollins.co.uk/green

For my father, Ron Freeman,
and my Grandma Sala

'Getting this hysterical about [anti-Semitism] on the other side of the world is sane?'

'When she talks about it, it's not on the other side of the world, it's on the next block.'

'And that's sane?'

'I don't know what it is! I just get the feeling sometimes that she KNOWS something, something that . . . It's like she's connected to some . . . some wire that goes half around the world, some truth that other people are blind to.'

ARTHUR MILLER, *Broken Glass*, 1994

CONTENTS

FAMILY TREE

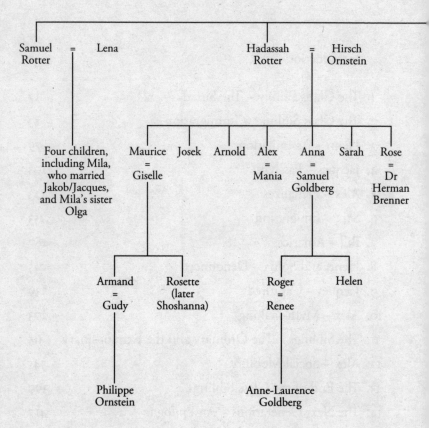

Samuel Rotter = Lena

Hadassah Rotter = Hirsch Ornstein

Four children, including Mila, who married Jakob/Jacques, and Mila's sister Olga

Maurice = Giselle

Josek

Arnold

Alex = Mania

Anna = Samuel Goldberg

Sarah

Rose = Dr Herman Brenner

Armand = Gudy

Rosette (later Shoshanna)

Roger = Renee

Helen

Philippe Ornstein

Anne-Laurence Goldberg

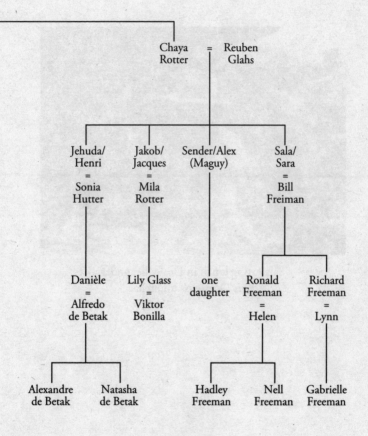

Sala eating lunch in Deauville, under
Alex Ornstein's umbrella.

INTRODUCTION

I STOOD UP to shut the closet door and that's when I spotted the shoebox, right at the back, behind a pile of leather handbags. It was burnished red, although it looked almost grey, covered in over a decade's worth of dust. Surely, I thought, it would just contain another pair of slightly battered kitten-heeled sandals. But still, I'd come all this way, I might as well look inside. So I sat back on the floor, pulled it out and opened it. I did not find shoes. Instead, it was filled with the secrets my grandmother had managed to keep all her life and some years beyond.

The road that led me to rifling through my grandmother's closet a dozen years after she died began, for me, twenty-three years earlier, in 1983 when I was five years old. That was the year my parents took me to Europe for the first time to meet my French family: my grandmother's oldest brother and his wife, Henri and Sonia Glass, another brother, Alex Maguy, and their last surviving cousins, Alex and Mania Ornstein. My grandmother, Sala, also joined us there, flying over from her home in Florida, where she lived with her American husband, my grandfather, Bill.

My dad was keen for us to meet them all, perhaps to balance out our family tree: where my mother's side was fruitful, with its abundance of American aunts, uncles and cousins scattered generously around the United States, from Washington DC to Cincinnati to Seattle, my father's side was comparatively barren. Until this trip it had consisted in my mind solely of my grandparents and my uncle, my father's younger brother, Rich, all clustered together in Miami. I knew my grandmother had had to leave her relatives behind in France when she escaped what was vaguely described to me as 'the war' and this, my father said, was why I didn't have much family on his side. He didn't explain where the family was on his very American father's side, and I was too young then to think to ask why.

My mother's family was warm, rambunctious and close, and I always looked forward to seeing my cousins, who I thought of as quasi-siblings. But when we visited my paternal grandparents, they snapped at one another continuously, which scared me because I never saw my parents fight. Also, for reasons I was in no way capable of articulating then, I found my grandmother difficult. If pressed, I would have said she was 'weird', but what I meant was that she seemed sad, and sad adults are confusing for children, especially ones as sheltered as I was. When we visited them in Miami, my grandfather, in his white trousers and golf shirts, would sit with us by the hotel pool on the candy-coloured sun loungers, enjoying the sunshine, letting my sister and me twirl his enormous moustache. My grandmother would sit under an umbrella, separate from us. She was further protected from the sun by a wide-brimmed hat, various Hermès – or Hermès-esque – silk scarves wound in complicated knots around her neck, mini Dior handbag in her lap. She looked as distinctly French as my grandfather looked American, with the naturally soft, elegant looks of a Renoir painting but now overlaid with the melancholy of a Hopper one.

Often by the pool she would read the French fashion magazines her brothers sent her from Paris, and despite having lived in America for forty years by the time I was born, she clung on tightly to her French accent. So it made sense to me that she would come with us to France. After all, she was, emphatically, French.

I flew with my parents from New York to Paris, and then took a train to Deauville, a seaside resort in Normandy. Deauville looked then and still looks now frozen in the mid-twentieth century, with its grand hotels and long beach dotted with large, colourful beach umbrellas, to which liveried waiters brought three-course meals on silver trays. We went there to meet the French relatives because that is where they liked to go on holiday from their homes in Paris, albeit rarely with one another.

Even though I was only five at the time, my memories of this holiday are clearer than of ones I took in my teens and twenties. Partly this was from the novelty of being outside of America for the first time, and the experience was as jarringly formative as the first day of school, or my first job. But it's also because my family takes so many photos, and more photos were taken of this holiday than of most people's weddings, mainly by the family photographers, my grandmother's brother, Henri, and my father. We are also a family of anecdotalists, and it is impossible for me to separate now what I actually remember about this trip, and what I remember from the photos and stories told afterwards. Am I remembering actual memories or are they memories of memories? In my family, the line between the two is not always clear. But everything I have written here about this trip has been corroborated by those wise enough to make this distinction better than me (my parents, in other words).

ON OUR FIRST NIGHT in Deauville we arranged to meet everyone at the front of the hotel dining room before dinner. I assumed that my French family would turn out to be like my American one, and I'd be running up and down the beach with my new relatives the way I ran around Cincinnati with my cousins, because in my five years of experience that's what extended families were like. But when we arrived in the dining room, a group of impossibly old people was waiting for us, none of whom looked predisposed to run anywhere. Only two of them could speak English, Alex Maguy and Sonia. The rest just smiled and nodded at me and I, gripping my mother's hand, shyly did the same back. Deauville, it turned out, was nothing like Cincinnati. So it was with some relief that I saw my grandmother arriving, the last of the group – at least I knew her and she spoke English. But instead of joining us, she hung back, watching her siblings and cousins. Just as I was about to go over to her, I noticed something I'd never seen before: she was crying. And then she turned around and rushed out of the room.

'What's wrong with Grandma?' I asked my mother, but she shook her head at me and held her finger to her lips. I looked up at my father for an answer but he was looking towards where his mother had disappeared and went after her.

Alex Maguy – whose real surname was Glass, like Henri and Sonia, as well as my grandmother originally, and it didn't occur to me to ask why he'd apparently changed it – had a cabana on the beach, and my parents said I could use it to change in and out of my swimsuit. Having one's own cabana seemed to me the absolute pinnacle of cool, but that was before I saw what Alex Ornstein had on the beach: his own giant umbrella, red with a blue flag on top, and every day we would all meet under it for lunch, attended to by smartly dressed waiters. Even though it was Alex Ornstein's umbrella, Alex Maguy dominated those lunches. He was small, bald and tough like a bullet, but he loved talking with my father, as well as with his cousin, Alex Ornstein, who he occasionally embraced fondly. He didn't give hugs to my sister or me, but he seemed to enjoy talking with us, telling us about the famous artists he knew, none of whom we'd ever heard of, because we were, respectively, three and five years old. When I got lost on the beach one day, it was Alex Maguy and his cabana I looked for, because I knew he'd know how to get me home.

Like my grandmother, Sonia was short and had red hair, but where Sala was thin, quiet and melancholic, Sonia was a solid ball of vibrating energy. With her bright hair, pink lipstick and blue eyeshadow, she looked like a firecracker. She taught my sister and me how to play bridge and introduced us to *pain au chocolat*, which was even more exciting than bridge. In the mornings she would meet us in the hotel lobby and walk us onto the beach, where she seemed to know every person on the boardwalk.

'Who was that?' I asked once, after she'd had a long, involved conversation with an older American lady about their respective dogs.

'I have no idea,' she replied, marching onwards.

Sonia's husband Henri was, at 6 feet, about a foot taller than his wife and siblings, but gentler than them, and at eighty-three still strikingly handsome. He would catch my eye across the table and make apologetic smiles for not being able to speak English, and he would often hold my grandmother, stroking her hair like she was still his baby sister. When Sonia and Alex Maguy argued viciously over lunch Henri would just sit back, letting it blow over. We all knew you shouldn't get between a firecracker and a bullet.

Alex and Mania Ornstein were the frailest and in many ways the easiest-going members of the groups, often acting as peace-brokers between Sonia and Alex Maguy. Being an Ornstein seemed to be less complicated than being a Glass.

Hadley in Deauville, next to Alex Ornstein's umbrella.

Despite Deauville's differences from Cincinnati, I had a wonderful holiday. I was introduced to French culture essentials, such as triple-scoop ice-cream cones and baguettes. But the grown-ups occasionally seemed to be grumpy, especially Sonia and Alex Maguy, who were barely able to sit at the same table by the end of the holiday. This was the first time in decades that they had all spent any time together. It was also to be the last.

At the end of the week, I went back to the United States with my parents and sister and soon after, slowly, inexorably, everyone I met in Deauville died. My grandmother died in 1994, when I was sixteen. She had made a life for herself in America but she never stopped seeming sad to me, and her sadness never stopped unnerving me. As a result I never let her get close to me. By the time she died, I was closed off in my own sadness, hospitalised for anorexia, which kept me from her funeral. For years afterwards, thinking about all this made me feel things I still couldn't articulate so, again,

I probably would have said it made me feel 'weird', but what I really meant was that it made me feel terrible. So I deliberately didn't think about her, or any of my French family, at all.

But when I became an adult, I suddenly couldn't stop thinking of them. Moments I had barely noticed at the time, yet which had made enough of an impact to leave a footprint in my memory, began to surface: my grandmother reaching out for Henri's hand in Deauville, as if he – or she – were about to drift away; Alex all alone in his grand apartment in Paris in the 1990s, surrounded by Picasso and Matisse paintings; Sonia and Alex not even speaking to one another at my bat'mitzvah, despite living almost their whole lives as neighbours in Paris. I was ashamed of how I'd pushed my grandmother away, and that I'd never asked my French relatives about their pasts when they were all alive. But then, no one else did either: my father, my uncle Rich, and Henri and Sonia's daughter Danièle hardly ever talked to their parents about their pasts.

We all knew lightly pencilled outlines of stories, but nothing concrete, and certainly nothing that seemed provable. I knew that my grandmother, along with her mother and brothers, lived in Paris in the 1930s. At some point, through Alex Maguy, she met my American grandfather and went with him to the States. I knew that Alex had fought in the war, and was then captured and sent to a concentration camp, but somehow escaped, and I knew he had worked as a fashion designer and then an art dealer after the war. I knew there was also another brother who had not survived the war. About Henri and Sonia's past, I knew almost nothing.

It felt increasingly apt that the one time I had met them all was in Deauville, because Deauville is a picture-perfect image of an idealised French past. My grandmother – with her chic French fashion, her home full of French art and magazines – was herself an image of idealised Frenchness and, in her obvious homesickness, embodied a longing for the France of her past. I knew there was a story, but even thinking about it felt like touching a bruise and I started alternately tapping this sore spot and then running away in horror at what I was doing. Just an afternoon trip to an archive to look for the Glasses' birth certificates, for example, would exhaust me so much emotionally I'd have to take a two-hour nap afterwards. I hid my early files and notebooks in the backs of various cupboards around my flat, kidding myself that I wasn't doing what I was, in fact, starting to do.

When I was in my mid-twenties, I came up with an idea of how to write about my grandmother in what seemed like a painless way: I would write about her relationship with fashion. By now, I was working as a journalist in London, and my grandmother had used her wardrobe to make a defiant statement about her identity. While other Jewish grandmothers in Miami wore shapeless shift dresses or badly fitting clothes in garish prints, my grandmother always looked like she was going to a fashion show, even if she was just going to the supermarket. Her hair and make-up were always impeccable, her accessories exquisite. She wore distinctly French styles – Yves Saint Laurent-like peasant tops, Chanel-esque jackets – proudly emphasising her non-Americanness through her clothes.

At this point, my uncle Rich was living in my grand-parents' former apartment and, fortunately for me, he hadn't thrown away any of her old things. So I flew there, simply intending to go through my grandmother's closet and describe her wardrobe, using it as a sort of meta way to write about her, because writing simply about her without any proxy still felt like staring straight into the sun. And so, after arriving at what was now my uncle's apartment, I opened her closet door and began.

Her dresses were still carefully preserved in the dry cleaners' plastic wrap, and still smelled of her mix of Chanel perfume and Guerlain face powder (even her cosmetics were strictly French). I sat on the floor, making sketches of her shoes, her bags, her scarves, until I'd filled up my notebook. And then I saw the shoebox at the back. This is what I found inside:

a small photo album with a carved wooden cover, filled with pictures of Henri and Alex looking younger than I'd ever seen them. There were also several photos of my grandmother as a child. Later in the album there were photos of her as a young woman embracing a man whose face had been scraped out by someone's – presumably my grandmother's – fingernail;

a professional photo of my grandmother in her late twenties that someone had ripped into quarters, and taped back together, but missing one quarter;

a couple of photocopied pages from a book titled *Dressmakers of France*;

three letters from someone called 'Kiki', all dated during the 1940s and sent from Los Angeles, but in French;

photos of a balding man in round spectacles I'd never seen before, including one in which he was in army uniform, and two in which he was with a group of men. On several of the photos my grandmother had written in her distinctive cursive '*Jacques*';

a pencil drawing of Jacques, mounted on cardboard, on which the artist had written '*Camp de Pithiviers, 22.VI.1941*';

a rectangular metal plate on which the words '*GLASS, Prisonnier Cambrai, 1940*' were written;

a photocopied note on which someone had written, in French, that '*la famille Glass*' was hiding in Paris under an assumed name;

a telegram from the International Committee of the Red Cross, apologising for the 'distressing news contained within';

photos of Henri, Sonia and Danièle when she was a baby;

newspaper clippings about Alex Maguy;

several photos of Alex with Pablo Picasso;

a scrappy piece of paper folded into quarters on which someone had drawn a man, pointing a gun at his own head, and the tip of a cigarette had burned through the paper where the gun was pointing at the man's head. It was signed '*Avec amitié*, Picasso'.

I put everything back in the shoebox, the shoebox in my bag and flew home the next day. I knew I had a story now, and it wasn't about fashion.

Over the next decade, I followed these clues to trace the lives of my grandmother and her brothers. Sometimes they confirmed and filled in stories I'd already vaguely known, sometimes they told me things I'd never have imagined about my family. In some cases I uncovered truths that I know were meant to be hidden for ever, and I then seriously questioned the morality of what I was doing, rummaging around in my relatives' closets that they'd long ago closed for the last time. After all, that I had found my grandmother's shoebox of tokens from the past was not, I knew, a sign that she had wanted it to be discovered: it was a testament to how quickly she was incapacitated by her stroke that she was unable to destroy it before she died.

Yet I also knew that the stories I found could not be allowed to fade away, like a black and white photo in the back of a closet. The more I researched, the more the story

Sala and Bill in Long Island in the 1950s.

went beyond the personal past to the political present, and it is probably no coincidence that I finally committed to writing this book in the shadow of the Brexit referendum and Donald Trump's 2016 election. Neither of those political shifts was about keeping the Jews out, but they were about keeping out vaguely defined 'outsiders'.

Alongside that, open anti-Semitism was on the rise throughout Europe in a way I never thought I'd see in my lifetime, from the far right and the far left. A 2018 survey found that one in four Europeans believe Jews have 'too much influence in conflict and wars across the world', and one in five think they have 'too much influence in media and politics'.[1] In France, which is where most of my family's story is set, anti-Semitic acts rose by 74 per cent between 2017 and 2018;[2] meanwhile in America, the Anti-Defamation League reported that in that same period anti-Semitic attacks doubled.[3] Of course, it's easier to ignore the lessons of the past when the past itself has faded to nothing: according to two recent surveys 41 per cent of Americans do not know what Auschwitz is[4] and one in three Europeans know 'little or nothing' about the Holocaust.[5] Reading these news stories quashed any concerns I had that writing about the past, or my family, was self-indulgent.

But my obsession with this story had little to do with political prescience on my part. Instead, it was because of the people involved, each one such an extraordinary force of personality that I couldn't shake them off decades after they died.

My grandmother and her brothers, once so close, took very different paths during the war, and each of their stories represents a separate strand of the Jewish experience through the twentieth century. Learning about them provided me with not just a map for what was behind me, but one that explained where we all are today. 'If you don't know the past, you can't understand the present and plan properly for the future,' Chaim Potok writes in *Davita's Harp*. What I found about the past and present is in this book.

Sender, Sala (centre) and an Ornstein cousin
in Chrzanow in about 1916.

I

THE GLAHS FAMILY –
The Shtetl

Austro-Hungarian Empire, 1900s

HENRI, JACQUES, ALEX AND SARA GLASS loved being French, and the reason was that they weren't French and their names weren't Henri, Jacques, Alex and Sara Glass. They were born Jehuda, Jakob, Sender and Sala Glahs in what is now Poland but was then still Austria-Hungary. This caused further confusion about the nationality of the Glasses in life and death: Alex was often described in newspaper articles in his lifetime as 'Austrian' and Sala's death certificate states her place of birth simply as 'Austria'. This was echoed by several of her friends from later life who told me that she spent her early years 'in Vienna, I think'. In fact, Sala grew up more than 400 kilometres away from Vienna and the Glahs family probably never visited what is now Austria at all. They were from Chrzanow, once a busy market town whose name derives, with a memorable lack of romanticism, from the

Polish word for horseradish ('*chrzan*'), a local speciality. Its region was more elegantly named, Galicia, in what is now Poland's south-west corner.

Chrzanow was a typical early twentieth-century eastern European shtetl, or Jewish village, the kind that's so familiar from popular culture that even those who lived there describe it through the prism of art, flattening reality to something close to cliché. The very few times my grandmother referred to her childhood she talked about it in reference to *Fiddler on the Roof*, and the memoir of a townsperson who lived there at the same time as the Glahs siblings described its picturesque side streets as looking 'like those in Chagall's paintings, poor and crooked'.[1] When I visited Chrzanow in 2018 my guide compared it to the towns in stories by Isaac Bashevis Singer. But Chrzanow has its own unique qualities that lift it beyond the generic. Back when the Glahses lived there it was known for its surrounding dark forests of densely packed silver birch trees where the children would hide to avoid their parents and school teachers. It also had an exceptionally pretty central square, fringed with colourful houses and shops, where people from miles away would come to do their shopping. Today, it is better known for the more dubious accolade of being only 20 kilometres from Auschwitz, so close the two towns considered themselves to be sisters.

None of the Glahs siblings ever spoke about their childhoods, and if they mentioned Poland at all they'd spit with disgust and move on, no elaboration necessary. So without personal anecdotes to act as my starting point, I turned to historical documents. If my family had been one of the famous Jewish dynasties – the Rothschilds, say, or the Freuds, or even the Halberstams, a wealthy family who lived in the region at the time – this would have sufficed. But they were not, and it did not. There aren't many records of the individual billions of poorer lives from Europe's past, people who leave only footprints in the sand that blow away as soon as they are buried; people who leave, at most, unidentifiable black and white photos behind them, their faces blankly solemn for the photographer's studio, the flash bleaching them of personality; or perhaps a brief mention in a census locked away in an obscure government vault that proves they once existed and nothing more. These people are merely referred to by history as 'the poor', 'the peasants', 'the illiterate', even though their lives are far more revealing of the times in which they lived than those of the grander families whose lives are faithfully recorded ever after by historians.

My father mentioned that back in the 1970s my great-uncle Alex claimed to have written a memoir, which was never published, but my father couldn't remember if he'd even ever seen it, let alone read it. If it existed at all, it had surely long been thrown away, but it seemed more likely that this was another one of Alex's many implausible boasts, that he once wrote a memoir that somehow no one had ever seen. The idea that Alex could ever have had the patience to sit down and write an entire book seemed about as likely as me hanging out with Picasso. But one day in 2014, my father's younger brother, Rich, emailed from Florida: he had found Alex's memoir among my grandmother's possessions. A week later it arrived, a bulky FedEx package, the pages untouched for at least twenty years, since my grandmother died. It was typed in French on loose-leaf paper and Alex had almost certainly dictated it to an assistant who then typed it up, because it read just as Alex talked, in his gruff, colloquial, rat-a-tat stream of consciousness: 'I still have my Yiddish accent. I've never tried to correct it. I love Yiddish. It is my mother tongue. The language I spoke when I knew hunger. When I fought those degenerate Poles who wished me dead,' he wrote on the first page. It was like he was standing in front of me in his flat in Paris, shaking his finger wildly, jabbing it at invisible opponents. (The first time I saw Joe Pesci in a movie I nearly fell off my seat in shock because, if you swap the Italian heritage for a Jewish one, Pesci looks – and talks, and swaggers and gesticulates – a lot like my great-uncle Alex did.) My father, with characteristic heroism, translated all 250 pages of Alex's memoir for me from French to English (my French is fine but in no way is it strong enough to handle Alex's punchy slang with occasional swoops into Yiddish). But before he sent the translation back to me, he warned me to read it with at the very least a sceptical eye: Alex's tendency towards self-mythology was infamous, and not even those closest to him ever really believed what he said about himself. So while this memoir was an astonishing find, I opened it expecting to read a somewhat deadening litany of Alex's triumphs. Instead, I was amazed to discover that the first thirty or so pages were a detailed and humble account of his childhood in Chrzanow, a period of his life he certainly never discussed with any of us. Instead of focusing on himself and his glories, he wrote heartfelt descriptions of his family and their struggles, and lives that had been hidden in darkness for over a century burst into the light.

Jews had lived in Chrzanow since 1590, when the town's first Jew, a man called Yaakov, settled there.[2] Yaakov clearly had quite an impact because by the beginning of the twentieth century more than 60 per cent of the town's inhabitants were Jewish,[3] and one of its main industries was manufacturing Judaica, such as Torah scrolls and mezuzahs.[4] The town square was bordered by 120 specifically Jewish shops, their signs written in both Hebrew and Yiddish, while the open market within was where women shopped for kosher food and headscarves. When the Glahs children were born, Chrzanow even had a Jewish mayor, Dr Zygmunt Keppler, a lawyer. From its top office to its lowest social order, Chrzanow was a Jewish town.

This was the tail end of what was a brief and relatively golden age for Jews in the Austro-Hungarian Empire. Anti-Semitism certainly existed there, most infamously in the Hilsner Affair, a series of trials that took place in 1899–1900, in which a Jew, Leopold Hilsner, was accused of blood libel and spent nineteen years in prison before finally being pardoned. But Emperor Franz Joseph I had a fondness for the Jewish religion, and under his rule, Austro-Hungarian Jews emerged from the ghettos and became part of society as the emperor gave Jews equal rights, and financed Jewish institutions. This is why there seems to have been such a flourishing of Jewish productivity in the Austro-Hungarian Empire between 1848 and 1916, from such people as Theodor Herzl, Stefan Zweig and Sigmund Freud: it's not that this generation of Jews was uniquely talented compared with previous ones, it's that they were granted a then unique amount of freedom.

The Chrzanovian Jews were mostly poor, but their lives were better than they had ever been or would be again. They had a friendly relationship with the Catholic Poles in the neighbouring countryside, who came into town to go to church, do their shopping and take their children to school, where they were taught alongside the Jewish children.[5] Chrzanow was situated close to the Three Emperors' Corner, the border dividing Russia, Germany and Austria, and the city lay on the main highway that connected eastern and western Europe, meaning traders from all over came through it. So although it was a very Jewish town it was also a very international one, and the townspeople regularly mixed with many other ethnicities and nationalities. Back then, this was a wonderful financial advantage for the town's Jews; very soon, it would become one of their greatest misfortunes.

One person who never trusted her neighbours was Chaya Rotter. Born in 1873 and the youngest of three children, she grew up in Chrzanow. Despite her lifelong closeness to multiple other countries, she spoke only Yiddish and Polish. She had little interest in mixing with anyone but her own kind.

On 13 March 1898, when she was twenty-five, she married someone who was, ostensibly, her kind in a wedding arranged by her parents. Reuben Glahs was a Jewish scholar five years younger than her and also from Chrzanow. But in truth, they were a deeply unlikely couple, in looks as much as temperament. In the very few photos that remain of her it is clear she was a large woman, solid rather than fat, with much-remarked-upon large feet and a face not even a poet could describe as beautiful. But her most extraordinary feature was her eyes. On her medical notes later in life they were described simply as 'blue/grey', a description that suggests either enormous self-restraint or irony on the doctor's part. In fact, they went in two different directions at the same time, which made her look both wild and watchful.

Reuben, by contrast, was dark-haired, delicate, shorter than Chaya and strikingly handsome, like a young Adrien Brody. Unlike Chaya, he was fluent in multiple languages – German, Polish, Russian, Yiddish – and the only person in Chrzanow other than a rabbi who could read and write Hebrew. Where Chaya was tough, practical and energetic, Reuben was gentle, scholarly and slow. In his memoir, Sender – Alex as I knew him – draws frequent comparisons between his parents (invariably to his mother's disadvantage, no matter how neutral the differences he was describing): she liked to debate furiously in the market square, washing the family's dishes around the central well where the towns-women gathered, while he preferred to sit with his friends in the cafés, listening and nodding and drinking coffee. She was ambitious for more whereas Reuben thought you should be happy with what you have. Between them, they represented the different attitudes peasant Jews had about their place in the world at that time: should you fight for a better life than the one you were born into, or should you meekly sit back and be grateful for what you were given? Chaya and Reuben never really resolved this difference, and their marriage was less than blissful.

'She believed herself, quite falsely, to be from a higher social class than his. So she treated my father with indifference. I saw her coolness to him. It pained me, for my father was a man of deep goodness, of noble heart and intelligence,' Sender wrote in his memoir, in one of many passages setting out at length his mother's flaws and his father's perfection.

As the daughter of a poor tailor, it's unlikely Chaya really thought of herself as being in a higher social class than anyone else, and Sender's allegation almost certainly says more about his feelings for his mother than it does about Chaya's feelings for Reuben. (And these feelings were also somewhat ironic, given that, in temperament and ambition, Sender was much more like his mother than his father.) But it is also likely that Reuben was a disappointment to her. When they met, he was a handsome man celebrated in the town for his intellect, but Chaya soon learned you can't eat intellect. He worked diligently from the day of his wedding, but life only got harder for them, because of his unfailing inability to earn any money. He tried his hand at being a tailor, a glass blower, a potato picker, a translator and, finally, a Singer sewing machine travelling salesman, and each career was less successful than the last. They were desperately poor, and became more so with each child born. After an initial still-birth in 1900, Jehuda, Chaya's favourite, was born in 1901, followed shortly by Jakob in 1902, then Sender in 1906, one more stillbirth, then a little girl, Mindel, in 1908, who died from illness as a child, and finally Sala in 1910. For a decade, Chaya was almost continually pregnant, and hungry.

The children's early years were both difficult and blissful. They were in a constant state of near starvation, dreaming of food that wasn't even available to buy, not that they could have afforded it anyway. One day, a piece of cheese appeared in the window of one of the shops in the town square, beneath a glass bell. The town's children, including Jakob and Sender, stared at it in wonder: cheese! With holes! Several centimetres thick! No one had ever seen such a marvel, and they watched, longingly, as one of the wealthy Chrzanovians from the town's poshest street, Aleja Henryka (Boulevard Henry), went into the shop, bought it, bagged it and walked home with it, without giving any of them even a crumb. But Sender got his own back on his rich neighbours: whenever he smelled good cooking in one of their houses, he would sneak around the back, look through the kitchen window, wait for the cook to step away, then climb in, pocket a meatball and run into the forest to eat his prize. His mother, secretly pleased at her youngest son's pragmatic approach to life, pretended not to notice the grease stains on his trousers.

They lived on a street called Kostalista in a ruin of a building, in a two-room apartment on the second floor, so dark you could barely see more than 3 feet in front of you in the daytime (Chrzanow didn't get electricity until 1912). The windows looked out onto a barren courtyard filled with firewood for the long, bitter winters. The apartment was cold, dirty and dangerous, and the children, particularly Sender, occasionally fell out of the unprotected windows, crashing down head first onto the paving stones outside.

Despite all the hunger and near-death tumbles, life for the children was happy. Little Sala, sickly from birth with weak lungs, would stay at home with her mother during the day, contentedly cooking and sewing. Sometimes when she was allowed out, she would play with her pretty cousin, Rose Ornstein, who was about the same age as her, and the two would make dolls out of clothes-pins. The boys nominally went to the local grammar school with non-Jews in the morning and then Hebrew school in the afternoon, but only Jehuda actually attended classes. He especially liked his Catholic Polish teacher, who taught him in the morning, and the teacher liked him, even coming over to the Glahses' home for a kosher dinner from time to time. But Jakob and especially Sender preferred to run through the streets and play football with their Ornstein cousins, Rose's brothers, who were roughly the same ages as they were: Maurice, the eldest and therefore the leader; Josek, who was two years younger than Sender but so brave when it came to stealing food that Sender graciously considered him an equal; quiet and shy Arnold; and Alex Ornstein, the baby of the boys. (As well as Rose, there were two other Ornstein girls, Anna and Sarah.) The Ornsteins were the children of Chaya's older sister, Hadassah, who managed to produce seven children in a decade,[6] all sweet-natured and easy-going, despite having to fight for a spot round the dining table at every meal. They lived around the corner from the Glahs family, on Aleja Henryka, named after a converted Jew,[7] because their father, Hirsch, was comparatively wealthy. But Sender never mentions feeling socially inferior to, or jealous of, his cousins in his memoir. Instead, he describes the thrill of dashing up Aleja Henryka with his brother and cousins, Sender and Josek, pocketing some meatballs on the way and heading into the birch tree woods, where there was a large sand pit, a stone quarry and a lake. They would eat Sender and Josek's takings and hide from their parents for hours, playing make-believe and kicking a football that was a rolled-up bunch of rags.

The Glahs family kept kosher and Reuben, like all the Jewish men in Chrzanow, went to prayers every Shabbat and on holy days, walking to the Great Synagogue off the market square around the corner from their home. They were Orthodox but not ultra-Orthodox, unlike many of their fellow townspeople who dominated the local politics, in their heavy black clothes, long beards and side curls. In the very few surviving photos of the Glahs children from this period, which I found in Sala's and Henri's albums, the boys often wear yarmulkes, but they don't have side curls or

27

wear traditional clothes, and Sala is generally wearing pretty frilly dresses, while Chaya never covered her hair, as ultra-Orthodox women do. Their lives were informed by Judaism, but not controlled by it, and compared with many of their neighbours they were almost scandalously modern.

Throughout Galicia at this time there was a growing schism among the Jews regarding tradition versus progress, with the heavy-coated conservatives on one side, and the less tradition-bound Jews on the other. The latter argued for a modern approach to Judaism, influenced by the Haskalah, the Jewish enlightenment, which emerged in the late eighteenth century and argued that Jews should maintain their secular distinctiveness, but should also take more part in the modern world, such as adopting modern dress and broader education. It looked at Judaism as an evolving cultural identity rather than a restrictive religious one. Ironically, this ideology that pushed for integration would later contribute to the rise of Zionism, partly because many Jews later realised that, no matter how much they assimilated, they were still persecuted, and therefore Jews needed a Jewish homeland.

But in Austria-Hungary in the early twentieth century, the idea of a Jewish state was so far away it might have been on the moon. Given that traditional Jews far outnumbered progressive ones in Galicia in general and Chrzanow in particular, the whole debate was ostensibly moot for Chrzanovian Jews. But Jehuda, a talented scholar from an early age who would likely have read about the Haskalah, argued for his family to adopt a more progressive approach to Judaism.

In his memoir, Sender describes, with palpable retrospective awe of his big brother, how at the young age of twelve Jehuda urged his parents to be less obviously Jewish and to assimilate more with the Germans or Poles – to try to speak their language more instead of always relying on Yiddish, for example. Chaya waved her son away and continued to speak Yiddish loudly in the town square. Reuben similarly couldn't countenance giving up what he saw as his primary identity. But as a compromise, he allowed himself to be persuaded by Jehuda to change the spelling of their surname from Glahs to the more westernised Glass – something simultaneously strong and fragile, able to withstand pressure but prone to breaking. Jews' names as a whole in this period were unfixed, mutable – a sign it seemed to them at the time of their adaptability. But it was also an indication of the instability of their lives, and was seen as part of their 'rootlessness' that would soon be used against them.

All four children idolised their gentle, loving father, who raised his hand only once: to Sender (of course), when he announced at age four, on the way to synagogue, that he didn't believe in God, and the strike was so half-hearted it felt more like a pat. Although Chaya was undoubtedly the more assertive parent, it was Reuben's looks that were dominant. Jehuda, Jakob and Sala all inherited Reuben's delicate, pretty appearance; Jakob in particular, who Reuben named after his beloved late father,[8] looked so similar to him the neighbours used to joke they probably had the same fingerprints. He was also the most like his father: gentle, passive and easily pushed around – Jakob skipped school only because Sender told him to do so. Jehuda, quiet and self-contained, inherited his father's intellectual curiosity, but he was more reliable and practical. As for baby Sala, her father loved to buy pretty dresses for his little daughter, while Chaya, judging from photos, would not have recognised a pretty dress from an ugly one if it hit her in the face in the market place. But Reuben always took care over his appearance, even when he was reduced to wearing almost literal rags. The Glahs children all inherited his appreciation of aesthetics, and for the rest of their lives they dressed carefully and stylishly, a lifelong show of love for their father.

The only child who resembled, and acted, like Chaya was Sender. According to family lore Sender was 'born fighting', because when he came out of his mother he was silent, so the midwife slapped him. It was the last time in his life Sender lost a fight. From the age of six he was getting into scraps at school, daily. He wasn't bothered by the blood and bruises as long as he won the battle, and he always fought until he won. Sender was born on 25 December and his mother referred to him as 'little Jesus', a teasing reference to his dominating personality, which was in inverse proportion to his physical size. Unlike his brothers, Sender was short, something he later put down to 'deprivation', although he never explained why his brothers both grew to over 6 feet, about a foot taller than him. But Sender wasn't just a stubby little fighter – he was also a dreamer, and what he dreamed of was escape. He loved to hear his father describe places he'd read about, such as Paris, London, Venice, cities of such beauty they made the Chrzanow synagogues look like nothing, Reuben said. Sender loved his father, but he would never be like him, slaving away for no recognition. What was the point of working hard without reward? At the age of eight, Paris was far beyond his reach, so he came up with a plan to go to the closer and yet almost equally exotic Trzebina, a town 7 kilometres away, where people from Chrzanow went when they needed a dentist. Sender told his mother he had a terrible toothache and Chaya let him take the train on his own with his favourite cousin, Josek Ornstein. The town itself was something of a disappointment, but the freedom of travel thrilled Sender so much he was, for once, almost speechless. Even though it meant the boys had to suffer a hideously painful tooth extraction by the dentist, the journey was worth it. So much so, they did it again, costing them another tooth. Still worth it.

'It was a world of superstitions, of quarrelling rabbis, quarrelling Hasidim, where thousands of Jews lived, twenty synagogues, where the air was so fresh. I sometimes felt, in lieu of food, I was nourished by the Carpathian air,' Alex later wrote. But then the First World War started and everything that had been good about the children's lives instantly turned very, very bad.

WHEN CHAYA WAVED her husband off to war she must have had few hopes of ever seeing him again. Reuben couldn't even walk up Aleja Henryka without losing his breath, and that one time he gave Sender a smack he, rather than Sender, had cried – how on earth was such a man going to survive life in the Austro-Hungarian Army? But like many Jewish men, Reuben felt intense loyalty to the Emperor Franz Joseph I because of his kindness to the Jews. An educated man like Reuben would have been all too aware that it was very much in his best interest, as a Jew, to defend the emperor. So he signed up to fight pretty much as soon as his country declared war on Serbia. But there were, surely, few more unlikely soldiers than Reuben Glass.

Chaya was now, essentially, a single mother at the age of forty-one, with four children, aged thirteen, twelve, eight and four. There was no way she could look after them on her own. Her older sister, Hadassah, was busy enough with her own seven children and her brother, Samuel, was busy with his four. No, she needed a man to take charge of the household, one who would look after the family and look after her. She didn't have to search too far to find just the one she needed.

Jehuda was only thirteen, but when his father went off to war he became the head of the household. Chaya relied on him, not even like a wife on a husband but a daughter on a father, and this was to be their dynamic for the rest of their lives. It was an obligation Jehuda quietly shouldered with enormous patience. 'Jehuda,' Chaya would say proudly to her children and, later, her grandchildren, '*iz die beste.*' (Sender, on the other hand, she would describe as alternately a '*Pshakrev*' – dog's blood, or a Polish curse – or '*mitzvah*', a blessing, depending on both of their moods.) Despite still being at school, Jehuda, as he later recounted in his own notes, supported the family, working for the library in the evenings and at weekends, and he tried, with minimal success, to get his brothers to go to school. He, too, started missing school: his 1916/17 school report says he missed 145 hours that year, but he still got straight As. However, as Chaya became more demanding, and life in Chrzanow became more difficult, what he really wanted was to leave. Whereas Sender looked to schemes and tooth extractions as his means of escape, Jehuda realised academia might be his ticket.

Food became increasingly scarce in Chrzanow as the war went on and the Jews were used as the scapegoats for everyone's suffering; Polish authorities started confiscating their goods, claiming, falsely, that they were trading on the black market. The local halls in town, where the Jews had often held cultural committee meetings, were suddenly off-limits to them.[9] Both Sender and Jehuda watched all this, and began talking more openly about leaving the town. Jakob laughed at their concerns, and insisted the Jews would be safe in Chrzanow, as they always had been. Little Sala, who had Jehuda's quietude and Jakob's gentleness, revered her three older brothers, and agreed with whichever one seemed to be taking charge, which was generally Jehuda. But any talk of leaving Chrzanow could only be talk for now: they weren't going anywhere until the war ended and their father returned.

However it was becoming almost impossible for them to stay. In late October 1918 there were rumours that a pogrom was being planned, organised by the Polish authorities. On 5 November 1918, six days before the end of the war, the first town in the newly liberated Poland to suffer such an attack was Chrzanow.[10]

They came at night. The townspeople heard them before they saw them, 'a savage screaming crowd that seemed like a monster. They were attacking animals, wild beasts from the guts of hell. From their distorted snouts came cries of a horrible hatred which I found impossible to understand,' Sender wrote. Polish men and women tore through the town, ransacking the synagogues, smashing the Jewish shop windows. The Jews ran to their homes, frantically locking the doors behind them. The Glass family hid under a bed, both Sala, who was eight, and Chaya, forty-five, clinging to seventeen-year-old Jehuda in terror. After an hour or so of listening to the frightening noises outside, twelve-year-old Sender scrambled out from under the bed and, ignoring the cries of his family, ran out to join the few Jewish men who were attempting to fight back. In the dark, he tried to make out the faces, but they were so obscured by hate and fury they looked more like wild boars than humans to him – except one. As he watched the group charge up his street he looked at the leader and realised he recognised him: it was Jehuda's former tutor, the Christian Pole who came over for dinner occasionally. As he looked closer, he recognised some more: people who came in every Sunday to go to church, the man who sometimes gave him a bit of cheese in the market, women who had bought sewing machines from his father. He saw a well-respected judge, Court President Wierszbyicki, he saw scholars, and he saw peasants and thugs – representatives of all sectors of Polish society and here they were, beating up his friends, trying to burn down his house and kill his family.

'Something in me died in the face of this inhuman explosion of savagery,' he later wrote. 'From that day, my childhood was over.'

The pogrom lasted twenty-four hours, and Sender did as much as a young boy could to fight back, tripping the men as they charged in to ransack the empty stores, kicking their horses. At one point he was slashed across the forehead with a knife and, decades later, Sala could still remember her terror when her brother stumbled through their door in the morning, blinded by blood pouring into his eyes from his deep head wound, half-crazed with adrenalin; for the rest of her life she associated Poland with that vision of violence. In one night, almost all the town's Jews were left destitute, their money and livelihoods taken from them by their own countrymen. When the war ended six days later, few celebrated.

From then on, attacks on Jews became common in Chrzanow and in the surrounding area, especially from the so-called 'Polish liberation army', which emerged after Poland's liberation at the end of the war. Its members were known as 'the Hallerchiks' in honour of their leader General Haller, and they would roam through Chrzanow ripping the beards off any Jews they encountered, tearing the skin and laughing at the bloodied faces. If they came across a clean-shaven Jew, they would beat him for his lack of religiosity. They justified these attacks by citing the increasingly popular theory that Jews were not loyal to Poland, but were instead Bolsheviks, plotting to overturn the government. Neither the Hallerchiks nor the Chrzanovians could have known it at the time, and certainly the Glass family didn't, but they were at the emerging forefront of a relatively new kind of anti-Semitism, one that would shape the twentieth century, and their own lives. And it would linger, like a strange stray black cloud, over the lives of their children and grandchildren.

The theory that Jews are political destabilisers, working against whatever country they live in, is a more modern and politically inflected form of anti-Semitism than the traditional and religiously based one, which held Jews responsible for Jesus's crucifixion. It emerged in the eighteenth and nineteenth centuries as a reaction against the social and economic changes in Europe, stemming from the French Revolution, when the old monarchical hierarchies were toppled, followed by the spread of industrialisation and urbanisation across the Continent. These two enormous shifts combined to create a new liberal, capitalist social order, one in which citizenship was based on civic participation and equality, as opposed to bloodline and history – forward-looking rationalism over backward-looking nationalism.[11] Thus, Jews could be seen as citizens as opposed to outsiders. Opponents of the Enlightenment, however, argued for national purity, celebrating a country's heritage as opposed to its modern future, and during the nineteenth century there was a rise in anti-Semitism, as those who failed to benefit from the new economy blamed the Jews. In 1845 the French writer Alphonse Toussenel claimed in *Les Juifs, Rois de l'Époque*: 'Protestants and Jews . . . have controlled public opinion in order to favour trafficking and rigging the market, blocked every defence of royalty and of the people, put the producer and the consumer at their mercy so that in France the Jew reigns and governs.'

These beliefs were validated by the infamous 1903 document, the *Protocols of the Elders of Zion*, which emerged just as the Glass children were being born. It claimed that a mysterious Jewish cabal was controlling governments and the media, and even though the *Protocols of the Elders of Zion* was quickly exposed as a hoax, it helped to forge the dominating anti-Semitic narrative of the twentieth century. This really began to take hold after the First World War, when nationalism escalated in response to the economic devastation across the Continent, although specific takes on it differed slightly. In one version of this theory, Jews are greedy money-hoarders who control a country's government through their connections and wealth, puppet masters pulling the strings. In the other version, the one promoted by the Hallerchiks, Jews are communist revolutionaries looking to overthrow a country's government. But the message of both versions is the same: Jews are political disruptors working against the people and for themselves, which is just a new take on the old idea that

Jews are not really citizens of the country in which they were born, so cannot be trusted. In other words, anti-Semitism becomes another form of xenophobia.

This theory has retained a tenacious hold on the popular imagination, despite everything Jews endured in the twentieth century. In the twenty-first century it can be seen in, for example, the right wing's demonisation of George Soros, the Hungarian-American philanthropist and Holocaust survivor who has been vilified by the American,[12] Hungarian[13] and British far right[14] as a suspicious manipulator plotting to control the global order and bring chaos into the lives of peaceful citizens.* †

* President Trump repeatedly implied in October and November 2018 that Soros was funding the so-called 'migrant caravan', a group of thousands of desperate Central American migrants seeking asylum in America. Various other Republicans and far-right commentators also pushed that allegation, and many people believed it. One believer was US citizen Robert Bowers, who reposted a comment that said, 'Jews are waging a propaganda war against Western civilisation and it is so effective we are heading towards certain extinction.' On 27 October Bowers shot and killed eleven Jews in a synagogue. This did not stop President Trump from continuing to endorse the entirely unfounded theory that Soros was funding the caravan. (John Wagner, 'Trump says he "wouldn't be surprised" if unfounded conspiracy theory about George Soros funding [migrant] caravan is true,' *Washington Post*, 1 November 2018.)

† And this mentality is not limited to the right. The former leader of Britain's Labour Party, Jeremy Corbyn, has been repeatedly criticised for what many see as flirtations with anti-Semitism. One especially egregious example hit the news just as I was starting to write this book in 2018, when it emerged that in 2012 he appeared to express support on Facebook for a mural that depicted stereotypically Jewish-looking bankers

The campaign for Brexit – which went on near simultaneously with the vilification of Soros, and crossed left and right party lines – would probably have appealed to the Hallerchiks, with its dreamy-eyed talk about hard borders, heritage and national purity. Nigel Farage, Brexit's most influential architect, has long talked darkly about 'the new world order' and argued that 'globalists have wanted to have some form of conflict with Russia as an argument for us all to surrender our national sovereignty and give it up to a higher global level.'[15] It takes some effort not to hear the echoes of the Hallerchiks' insistence that Jews, those citizens of nowhere, were working against Poland for some kind of greater global domination, but Farage determinedly stuck his fingers in his ears and insisted any suggestion of anti-Semitism was 'wide of the mark'.[‡] From 'Bolsheviks' in the 1920s to 'globalists' in the 2010s, the euphemisms for anti-Semitic and nationalist beliefs might shift over time, but the underlying stories remain remarkably constant.

playing Monopoly on the backs of slaves. (Corbyn insisted that he 'did not look more closely at the image'. 'Jeremy Corbyn regrets comments about "anti-Semitic" mural', *BBC*, 23 March 2018.)

‡   Similarly, in her first Conservative conference speech after becoming Prime Minister soon after the referendum, Theresa May attacked 'global elites' and claimed, 'If you believe you are a citizen of the world, you are a citizen of nowhere.' Vince Cable, the leader of the Liberal Democrat Party, said at the time, 'It could have been taken out of *Mein Kampf*. I think that's where it came from, wasn't it? "Rootless cosmopolitans"?' 'Vince Cable: Theresa May's Tory conference speech "could have been taken out of Mein Kampf"', *New Statesman*, 5 July 2017.

CONTRARY TO EVERYONE'S EXPECTATIONS, his wife's presumably most of all, Reuben did return from the war, but only barely. He had fought in the Second Battle of the Piave River in June 1918, in which the Italian Army crushed the Austro-Hungarian Army. This battle was the beginning of the end of the Austro-Hungarian Empire, in which almost 230,000 men were killed, but Reuben survived. He was, however, badly gassed, and his lungs damaged irrevocably. Somehow, he limped through the rest of the war, further depleting whatever strength his lungs had left, and returned home, where he walked in the door and collapsed in the front room.

When Reuben realised how poor his family had become in his absence, with Sender stealing food for the family table and Sala wearing rags, he forced himself to return to work. Reuben didn't have a pension from the army, and the family desperately needed money, so he went back to hawking Singer sewing machines around the countryside. But there are few worse careers for a man with broken lungs than that of travelling salesman, schlepping through sooty towns on dirty trains in cold nights.

'My father was very, very ill, and there was no medicine for him. As if we could afford medicine. He had to return to work, to continue his endless travels as a sewing machine salesman for a miserable little salary. Great sadness infected our home,' Sender wrote.

Reuben did not last long at his job, but the sadness did. One night Reuben came back to the apartment after another trip, went to bed and never got up again. For the next few years he lay there, sick, in horrendous pain, racked with a violent cough that seemed to rip his lungs apart with every hack.

After the war the Glass family were still in their old home but in an utterly unfamiliar land. The deeply anti-Semitic National-Democratic (ND) Party was on the rise in Poland. At the Versailles Conference in January 1919 the Polish delegation, co-led by Roman Dmowski, co-founder of the ND Party, fought unsuccessfully against signing the minorities protections section of the Treaty of Versailles. Dmowski and the Polish politicians complained that it suggested Poland and the Polish people were oppressors as opposed to victims, which was how they saw themselves, and not without some merit. Poland was decimated after the war, after German, Austrian and Russian troops had marched back and forth across it, destroying railways and agriculture, and the ensuing poverty led people to look for targets to blame. Dmowski insisted, in familiar rhetoric, that 'international Jewry' was plotting Poland's destruction, and the Catholic Polish media repeatedly and openly associated Jews with evil.[16] This did little to stem the attacks against Jews in Poland.

The Ornstein cousins had already left Chrzanow for Paris, and after the first pogrom the Glass family knew they had to go too. Like a strikingly high number of Jews in the early 1920s, Jehuda went to Prague to attend university,[17] which the family somehow managed to pay for. So Jakob was the first of the family to go to Paris, in 1920 when he was eighteen years old, followed shortly thereafter by fourteen-year-old Sender. But Chaya and Sala stayed behind with Reuben, as he could not survive the journey, and the three of them alone endured the terror of multiple pogroms and increasing anti-Semitism. Finally, in 1925, after years of pain, Reuben died.

For the rest of their lives, the Glass children referred to Reuben's death as one of their most formative and traumatic experiences, despite all they later endured. Jakob and Sender were both living in Paris at this point, and the former wept for the only adult he knew who never berated him for his deficiencies, while Sender, who idolised his father, both despite and because he was so different from him, raged with fury against his death. Fifty years later, he dedicated his memoir to his father, 'the man I loved most in my life'. Sala, still then only fourteen, cried for her father who had made her feel pretty and loved and safe. Chaya leaned on Jehuda more heavily than ever, demanding he come home from university to help her.

Jehuda didn't cry when his father died. Instead he tucked his grief behind his implacable exterior, like the creased photo of his father that he hid inside his stiff wallet for the rest of his life. Almost thirty years after Jehuda died, I found that wallet, in a storage box in the basement of his daughter Danièle's building. It had slipped into the lining of an old suitcase and I happened to discover it by accident. I pulled it out and looked through it, hoping to find something that would reveal a little of Jehuda's later life: receipts, perhaps, or scrawled notes. But the only thing in it was the photo of Reuben, a century old by that point, the only memory Jehuda kept on him at all times, until he, too, was a memory.

Almost as soon as Reuben died, Chaya and Sala went to Paris. The world in which the Glass children had grown up, the eastern European Jewish shtetl, based on community but also dependent on peaceful interactions with outsiders, was dying. Like Reuben, it had no place in this harshly emerging modern era. So both he and it were buried in Chrzanow's Jewish cemetery, filled with other Jews whose families, if they were lucky, were forging new lives across Europe, leaving behind neglected gravestones and much more.

None of the Glasses ever returned to Chrzanow, except one, once. In the 1970s, Sender – now known as Alex – visited Poland on a trip organised by some of his fellow veterans from the Foreign Legion. He went, very reluctantly, back to a country he associated only with death, pogroms and hunger. But he went because he was interested to see how many Jews were left where he grew up, and how they were living. What he saw devastated him. The town, which he remembered as surrounded by forests and countryside, was, he wrote, now 'an open, heavily polluted field'. The only things he recognised were 'the brutish mugs' of the Polish people he saw in the market place – otherwise, everything from his childhood was gone: his home, the synagogues, the Jews.

Chrzanow fell into German hands almost the day the Second World War was declared, 1 September 1939. This was not a surprise to the Chrzanovians: the month before they'd watched the long caravans of desperate people marching down the long highway between Katowice and Krakow, which ran through Chrzanow, as civilians who lived near the German and Polish borders fled into the countryside for safety. Adolf Hitler had been pushing the myth that communism was a Jewish plot for almost a decade, borrowing the story from anti-Semitic nationalist movements in various countries, including Poland. Meanwhile, the theory that Polish Jews were working for the Soviets, and had even been responsible for the Great Purge of 1936–8 in which up to 1.2 million people were killed in Russia, had become so widespread it was generally assumed to be fact, and Polish nationalists referred to Jews collectively as traitors.[18] Chrzanow was infused with panic, and the wealthier and cannier sent their female relatives, children and valuables out of the city to safety.[19] But many did not. Because so many of the town's Jews knew and did business with the Germans, they refused to believe that the Germans would actually hurt them, their long-time neighbours, friends and colleagues.[20] For neither the first nor the last time, the Jews were over-optimistic about the benevolence of outsiders. On 4 September 1939 the Nazis entered the city and immediately began to terrorise the Jews. But as much as the actions of their neighbours and former colleagues shocked them, an even bigger surprise to the Chrzanovian Jews was how keen their countrymen, the Poles, were to betray them.

'They were the ones who pointed out the Jews to the German soldiers, who couldn't tell the difference between

Jews and Poles. They didn't know any German but with sign language they pointed out "Jude!"', one resident of the town later recalled.[21] More than 15,000 Jews – almost the entirety of the town's Jewish population[22] – died in the Holocaust, rounded up and sent just down the road to their sister town, which many of them would have visited before, where they were murdered.[23] Ironically, the pogroms that had so terrified my grandmother and her family had actually saved their lives, because they propelled the family out of Poland before the 1930s. Had they stayed, they almost certainly all would have been killed.

I WENT TO CHRZANOW in the spring of 2018, forty years after Alex visited, almost exactly a hundred years after the Glass family started to leave. My father travelled there with me, as did our relative Anne-Laurence Goldberg, Anna Ornstein's granddaughter. Chrzanow itself wasn't quite as grim as when Alex had visited, when it was still under Communist rule: there were typical eastern European tower blocks around the outside, but also pretty streets in the centre, bordered with houses freshly painted in dusky pinks, yellows and greens, as they had been back when the Glasses lived there. Yet it still feels like a town from which something's been sucked out, and what's been sucked out are the Jews. In 1920 Jews represented 55.5 per cent of the town's population. Today, they officially represent less than 1 per cent, although our guide admitted that number was more likely to be closer to zero.

My father, Anne-Laurence and I walked around the town, retracing the stories Alex told in his memoir. The square, where Chaya used to wash the dishes and do the shopping, is still there, but all the Jewish shops that bordered the square have gone. Of the town's twenty synagogues not a single one remains. The Great Synagogue, where the Glasses prayed, was destroyed in the 1970s to make room for a car park. All that remains of it is a broken concrete wall, heavily graffitied. In fact, the Jewish cemetery where Reuben is buried, which somehow survived the war, is pretty much the only sign that Jews ever lived there at all. He lies in a quiet corner, shaded by the former Galician forest where his children once ran. He is near his daughter Mindel, who died as a child; his father Jakob's gravestone lies on the other side of the cemetery, next to the great family tomb for the wealthy Halberstam family, like a humble sentryman keeping guard. Reuben was not one for making public statements in life, but in death the deeply carved Hebrew letters on his tombstone act as an uncharacteristically defiant show of Chrzanow's Jewish legacy.

The week before my father and I booked our tickets to go to Chrzanow in 2018, the Polish President, Andrzej Duda, signed into law an anti-defamation bill, making it illegal to attribute responsibility or complicity for the Holocaust to the Polish state.[24] This law, President Duda said in a national broadcast, 'protects Polish interests . . . our dignity, the historical truth . . . so that we are not slandered as a state and as a nation'. In a century-spanning echo of

Dmowski's complaint in 1919, Duda objected to the idea that Poland was ever an oppressor. Instead, he said, stories about Poland during the Second World War should focus on Poland's suffering and glory.

This bill was not a surprise to anyone who had followed the Law and Justice Party since they came to power. In 2016 President Duda threatened to take away a national honour from Jan Tomasz Gross, an American citizen born in Poland and one of the world's experts on the Holocaust.[25] Gross wrote in an essay that the Poles 'killed more Jews than [the] Germans [did]', a claim other historians have backed up as correct. Yet Duda insisted this was 'an attempt to destroy Poland's good name', and while in Poland Gross was hauled in for five hours of questioning.[26]

No doubt, Poland endured one of the most brutal occupations of any country invaded by the Germans, and the Poles, who the Nazis considered to be *Untermenschen* (inferiors), suffered horrifically. Yet it is also true that part of the reason 90 per cent of Poland's Jews were killed during the war, one of the highest percentages in Europe, is that they were denounced, hunted and killed by the Poles themselves, before, during and even after the war. Just one year after the end of the Second World War, on 4 July 1946, soldiers and civilians led an attack on the Jews in the Polish town of Kielce, killing more than forty Jews. They had survived the Holocaust, returned to what was in many cases their homeland, only to be then killed by their fellow citizens. After what became known as the Kielce pogrom, many of the surviving Polish Jews left the country and few have ever returned. Before the Second World War, more than 3 million Jews lived in Poland, the biggest Jewish population in Europe; today it is estimated to be about ten thousand. By comparison, more than fifteen thousand Jews live in Miami Beach and more than fifty thousand Jews live in the north London borough of Barnet.

Poland had been a deeply anti-Semitic country long before the Nazis turned up, as the Glass family knew well. So while there certainly were brave Polish individuals who tried to help the Jews during the war, they were very much the exception.[27] Even after the war, many in eastern Europe, including Poland, continued to refer to Jews as Bolsheviks, suggesting that what happened to them was in some way their fault, and certainly not Poland's. That mentality still exists today: by outlawing suggestions of Polish complicity President Duda and his Law and Justice Party are trying to create 'a narrative of heroic Polish victimhood', the *New York Times* said,[28] one that absolved them of any wrongdoing in the Second World War. An official to the President said any Jews who criticised the law, who claimed that Polish anti-Semitism helped to enable the Holocaust happening on Polish land, were merely 'ashamed [that] many Jews engaged in collaboration during the war'.[29]

Just down the road from Chrzanow is the Auschwitz-Birkenau Museum and Memorial. While my father, Anne-Laurence and I were in Chrzanow, the nationalist and pro-government Polish media was accusing the museum of downplaying the deaths of Poles in the camp and focusing instead on what was described as 'foreign narratives' – in other words, the Jewish stories.

'Foreign, and not Polish narratives reign at Auschwitz. Time for it to stop,' wrote Barbara Nowack, a former local councillor for the Law and Justice Party. The home of at least one guide at the site was vandalised in March 2018, with someone spray-painting 'Poland for the Poles' across the outside alongside a Star of David equated with a swastika.[30]

None of this would have surprised the Glasses. It did, however, surprise me. Because I went to Auschwitz-Birkenau before visiting Chrzanow with my father and Anne-Laurence (whose grandparents, Anna and Samuel Goldberg, had been killed there), what struck me was how much emphasis was placed on the Polish victims. Seventy-five thousand non-Jewish Poles were killed in Auschwitz, which is shocking, but so were the 1.1 million Jews, and looking around at the exhibitions, signs and tours it felt like the memorial was suggesting some kind of equivalence between the Polish and Jewish suffering in the camp. There is even a gift shop – yes, a gift shop – in the car park outside, run by the local municipality, which sells Polish tourist tat. Because nothing makes one more desirous of buying an 'I Heart Poland' coffee mug than a trip to Auschwitz. 'An Auschwitz gift shop' is surely the ultimate Jewish joke, and its intention is clear: Auschwitz, it is saying, is about Polish victimhood and triumph. The Jews were a side issue.

'In all Holocaust sites there is a tendency to emphasise the nation's suffering and German culpability,' Martin Winstone from the Holocaust Educational Trust told me in 2018:

> Auschwitz was one of the very few concentration
> camps where non-Jewish Poles were killed, so it's
> not surprising Polish suffering is emphasised there
> – although, of course, far more Jews were killed
> there. But so much depends on political and social
> climates. Even just five years ago people would have
> said Poland was being really honest about its history.
> But with this government in power they are trying
> to limit discussions of Polish culpability, and these
> efforts aren't actually aimed at the international
> community, but at the people in Poland – teachers,
> academics – who are trying to tell the true story.
> A huge amount of Polish identity is based on
> the idea that Poles were victims of the German
> occupation, but that doesn't mean some of them
> didn't also perpetrate it. Every country wants to have
> heroic narratives of the war, and what this all shows
> is how vulnerable historical truth is.

Back in Chrzanow, we found the building where Anne-Laurence's grandmother, Anna Ornstein, and the rest of the Ornstein cousins lived on Aleja Henrika. It was large and imposing, with fretted ironwork around the balconies, preventing any children from rolling off. It was painfully different from the crumbling semi-death trap where the Glasses lived, as described in Alex's memoir. We eventually found the Glass family's street, after figuring out it had been renamed from Kostalista to Lipstada. Their house had long since been torn down, which wasn't a surprise – I hardly expected a condemned building from a century ago to still be standing. But what I saw around the corner made me stop and stare. There, on the side of a building just behind where the Glasses once lived, was fresh graffiti: '*Anty Jude*'. This was a tag from a fan of the Wisla football team, whose supporters refer to themselves as the 'Anty Jude Gang', in opposition to the Widzew team, which is associated with the Jewish community in the way Tottenham Hotspur Football Club is in England. The Anty Jude label is defended by supporters as mere larky banter – only the most po-faced seeker of victim status could confuse it with *real* anti-Semitism, they say. At a Polish league game in 2013 between Wisla and Widzew, there were chants of 'Move on, Jews! Your home is at Auschwitz! Send you to the gas chamber!' A Polish municipal prosecutor decided these were not criminal offences.[31]

Not even being less than 20 kilometres from Auschwitz made this graffiti artist rethink leaving this tag. If anything, it may have encouraged them. My father winced when he saw it and looked away, but I think the Glasses would have appreciated the aptness of seeing this on their neighbour's building in 2018. Almost a century after they left everything they had and knew to go to France, their old town – their old country – was still very much vindicating their decision.

Sala in France, 1929.

2

THE GLASS SIBLINGS –
Immigration

Paris, 1920s–early 1930s

OF COURSE, to the Glasses, their decision to move from Poland to Paris in 1920 felt utterly personal: their home town was suddenly under threat from violent pogroms; the Ornstein cousins were already in Paris so could help them once they arrived; Paris wasn't unreachably far from Poland. This random set of circumstances, it seemed to them, happened to blow them towards the French capital.

But as is often the case with events that feel specific to us in the moment, the Glasses' move was wholly typical of both their time and their demographic. Between 1880 and 1925, 3.5 million Jews left central and eastern Europe and 100,000 of them went to France,[1,2] most for exactly the same reasons as the Glasses: they were fleeing the pogroms, and they knew people in Paris. Between 1900 and 1935, the number of Jews in France tripled,[3] and by the end of that decade Paris had the third largest Jewish community in the world, surpassed only by New York and Warsaw.[4] So not only were Jews likely to feel at home there, but they were also likely to have relatives there who would help them settle in, as the Glasses did. New York was too far away for many eastern European immigrants, and Warsaw too close to the danger from which they were fleeing, so Paris was the logical third option. Even more appealing for immigrants in the 1920s was that, at this point, France – unlike the United States or the United Kingdom[5] – had never imposed an anti-immigration statute that capped the number of (primarily Jewish) immigrants allowed in. Instead the country was known as *une terre d'asile* (a nation of asylum), and as a result, by the late 1930s, Paris had a Jewish population of 150,000, of whom 90,000 were immigrants from eastern Europe, including 50,000 Poles.[6] France, these Jews imagined, would be their salvation, away from pogroms and rampaging peasants. There was even a popular Yiddish phrase suggesting as much: *lebn vi Got in Frankrykk*[7] (live like a king in France). Although seeing as there was a similar phrase about Poland, describing it as a *Pardisus Judeorum* (a Jewish paradise),[8] the Polish Jews at least ought to have known better than to put too much faith in old Yiddish sayings.

France's appeal to fleeing Jewish immigrants went deeper than mere pragmatic considerations. In 1791 it became the first country in western Europe to liberate Jews[9] and so was associated in many Jews' minds with liberalism and tolerance. Immigrant Jews weren't especially bothered by the

Dreyfus Affair,[10] the notorious case in which Alfred Dreyfus, a Jewish artillery officer, was accused of passing confidential French military documents to the Germans and was unanimously found guilty by seven judges of treason in 1894. He was finally exonerated in 1906 after another (non-Jewish) Frenchman, Ferdinand Walsin Esterhazy, was proven to be the culprit. The French Army had mounted a massive cover-up to obscure Dreyfus's innocence and, more than a century on, the case remains one of the most notorious examples of anti-Semitism. Many eastern European Jews at the time, however, saw it differently. At least, they reasoned, in France these arguments happen in the public sphere, an improvement on what they saw in their own countries, where their relatives and friends were lynched and dumped.

'We saw the Dreyfus Affair as part of history, and touching only on a part of the populace, the military. It seemed to us a sort of literary anti-Semitism, the product of old, reactionary fanatics. What had really touched us was the Beilis Affair. For us poor Jews, the Beilis Affair had a terrifying resonance when the pogroms began, because it seemed like it could happen anywhere,' Sender wrote, referring to the vehemently anti-Semitic 1911 case in Russia, in which Menahem Mendel Beilis, a Hasidic Jew, was falsely accused of killing a thirteen-year-old Ukrainian boy, and the murder was associated with the blood libel. West, in other words, was infinitely preferable to east.

And in the main, France was happy to have the Jews. After the Dreyfus Affair, which exposed systemic French anti-Semitism under the shaming bright lights of publicity, anti-Jewish feelings subsided.[11] The anti-Semitic newspaper *La Libre Parole*, which once had a circulation of over 300,000 copies, folded, and even Maurice Barrès, one of the leaders of the anti-Semitic right at the end of the nineteenth century and during the Dreyfus Affair, wrote in his 1917 essay, '*Les diverses familles spirituelles de la France*', that Jews should be considered one of France's 'spiritual families' because of their courage during the war.

But there was a practical element to France's embrace of Jews as well as a moral one: 1.4 million Frenchmen died in the First World War, and the country desperately needed workers. So much so that in 1927 the Naturalisation Act was introduced, reducing the requirement for naturalisation from ten years to three, making it even easier, and quicker, to get immigrants into jobs.[12] The eastern European immigrants were shunted into industries that were seen as Jewish, such as the textile and garment trades, furniture-making and watch and jewellery repair. Most of these were based in or near the Marais, the Parisian quarter that was once chic but had become something of a ghetto. Just a few years before the Glass family arrived, New York's Yiddish newspaper *Der Forverts* ran an article about the Marais: 'The alleys are frightfully dirty, the houses mostly old ruins . . . Without exaggeration one can find from twelve to fifteen persons living in two small rooms . . . The largest and best room serves as the atelier; one eats where one can and sleeps in a dark hole without a window.'[13] This was where many immigrants settled, and it was so popular with Jewish immigrants it became known as the 'Pletzl' – Yiddish for 'little place'.

Jakob was the first to arrive in Paris, when he was just eighteen years old, and he adhered so faithfully to the trends of his demographic that the outlines of his story at times veer towards textbook. He rented a small flat near the Pletzl, on rue de Cléry, because it was close to his Ornstein cousins, and he got work as a furrier in the Pletzl, not because he knew anything about fur but because his cousin Josek, the second-oldest Ornstein, worked in the fur trade and helped him find a job. Jakob spent his days in the Pletzl, tending to animal skins in a darkened room, and he loved the simplicity of his work and life. In the Pletzl he could live as he had always done, surrounded by Poles and Yiddish speakers. If he never left his neighbourhoods, and there was rarely any need to do so, he barely had to remember he had left Chrzanow at all.

Sender, however, felt very differently. The fourteen-year-old arrived not long after Jakob, on a train full of other eastern European immigrants. His clothes and speech immediately marked him as a foreigner, so he was shunned by the French commuters around him as he walked through the train station. It was there that he saw and learned his first French word: '*sortie*' (exit). Following Jakob's instructions, he caught a bus from the station and stared out of the window in astonishment at the beauty of Paris. His occasional trips to the dentist in Trzebina hadn't prepared him for anything like this. He stared out of the bus window at the elegant architecture and even more elegant people in gleeful amazement. When he arrived at his new neighbourhood next to the Pletzl his heart sank into his shoes. It looked to him like Jakob had found the one ugly part of Paris, and was making him live there. He walked through the dirty and noisy streets looking for rue de Cléry, and when he saw Jakob's poky flat, he understood how little Jakob had changed his life, whereas Sender had come here to change everything. He also grasped that he was expected to become a traditional immigrant Jewish tailor like his brother and beloved Ornstein cousins, but he knew that he would never, ever do that. He loved few people more than Jakob, and no one more than his father, but he looked at their lives of drudgery, and although there was a part of him that admired their humility, he knew life had more to offer, and he would grab it. Jakob and Reuben expected nothing from life; Sender demanded everything. He had not come all this way to continue living like a Polish peasant. Despite having had such a circumscribed childhood, Sender's ambitions were boundless, and from what his father had always told him, and what he had seen on his bus ride to the Pletzl, he knew Paris could provide what he sought. In his memoir he wrote:

In Paris there was such gaiety. It dazzled the eyes. In Paris, on the terraces of the great restaurants, people drank wine and were happy. It was the image of happiness on earth. 'This life is impossible. It must

be better, elsewhere': these words turned in my head
during the long Chrzanow nights. So, it was true.
Life could be marvellous. Paris is where I was reborn.

After rejecting the life of a tailor, spending his days sitting
on a bench in the Pletzl, Sender decided to be a couturier.
He wanted his name above the door of his own salon, like
those he saw on his daily walks around the city, when he
eagerly escaped the Pletzl to explore the ritzier neighbourhoods around rue du Faubourg Saint-Honoré and Place
Vendôme. Lanvin, Schiaparelli, Vionnet, Patou: that's who
he wanted to be like, not just another Jewish tailor. There
was, however, a small problem: he didn't even know how to
sew on a button.

Not for a second did Sender see this as a possible impedi-
ment to becoming a world-famous fashion designer. If
anything, that it was such an unlikely path for him to choose
only made him more determined to succeed. So, undaunted,
he found a job as an apprentice at a garment workshop
where he learned how to cut, sew and drape while working twenty-four-hour shifts. And when he finished a shift
he came back to his and Jakob's flat and practised sewing
for another twenty-four hours. It infuriated him that he was
so bad at it, and his anger drove him to work harder: he
wouldn't, he explained to his bemused brother, stop until
he became good. His cousin Josek was one of the few who
understood his ambitions, because, like Sender, Josek was
smart, but he considered himself too smart to take such an

absurd risk as trying to be a couturier, whereas Sender felt he was too smart not to.

'Life,' he wrote, 'was not going to pass me by any more.'

Over the next few years, while Sala and Chaya stayed in Chrzanow with Reuben, and Jehuda continued his studies in Prague, Jakob worked quietly as a furrier in the Pletzl and Sender, then in his mid-teens, threw himself into couture and Paris life. He slogged his way through the workshops and got apprenticeships with small couturiers around the Saint-Martin neighbourhood, making a name for himself as an exceptionally hard worker and a perfectionist.

Couture might seem like an odd career path for one who used to relax by getting into brawls in the streets of Chrzanow. But what fashion meant to Sender was beauty, and beauty represented the opposite of Poland. It was a bulwark against the suffering he saw his father endure. He wrote:

> In my little Chrzanow world, there were no
> paintings at all, no beauty. But I always felt a
> growing hunger inside me for it, and I arrived in
> Paris famished for this beauty. Different from other
> immigrants who came to France mainly to earn
> money, I wished to educate myself constantly, to
> continue the Jewish traditions but also to open
> myself to French culture. I participated in the life of
> the country. Everywhere I went something new was
> happening, and I hurried to make up for lost time.

I wanted to know everything, to devour life like a
man eating a big chunk of meat.

While he spent his weekdays learning how to make beautiful
clothes, he spent his weekends and nights learning how to
make a beautiful world. Jakob liked to hang out at the cafés
in the Pletzl with his cousins and other Jewish tailors. Sender
was not averse to cafés, but he wanted to find a new life,
not cling to his old one. Not long after he arrived in Paris
he met Marc Chagall, who was already an established artist,
at Café Koretz, a small hangout for Yiddish speakers in the
Pletzl with only five or six tables. Over dishes of stuffed carp,
cake and tea, the two would talk about politics and share
memories of their home towns that still haunted them both.
It was through Chagall that Sender became aware of modern
art and artists, and he was soon spending his weekends at the
Musée du Luxembourg, then Paris's only museum of modern
art. When Sender invited his brother to come with him at
weekends to look at the Cézannes and Monets, or to look in
the windows of the French couturiers on the Grands Boulevards, Jakob would wave him away.

'We don't know anything about painting, why would
we spend our weekends doing that? Let's have fun instead,'
he'd say. And when Sender stormed off towards the Louvre
on his own, Jakob would head to his local café to see his
friends, all of whom were also Jewish immigrants, to read the
Yiddish newspapers, to drink, to joke, to do nothing.

So Sender looked elsewhere for like-minded compan-
ionship. Through Chagall, he became increasingly close to
artists who, like Chagall and himself, were Jewish refugees,
such as Jules Pascin and Moïse Kisling, known to his friends
as Kiki. These three artists – Chagall, Pascin and Kisling –
were part of the École de Paris, a term coined by a critic
to refer to the sudden influx of immigrant artists who had
all, for reasons very similar to Sender, washed up in Paris in
the interwar period. ('École de France', on the other hand,
referred to French-born artists, who tended to be more traditional stylistically and they somewhat resented the attention
these new avant-garde foreigners got from the art critics.)
They were all several decades older than Sender, and it's likely
that Sender, the fatherless teenager in a new strange land,
saw them as paternal figures. Chagall would refer to Sender
fondly as 'our youngest friend' and if he was ever away too
long from the cafés, because he was working so hard, one
of the artists would come looking for him, bringing a cup of
soup in case he was ill. For the first time in Sender's life, he
had friends.

By 1925, Sender had earned enough from his apprenticeships to be able to send money for Chaya and Sala to come
and join them in Paris after Reuben died. They initially lived
with him and Jakob on rue de Cléry, four people crowded
into a studio flat barely big enough for one. Like Jakob,
Chaya loved the Pletzl for its reassuring familiarity. The local
bakeries sold challah, not croissants. The Polish synagogue
was only a few yards away. Chaya had managed to move

halfway across Europe without changing her daily life a jot, and in all the years she lived in Paris she never learned a single French word. Chaya had never trusted outsiders anyway, and after her experiences in Chrzanow, she believed if the French didn't see her they wouldn't hurt her.

But while Chaya and Jakob felt similarly about the Pletzl, Sala shared Sender's feelings about Paris. After living for so long in fear in pogrom-torn Chrzanow, its beauty amazed her, and although as a sickly teenage girl she was largely stuck inside, she longed to explore the city like her older brother. Sender had never paid much attention to his sister before, but when she arrived in Paris she was a fifteen-year-old beauty who looked, Sender realised, not unlike the models in the fashion magazines he had taken to buying whenever he had spare change. She had wavy dark hair, high cheekbones and large round eyes, and her family later said they seemed to get bigger in Paris as she tried to take in everything around her. Of equal interest to Sender was the fact that she idolised him, making her his only sibling who took his dreams seriously. When Sender had a day off, and if Sala was feeling well enough, he would take her with him around the city, and the two Polish teenagers walked together down the Grands Boulevards, staring through the big windows of the fashion salons, looking at the elegant French ladies choosing fabrics while the couturiers bowed and flattered them. Decades later Sala would describe those walks to her family, still audibly thrilling at the memory of seeing such elegance, and being with her brother.

Sender also took her to the museums and introduced her to art, which she had never seen before in her life. Sometimes he would also take some of his Ornstein cousins, in particular his favourites Josek and Alex, one tough like him and the other sweet-tempered and easy-going. (All his life, Sender was drawn to two types of men: either tough competitive men like himself and Josek, or calm and gentle ones like Jehuda, Jakob and Alex Ornstein.) He showed them his favourite designers and artworks, because the parts of Sender's character that he felt he had to suppress to get ahead in the world he expressed through art and fashion. He told his sister that he loved the Impressionists because 'of their femininity'. When they went to the Musée du Luxembourg together Sender would stand for hours in front of a Monet painting.

'This fills my soul with delight,' he told her.

Sala's soul was also delighted by Paris, with all its beauty, art and fashion. Her weak lungs, however, suffered wretchedly in the dirty Pletzl. Jehuda arrived in Paris later that year after a brief period in Danzig, following his studies in Prague, where he worked as an engineer to make some money, and when he heard his sister's chronic cough he took charge. For the next half-decade Sala was in and out of sanatoriums that her eldest brother found for her up in the mountains, physically recovering but mentally rotting in lonely solitude, time and life drifting away. They were isolating and disorienting, these giant white buildings up in the sky, so far from her new home and even further from her old home, too far for any of her family to come and visit her. They did, however, make her better and the doctors finally put a name to her suffering: she had pleurisy, an inflammation of the tissue layers in the lungs, and although they couldn't cure it yet, the rest and clean air began to soothe the pains in her chest she'd had so long she assumed they were simply part of the human condition. Until, one day, they lifted, and it was like clearing dirt from her eyes. Life didn't have to be obscured by pain after all.

Jehuda's feelings about Paris were much closer to Sala's and Sender's than Chaya's and Jakob's: as soon as he arrived he knew this city was home, because it didn't feel like his old home. The elegance of the people and architecture, the delicious food, even the waiters with their short vests and white aprons looked impossibly chic to him as they carried thin-stemmed glasses of wine to their patrons: it was all so different from the unrelenting drabness of Chrzanow, and he loved it all.

Jehuda was known in his family as the intellectual one, but he was also deeply aesthetic. He'd always loved western culture, especially the art, and as a student in Krakow he proudly if somewhat eccentrically wore a chimney sweep's hat, as tall as a stovepipe, much to his brother Jakob's bemusement and his brother Sender's admiration. Fashion allowed this shy young man to carve out some self-expression, and it wasn't until he got to France that this expression found its shape and flow.

Initially he stayed in a tiny one-room flat near the rest of his family on a loud and busy main road. Almost as soon as he arrived, he told his siblings they should all change their Polish names to the French equivalents, just as he once urged his father to change their surname. Jehuda understood, as he had known in Chrzanow, that shucking off their heavy Yiddish and Polish labels would only ease his and his siblings' paths in life, and this was when the young people born Jehuda, Jakob, Sender and Sala Glahs became Jules, Jacques, Alex and Sara Glass. Unfortunately, Jehuda hated the westernised version of his name, 'Jules', as he thought it pretentious, a quality he abhorred above all. So he found what felt like a legitimate way around this rule of his own making by adopting the French version of his middle name, Henoch. He could be who he wanted, but within certain self-imposed parameters, and so he became Henri. It sounded respectable and French to him and he liked it so much he instantly made the change official: in 1926 he received a certificate from l'Administration Supérieure Confessionnelle Israélite de la Paroisse stating 'Jehuda Henoch Glass shall hereon be known as Jules Henri Glass.'

And yet, despite the Glass siblings' eager embrace of their French names, they did not apply for naturalisation, even after the Naturalisation Act the following year in 1927. In retrospect, this seems like a baffling decision, and yet it was one many foreign Jews took. Like a lot of immigrants, the Glass family arrived in Paris with a wariness of local officials and a suspicion of registering one's presence with the state.

After all, being known as Jewish hadn't helped them much back in Poland. Of more immediate concern, applying for naturalisation involved a large amount of time-consuming paperwork and the assistance of a lawyer. To the cash-strapped Glass family, whose ability to read French was, at this point, patchy at best, this made it an impossibility. And so they opted to remain unnaturalised, relying on work permits and the goodwill of France to immigrants. There was no reason to doubt the latter would change, they believed. The French had let them in, after all.

However, being unnaturalised meant the Glasses couldn't vote, which probably didn't bother Henri much, and they had to carry identity cards, which very much did. As well as restricting immigrants to certain geographical areas, identity cards determined what professions they could pursue. Despite his degrees, Henri didn't have many career choices when he arrived in Paris, as the Ornstein cousins had warned him: Josek Ornstein was celebrated for his intellect back in Poland, but in Paris he worked as a furrier. Henri, the trained engineer, similarly learned to shrink his ambition and shelve his dreams, going into business with his brother Jacques. Neither of the two older Glass brothers were natural businessmen, let alone tailors, as was soon to become all too clear, but Henri managed to save up just enough to get his own apartment over the river, far from his family and among the native Parisians in the 7th arrondissement.

Eventually, all the Glasses found their own apartments. Alex was driven out of the apartment he'd shared for years with Jacques by his mother. Alex and Chaya, as alike in temperament as they were in looks, were utterly impossible flatmates and they fought viciously, usually about what Chaya deemed to be Alex's 'dissolute' lifestyle of staying out late and drinking alcohol.

'Get your own place if you want to live like this,' she said, according to Alex's memoir.

'This IS my place!' he snapped back. But Alex had had enough of living with his family, so he simply walked out of the Marais, bought a newspaper, looked in the property section and went to the first available apartment that he could afford, around the corner from the Gare de l'Est. He gave the landlord forged identity papers, so he wouldn't know how young he was, and because Alex didn't have enough money for a bank account, he got his more well-known employers and customers to provide references, hoping their names would dazzle the landlord. He was right. Alex was still only a teenager, and he looked at least four years younger because he was so small, but he already knew how to game the system.

Chaya moved out soon, too, to a little flat on rue des Rosiers, the central spine of the Pletzl, and Sara lived with her in between stays in the sanatoriums. Back then, rue des Rosiers was filthy and almost intolerably noisy (a terrible place, in other words, for someone to stay while recovering from pleurisy). Today it is a very chic street, partially pedestrianised so visitors can shop that little bit more easily at boutiques such as Lululemon and Annick Goutal. Few signs

Sara and Chaya in their apartment
on rue des Rosiers.

of the street's earlier Jewish life still exist – there is a Jewish
bakery at one end, although, alone on this street of high-end
shops, it feels more like a heritage tourist site than something
connected to the life of the area – fancy dress among the
fancy dresses. A more revealing remnant of the past can be
found next door at 16 rue des Rosiers: a plaque commemorating the memory of five former inhabitants, including a
twelve-year-old (Rosette Lewkowicz), a two-year-old (Viktor

Wajncwaig) and a one-month-old (Paulette Wajncwaig) who were killed in the Holocaust '*par les Nazis, parce que nés juifs. Avec la complicité active du gouvernement de Vichy*' (by the Nazis, because they were born Jewish. With the active complicity of the Vichy government).

The Glass brothers could now focus on building their lives in Paris. For Alex, this meant becoming a couturier. He lived on his own but managed to save up enough money so that after finishing his apprenticeships, instead of working for a designer as most other aspiring young couturiers did, he decided to achieve his dream: at the age of only twenty, he opened his first couture salon. He called it Alex Maguy instead of Alex Glass, and he gave varying reasons for this over the years. In his memoir he says Maguy 'sounded more Parisian'; he once told my father, Ronald, it was to make him sound like a typical Frenchman. He also claimed it was in honour of a friend's wife, who was called Marguerite. And maybe those reasons are true. But perhaps Alex was also making a further break between his new life as a Parisian couturier and his old life as a Polish peasant, and by taking an entirely new surname he was putting a definitive division between his new, independent life and the emotionally enmeshed one he had with his family. Henri was not the only sibling to understand that changing one's name was an effective way to break from the past.

Alex's salon was small and basic, a two-room former office space, a far cry from the plush silk-strewn luxury he and Sara had seen through the windows of Lanvin and

Patou. But the details were irrelevant because he had done it: he had his own couture company, at 29 rue d'Argenteuil, near the Palais-Royal and just around the corner from the great couturiers. He had never even been allowed in any of their showrooms, having been relegated to the back rooms with the other trainees and workers, but now he had one of his own. It was, by any measure, an incredible achievement, especially for a designer who was hardly more than a teenager. Few rushed faster to achieve their dreams than Alex: 'I had never been in a salon de couture and had no idea what they were like, but that was of no importance. I wanted to be Number One. The best,' he writes. In the encyclopaedic catalogue, *Paris Couture Années Trente*, the entry about Alex (who appears just before Mainbocher) begins: 'This house of couture was run by an extremely young man.' But the catalogue underestimates Alex in saying that his first show was in 1937. In fact, it was eleven years earlier as Alex sent out invites as soon as he moved into his salon, summoning potential clients and the press to see the first collection of 'the Napoleon of couture'. Of all the things Alex lacked at various points in his life – food, stability, support – self-belief was never one of them.

The only person who was more proud of Alex than Alex himself was his sister. Almost eighty years after Alex opened his house, I found among my grandmother's belongings several photocopies of the pages about Alex in the 1956 book, *The Dressmakers of France*, by Mary Brooks Picken and Dora Loues Miller. Alex had clearly sent the photocopies to my grandmother, even signing them proudly and grandly on the back, and she kept them for the rest of her life. It's easy to see why the entry about Alex appealed to them both, because it gives a real, and merited, sense of just how extraordinary Alex's achievement was:

> He started his house in 1926. And it was *his* house
> – he had no partners, no financial backers. *He* was
> his house. And that was rare, for the combination
> of designer and businessman is a difficult role to
> maintain successfully over a period of years. His
> passion had always been painting – and in his studio
> the walls were covered with truly unusual paintings.
> An intimate of the great Kisling, he was also a
> friend of most of the living artists of his day who
> were considered significant. Perhaps that association
> explains his continued inspiration for creation.
> Where he obtained or inherited his business ability
> is unexplained. Perhaps that came from his sympathy
> and understanding of many types of people –
> businessmen as well as artists.

Alex had grown up in a world as disconnected from couture as it was from space exploration, and given how bad his father – and brothers – were at business, Picken and Miller's comment about his business ability being 'unexplained' is quite an understatement. But Alex taught himself to be good at business, because he knew he needed to be so to succeed.

Beauty was an ideal but Alex had learned from his father's struggles that one cannot eat ideals. Fashion, it seemed to him, was a way of living in a world of beauty but also making money from it – an aesthetic practice but also a commercial one.

As well as being inspired by the paintings in his studio, which were mostly by his new friends, he got inspiration from the city where he lived, taking in all the Parisian elegance he saw around him, digesting it, and recreating it through clothes. He took the long dresses worn by the high-society women he saw in Renoir's paintings and subtly modernised them, getting rid of the corsets, raising the hems and cropping the sleeves. For his first show he riffed on the outfits worn by the jockeys at Longchamp, that most Parisian scene of high society; everything, for him, was about paying homage to the beauty of Paris and trying to add to it. The critics loved it: the journalist from *L'Officiel*, the upmarket French fashion magazine that is still popular today, described him as 'so talented' but worried that he would become disheartened with how hard the business was.

They were right to worry: not a single one of his outfits from his first collection sold. Although Alex had chosen the more ostensibly glamorous profession when he opted to be a couturier near Place Vendôme over working as a tailor in the Pletzl, he had actually picked the much more difficult job. As a tailor, he would likely have been working for a contractor, who would have been in charge of selling the clothes to department stores or smaller shops around Paris.[14] This was how Jacques worked, and it saved him from having to deal with retail issues, which he could never have done. As a couturier, and a young and unestablished one, Alex had to deal with everything: the designs, the sewing, the marketing, the customers and the production. As one historian later put it: 'Running a fashion salon [in Paris in the 1930s] took the skill of a military general; securing the assurance of a faithful following demanded the diplomacy of a minister of state.'[15]

But Alex had one thing in his favour: he never, ever admitted defeat. After he failed to sell any outfits from his first collection, he shed 'one tear of frustration' and then promptly gathered up his designs and sold them to the more established houses around the corner. Each of the houses asked if they were exclusive – in other words, no other house would have these patterns – and Alex unhesitatingly said yes, even while he had the money for selling the same designs to different couturiers in his back pocket. According to Alex's memoir, the ruse was quickly discovered by Nina Ricci, then working at the design house Raffin, and she summoned the young designer to explain himself. Anyone else would have run away in fear, or at least crawled in to the meeting cringing with contrition, but Alex was defiant.

'Alex, it was not nice of you to sell this design to other houses,' the fearsome, white-haired designer said to him.

'Please forgive me, but I am just starting out, what did you expect?' he snapped back.

Fortunately, Madame Ricci already liked Alex, having met him when he did an apprenticeship at Raffin, and she asked him why he wanted to be a designer, when it was such a hard career.

'Because I burn with new ideas – young ideas, which you don't see in couture,' he replied. 'I want to give a woman the most natural beauty possible, rid her of the straitjacket of corsets, to make her supple. I want to invent a new elegance in harmony with the modern world, dressing a woman as lightly as possible. I dream of Paris, and the legendary elegance of its women. I would be proud to make a contribution to couture!'

When he finally paused for breath Madame Ricci offered him a job at Raffin, but Alex refused. He was betting, against every possible odd, that he could make it on his own.

Henri and Jacques thought they were playing it safer than their younger brother by staying in the Pletzl, slogging it out in the garment trade. In the early 1930s, they were also running a wood-carving shop, although 'running' was something of an overstatement. By the spring of 1931 both their businesses were bankrupt and people were chasing them for debts. But while Jacques merely shrugged at this development, seeing it as yet another hurdle in a life from which he expected nothing but hurdles, Henri was completely mortified. He'd loved his father but he had not studied so hard to live on the edge of bankruptcy as Reuben had done, and, unlike Jacques, he could not bear the humiliation of being dragged through the legal system. His ambitions might not have been as high as Alex's, but he had a greater sense of pride than Jacques, and he hoped for more from life than

Sara Glass.

his brother. Otherwise, what had been the point in coming to Paris at all? There was, he was sure, a better life out there for him.

By the early 1930s, all the Glasses were living in Paris. Sara had come home from the sanatoriums for good, healthy at last, living with her mother on rue des Rosiers and starting to think about what she wanted from life. Henri was also figuring out what he wanted to do and, like Sara, was in a city so beautiful he hardly believed he could call it home. Alex was working as a couturier, just as he'd dreamed he would, and

Jacques was – occasional court appearance aside – working steadily as a furrier in the Pletzl, just down the road from his mother, which was as much as he'd ever asked of life. They were all, in their different ways, content, planning for what they imagined would be an uninterrupted future in France, working, living and maybe one day loving as they wished, and always within comfortable walking distance from one another. They had escaped what they thought were the worst of times and created lives for themselves in the most beautiful city in the world. Their story of immigration was, at this moment in time, successful. But in just a handful of years, everything that they had worked so hard to achieve would be taken away from them again by the same beast they had tried so desperately to escape.

Young Henri.

3

HENRI – Assimilation

Paris, 1930s

JUST AS LIFE was becoming good for the Glass family personally, it was getting extremely bad for Jews in Europe generally. By the early 1930s, the Great Depression crisis bit into France, travelling eastwards from the United States, while at the same time eastern European Jewish refugees were running westwards towards France for safety. This confluence of international disasters resulted in a resurgence of the French anti-Semitism that had been dammed back after the First World War, and the immigrants who were once so welcomed for filling the gaps in the workplace were now attacked for stealing French jobs. The Metz Chamber of Commerce declared: 'These foreign competitors, highly undesirable, have become a veritable plague for honest French merchants.' In 1931 the president of the French Medical Association complained about 'this legion of Jews' coming into the medical profession.[1]

Politicians and commentators pushed three lines of attack against the immigrant Jews in France: that they were taking jobs from the French, that they were Bolshevik revolutionaries determined to destroy France, and that they were diseased criminals. François Coty, the perfume magnate who owned two newspapers, *L'Ami du Peuple* and *Le Figaro*, was so horrified by the growing numbers of German Jewish refugees arriving in the city after Hitler's election that he suggested they were a German plot to destroy France from within, and his papers relentlessly pushed this theory.[2] In 1934 Gaetan Sanvoisin wrote in *Le Figaro*: 'Hitler has sent us some 50,000 German Jews who are, for the most part, extremely dangerous revolutionaries.'

Any immigrant Jew who arrived in Paris expecting to find some kind of kinship with the French Jews was disappointed. The two groups were miles apart from one another, mentally and physically. Unlike the immigrants, who were largely workers, the native Jews were more bourgeois and they certainly didn't live in the Pletzl. They lived in the posher parts of the city and worked in liberal professions, such as banking, medicine and law.[3] They spoke French, not Yiddish, many did not bother celebrating the Sabbath, and they looked at these immigrants as potential threats to their hard-fought efforts to be part of the French bourgeoisie.[4] In other words, they were assimilated, and to the eastern European immigrant arrivals the French Jews seemed to be even more foreign than the French Catholics; differences with those you expect to be on your side are always more shocking than those you know to be your opposite. To the French Jews, the immigrants were embarrassingly backward, and their reluctance to relinquish their old traditions was baffling. Hadn't they learned from the past that they needed to blend in? They knew these new arrivals would only exacerbate the anti-Jewish feelings in the city, and make life worse for them.[5] To differentiate themselves from these coarse newcomers, who were rapidly making up more than half of the city's Jewish population and thus becoming a highly visible representation of Judaism to the French, many native Jews pointedly defined themselves in opposition to them. They described themselves as French first, and they complained that the new arrivals were too dirty, too noisy, too loud with their Yiddish – too obviously Jewish, in short.[6]

How much of one's ancestral identity must one give up to live in the modern world? How much do the actions of one part of a group reflect on the whole? And is a refusal to blend in a show of strength or self-defeating rigidity? And must the choice always be between assimilation and self-ghettoisation? Could there not be an option of inclusion, which allows for acceptance of a minority group's differences without this being seen as a threat to the majority? Natives and immigrants, Jewish and otherwise, have argued these questions for centuries, with each other and with themselves, and they will do so for centuries more. In the case of the native and immigrant Parisian Jews, the debate was irresolvable, not least because the two groups largely stayed away from one another. The French Jews didn't want to be associated with the immigrants, and the immigrants reacted to that rejection in what would soon turn out to be the worst way possible: they remained separate from French life.[7] During the 1920s and 1930s immigrant Jews formed their own little communities in Paris, creating pockets of mini-Polands, -Russias and -Lithuanias, in the Pletzl and around Bastille and Belleville. Although this gave them a sense of community in their new country, its advantages were to prove brutally short term. Because the ghettos kept them separate from the rest of the city, the immigrants remained unknown, strange, not French and thus, later, easy to sacrifice.[8] But in a similar vein to what the Chrzanow Jews thought of the Poles and later the Germans, so the immigrant Jews in Paris believed of France: surely their neighbours would protect them. And again, like the Chrzanow Jews, they were to be proven wrong.

Chaya especially and Jacques largely typified the behaviour of immigrant Jews: they remained unassimilated and stayed among Polish Jewish immigrants. Henri, Alex and Sara, by contrast, were more on the side of the French Jews. To them, Poland was a backward pit of hate and ignorance. Next to cultured, beautiful Paris, where people weren't beating them up in the street, there was no question in their minds with which country they wanted to identify.

Alex and Sara had been happy to slough off their Polish identities as soon as they arrived in Paris. They were born in 1906 and 1910 respectively and so largely associated Chrzanow with the war and pogroms. But Jacques and Henri had lived there longer, and for that reason Jacques struggled more to shrug off his past entirely: he considered himself French but he remained rooted in the world of other immigrants, rarely mixing with native French people.

Henri, however, made a seamless chameleonic break. Strikingly tall – at least six foot two – and handsome, with a broad forehead and dark deep-set eyes, Henri set out to become a proper Frenchman. He learned the language quickly and while Alex proudly kept his Yiddish accent all his life, Henri soon sounded entirely French. His reasons were more personal than political: Poland to him represented his father's death, and his years away studying had taken him further, geographically and mentally, from the shtetl world. For Henri, Poland was the past, France was the future, and that meant assimilating.

Jewish assimilation had a complicated history long before Jehuda Glahs became Jules Henri Glass. Chanukah, now one of the best-known Jewish holidays, is a celebration of Jews who refused to assimilate, as it's a festival in memory of a small group of Jews who in 167 BC disobeyed their Greek-Syrian oppressors by not worshipping their gods. And yet the only reason Chanukah – always a minor holiday on the Jewish calendar – is so well-known now is because of its proximity to Christmas. As a result, Chanukah has turned into a quasi-Jewish Christmas and so, with an apt kind of Jewish irony, Chanukah itself has become assimilated.

And yet, especially after the Haskalah, the Jewish enlightenment in the late eighteenth and early nineteenth centuries, many Jews saw assimilation as a positive, progressive step;

being part of the modern world instead of hiding from it behind shtetl walls, disguised within thick black clothes. Assimilation meant, as it did to Henri, having more options than one's parents did. But others felt the cost of assimilation both too high and impossible. Jews would always be seen as the vilified outsiders.

Some of the most influential thinking about Jewish assimilation was inspired by events in Paris shortly before the Glass family moved there. After witnessing the Dreyfus scandal, Theodor Herzl, the Jewish journalist and political activist, rejected his earlier writings urging Jewish assimilation. Instead, he became the father of modern Zionism, telling Jews they would never be safe no matter how much they assimilated, so they should stay true to their identity and establish a Jewish homeland. Assimilated Jews loathed this theory, as they saw it as undermining all their efforts to become a part of their country's civic life. And yet these efforts were, in the eyes of others, pointless: many non-Jews then believed that Jews could never be truly assimilated into a western country, and the question of how much they could be, or whether they could be at all, was known as the Jewish Question. So Herzl's turnaround was, in the context of his time, pretty understandable.

Assimilated Jews could argue that Zionism was ultimately analogous to what German writers such as Theodor Fritsch, author of *The Handbook of the Jewish Question*, suggested when he argued that Jews should be kept separate, even banished, so as not to contaminate the Aryan race. This partly explains why some of the earliest and most enthusiastic supporters of Zionism were not Jews, but rather evangelical Christians and anti-Semites, and there was and is some but by no means a complete overlap between the two groups. Evangelicals believe that Jews returning to their homeland will hasten the return of the Messiah. Alongside this, Zionism still has enormous popularity among anti-Semites who are a lot less concerned with providing the Jews with a homeland than they are with simply segregating them.[9] Herzl saw where matters were heading for Jews in Europe long before others did.

France might have been known as *une terre d'asile* but the French most definitely did not see themselves as a nation of immigrants. Immigrants were expected to assimilate and those who kept themselves separate and retained their original identity were regarded as suspicious. Antipathy to what critics would call the self-ghettoisation of immigrants and what defenders would call immigrants' distinctive identity was prevalent on both the left and the right in France,[10] and this attitude was hardly unique to France or the early twentieth century. In pretty much every western country today there is a belief that people who come to a new country should assimilate, almost as a show of gratitude, or at the very least politeness. Today this is mainly – but not solely – voiced by the right and is aimed largely at black and Muslim immigrants rather than Jewish ones.

France had a particular interest in cultural assimilation because of the country's principle of *laïcité*, roughly translated as secularism. *Laïcité* was instituted in 1905 with the separation of Church and state, meaning that state funding was withdrawn from religions in order to place all faiths on an equal footing and protect schools in particular from the Catholic church. Whereas in America today the separation of Church and state means the state cannot interfere in religion, in France it means all signs of religion are banned in the public sphere, because Republic takes precedence over religion, or as the 1905 law puts it, 'the Republic neither recognises nor employs nor subsidises cults', but it guarantees the freedom of these 'cults', as long as they do not upset the public order. *Laïcité* remains a cherished principle in France today, even if it does cause occasional controversy, such as whether it encourages assimilation or further self-ghettoisation from those who do not wish to give up, say, their religiously ordained head scarves and clothes. For Chaya, it provoked the latter: aware that she was not part of or welcome in French bourgeois society as she was, she stayed firmly in the Pletzl. Henri, Alex and Sara, who had the active desire to assimilate, did otherwise.

Despite what right-wing politicians today suggest, assimilation is neither simple nor the answer. There exists, allegedly, a magical sweet spot where immigrants are assimilated enough so as not to offend natives with their jarringly exotic customs, but not so assimilated that they are stealing natives' jobs and diluting the culture of the country. Immigrants are blamed by the media and politicians for not locating this spot themselves, but no one else has ever been able to define its whereabouts either, primarily because its location shifts depending on a country's economic situation.

By the 1930s, growing numbers of French people came to see dangers in the idea of Jews assimilating, mixing among them unrecognised. After the relaxation of naturalisation laws in 1927, right-wing newspapers and politicians spoke doomfully about immigrants taking jobs as well as Jews corrupting French society with their Bolshevik ideas and infecting the people with their strange foreign germs. When it came to assimilation, Jews couldn't win: mix into the culture and they were condemned; stay separate and they were damned. The Jewish Question was becoming a seemingly irresolvable puzzle and it would not be long before someone offered up the Final Solution.

Today, Jewish assimilation remains controversial, and while you still hear anti-Semites warning against it, some of the most striking critics are ultra-Orthodox Jews, who use the same arguments as those advanced by the rabbinical traditionalists of the nineteenth century. (And their fidelity to those arguments is, in their eyes, the point.) According to a study carried out by the Rabbinical Centre of Europe in 2014, as many as 85 per cent of Jews in Europe are assimilated, leading one member of the Israeli Chief Rabbinate Council to lament: 'The assimilation in the shocking numbers that we see is worse than the Holocaust we saw.'[11]

You don't need to be assimilated, or Jewish, to find this statement repulsive. But it is true that recognisably observant Jewish people and communities are far less commonly seen in Europe today than they were at the beginning of the twentieth century. That's not just because the Holocaust killed off so many of them[12] and many of the survivors went elsewhere (Israel, mainly), although both of those factors are certainly part of it – it's because the successive generations have assimilated. Contrary to what Herzl and many others thought, Jewish assimilation has proven to be more than possible – it has become inevitable. As society has become increasingly secular, and Jews have made secure lives for themselves in western countries, often intermarrying with other faiths, the story of Jewish identity in the late twentieth century became a story of assimilation. Whether Jews are truly accepted depends on which Jew you ask, and how many times they've been accused on social media that day of being part of a Zionist conspiracy. But in terms of Jews living, working and socialising with non-Jews, this has become such a non-issue it's almost hard to believe there was a time when it was otherwise, although that time is still very much in living memory: my grandparents would have been horrified if my father had married a non-Jewish woman, while my parents could not have cared less about the religion of my sister's and my chosen partners. Jews have become more assimilated with each successive generation, and this is certainly borne out by my family. And for us, the path that led us here began with Henri.

All the Glass siblings were style-conscious, thanks to Reuben's influence, but Henri approached fashion the most methodically, because it was part of his process of becoming

French. He studied how his neighbours looked and he copied them, buying three-piece suits when he could find them second-hand; double-breasted wool coats with velvet collars; starchy white shirts and silk ties, and always a hat. Henri's style was yet another thing Alex admired about his brother, and whenever he could find the material, he made pocket handkerchiefs for him, which Henri would carefully iron and then fold neatly to stick out of his breast pocket. In everything, from his studies to his appearance, he was utterly meticulous.

He was also a very private person, so when I started to research him I originally worried he might be the lacuna in the book, as he never talked about himself.

'Did your father leave anything that might tell me about the past – an address book, perhaps, or even old calendars?' I asked his daughter, Danièle, the first time I interviewed her for this book in her flat in Paris.

'Oh yes, a couple of things. Come down to the basement, I'll show you,' she said mildly.

I followed her down the stairs, expecting, at most, some old birthday cards, perhaps a business card or two. She unlocked the door to her building's storage unit and there were four suitcases, each containing every receipt Henri ever got, every business transaction he conducted, every letter he received and every photo he ever took, all perfectly filed in perfect French. Henri's careful bookkeeping was a reflection of his naturally precise nature but also of his lifelong fear that the authorities would one day call him to account, because he wasn't truly French. As a result I probably now know more about the minutiae of his business affairs than I do about my own.

For Henri, there was one big hurdle to his assimilation into French society: his failing businesses with Jacques. By 1931 the letters from lawyers were threatening the brothers with jail, each one another kick at his dreams. A man who has the bailiffs chasing him couldn't be a respectable Frenchman, after all. At last, one spring day, the worst letter arrived, telling him to meet the lawyer's assistant in Gare Saint-Lazare, in la Salle des Pas Perdus – the Room of Lost Steps, the poetic French name for the hallway or waiting area in railway stations or courthouses – and she would serve him with bankruptcy papers. He dressed wearily that morning, putting on his three-piece suit, fully expecting this to be the end of his brief Parisian life. Instead, it marked the true beginning of it.

Sophie Huttner, also known as Sonia, was born in 1905 in Kopyczynce, a small city 500 kilometres to the east of Chrzanow, in what is now the Ukraine. Born into a middle-class Jewish family and exceptionally bright from a young age, she moved to Paris in 1928 to study at the Sorbonne,[13] but she really came to experience life, and she certainly succeeded in that. At the time she arranged to serve this tall, quiet man with bankruptcy papers, she'd had at least two boyfriends, a Prussian prince and a man from Barcelona, and she later hinted there had been more; Sonia had always been popular with men, and it was not hard to see why. Although

Henri and Sonia shortly after they
met in Paris, 1930s.

not beautiful the way Sara was – Sonia's features were earthier and less delicate – she was sexy, smart, funny and flirtatious, and she knew how to tip her head down and then look up at a man through her lashes with an irresistible little smile. As soon as Henri saw her, waiting for him in the Room of Lost Steps, he fell hopelessly in love.

Although both were Jewish and raised in Austria-Hungary, their backgrounds were utterly different. Henri's father had been a travelling salesman, whereas Sonia's father was a government official. Henri had to learn French when he arrived in Paris but Sonia had grown up speaking it, because her nanny had been a dispossessed French aristocrat. Sonia didn't even really have to work, and she lived comfortably on her family's money for her first few years in France. But she was too smart to sit around, and she had enough drive to power the whole of Paris. She was fluent in half a dozen languages: French, Polish, German, Spanish, English, Portuguese, and she could easily switch between them in conversation. So she worked as an interpreter at several companies and as a secretary at others, and it just so happened that she was working as a secretary in a lawyer's office when she was sent to serve papers at Gare Saint-Lazare.

Henri was thirty-one when he met Sonia, but I could find no record of any other girlfriends in his past – no names mentioned among his letters, no teasing references by Sonia during their long lifetime together. It is entirely possible she was his first girlfriend, and he was certainly besotted by her. Henri was a keen photographer and while he took, at

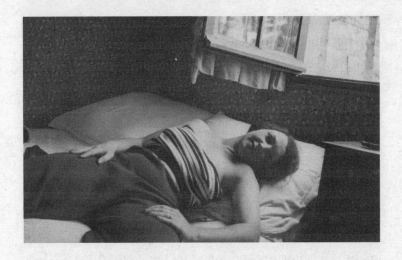

most, a few dozen photos of his family, he took hundreds of photos of Sonia during their courtship: here's Sonia looking up coquettishly on a bridge; here's Sonia in a beret, tight pencil skirt and sexy halter-neck top, plucking a leaf from a bush. Henri loved to photograph her, and Sonia loved to be photographed, posing with the ease of one who never lacked confidence about her looks. In one photo, taken in someone's room, Sonia poses by a bed in a pair of high-waisted trousers and jacket. In the second picture, she has taken off the jacket to reveal a skimpy vest top, and she is now sitting on the bed. In the last, she has rolled the straps of her vest off her shoulder and she is lying on the bed and spreading her legs, looking into the camera with a sexuality so frank it is unnerving. I found these photos among Sonia's possessions, twenty years after she died, and I let out a yelp when I got to the last one; you don't expect to find eighty-year-old evidence of your great-uncle and great-aunt's love life on an average Tuesday afternoon.

And apparently it was a very happy love life: Henri and Sonia got married on Christmas Day 1932, in Lwow, not far from where Sonia grew up, so her family could attend. Adolf Hitler would become chancellor of Germany just a few weeks later, but among the dozens of cards and letters the couple received from Sonia's relatives and friends back home, many of whom would be killed in the Holocaust within a decade, there was only joy and hope for the future: 'May you have a long and happy wedded life! Love, the Liebermans'; 'Wishing joy and long life, the Zygfryd Reizs'; 'God bless the newlyweds and their families on this happy day, the Koenigow Mlyniecs.' And in one of Sonia's scrapbooks I found a telegram from her new sister-in-law in France, dated 25/12/1932: '*Bonheur bonheur bonheur de tout coeur – Sara.*'

Henri didn't have as much money as the Prussian prince, and maybe wasn't as exciting as the man from Barcelona. But Sonia chose him because, as she explained to their daughter decades later, 'I saw he was a good son and brother.'

Which was not to say that she was wild about his family. Chaya she quickly got the measure of when Henri took her to his mother's flat on rue des Rosiers and she saw how much Henri longed to get some kind of independence from her. So she fashioned herself between them, stepping in whenever Chaya asked Henri to accompany her to synagogue or to do her shopping at the local kosher markets. Jacques, Sonia thought, was sweet, the sweetest of them all, only lacking in

Sonia and Sara.

backbone. Sara bemused her with her love of fashion. But Sara told her how happy she was to have a *real* sister – she'd had Mindel, but Mindel had died so long ago, and she had Rose Ornstein, but Rose was really her cousin. Sonia was her sister! She'd desperately wanted a sister, and Sonia, touched, told her she felt the same.

Alex was a different story: Sonia and Alex loathed one another from the moment they met. Alex couldn't believe that his idolised older brother – so tall and so handsome! – who, to his mind, could have had his pick of any French-woman in Paris would choose this short, dumpy Polack. Henri had been a father figure to Alex for pretty much all of his life, ever since Reuben went off to war, and he reacted to Sonia's arrival like a petulant child to a new stepmother. He thought she was ugly, fat and unworthy of his brother. And Sonia, who sized up Alex about as quickly as she did Chaya, saw in Alex an arrogant bully. Neither of them ever found cause to alter their first impression.

But family aside, Henri and Sonia were blissfully content newlyweds. Sonia had a much easier relationship with her past than Henri, because her childhood had been much happier. There were no tortured issues about identity, assimilation or non-assimilation for Sonia: she had grown up multilingual, so flitting between nationalities felt utterly natural to her, and her language skills were so good she was often mistaken for a native of multiple countries. And yet, even though Sonia spoke Polish and Yiddish, they almost always spoke to one another in French.

Henri, Sonia, Sara, Chaya and Jacques in Henri and
Sonia's apartment shortly after their marriage.

Soon after they were settled in their new apartment, on
rue Victor-Cousin, just next to the Sorbonne, they held a
housewarming supper for the Glasses, to compensate for the
fact that none of them could travel to Lwow for the wedding.
Henri took a photo of the evening to commemorate it, and
I found the picture, eighty years later, in a small envelope
on which he had written '*famille*'. Henri is the first one you
notice in the photo, because he is the only one standing.
In fact, he appears to be in mid-leap, as he has presumably
dashed into the photo frame after having set up the camera.
But even in his haste, his three-piece suit sits perfectly on him
and every hair is perfectly in place. The only difference about
him in this photo compared to previous ones is how happy

he clearly is: he is making an unabashed open-mouthed smile and both hands are resting gently on Sonia, who is sitting in front of him. Sonia looks a little more solemn, and with her drooping shoulders and slightly raised eyebrows she looks like she's asking the camera on the exhale, 'Can you believe I'm stuck with this lot now?' By contrast, Sara next to her looks absolutely delighted. She is twenty-two and a striking beauty; her confident pose, with her chin resting coquettishly on the backs of her fingers, makes her, for once, overshadow her usually more dominating sister-in-law. Chaya is seated next to her, a little in the shadows and, as usual, her eyes are going in two different directions, one looking suspiciously at the viewer, the other at Sonia. And finally there is Jacques, not quite as smartly dressed as Henri, but still stylish and very handsome, with the same finely drawn features as Sara. He is holding a French newspaper, whose front page bears a picture of Marshal Pétain, who had just been made Minister of War, and would in six years' time become the chief of state of Vichy France. He would have more to do with the direction of Jacques's life than Jacques could ever have imagined as he dangled the newspaper between his long thin fingers. Whereas everyone else in the photo is looking at the camera, Jacques is gazing off to the side, as if he was about to head in a different direction to the rest of them. Alex is not in the photo. Presumably he declined Henri's invitation.

'My father was brilliant, but he never had any success before he met my mother,' Henri and Sonia's daughter Danièle told me. And she was right. One of the first moves

Sonia made when she and Henri got together was to help him get off the bankruptcy charge, and the second was to extricate him from his business with Jacques. Henri felt enormous guilt about leaving his brother, but, as Sonia rightly perceived, Jacques didn't actually care that much about the business, and certainly didn't hold it against his brother for leaving it. At last, Henri was free of the work that had caused him so much anxiety, and brought him so little satisfaction. He could simply enjoy his happy marriage with Sonia. But he now had another concern: it was 1935, he was thirty-four, and worried.

'My time is running out,' Sonia later recalled him saying.

But fate already had a plan for him, one more befitting to his education than running a fur and carpentry shop. Henri, or quite possibly Sonia, had recently met a man who worked at the Sorbonne Science Faculty. He said that he needed a machine that could reproduce documents quickly and cheaply, and yet no such machine existed in the whole of France. Did anyone know a man who might be able to help, perhaps one with engineering and photography experience?

Henri had finished his engineering studies a decade earlier, but he had forgotten none of it. Sonia obtained a false identity card for him on the black market so, at long last, he could get a job that utilised his education, and he went to work in the Sorbonne, like the proper Frenchman he longed to be. He could finally leave the Pletzl behind and use the skills he'd studied so hard to acquire at university. And Henri wasn't just a good engineer, he was a truly original one.

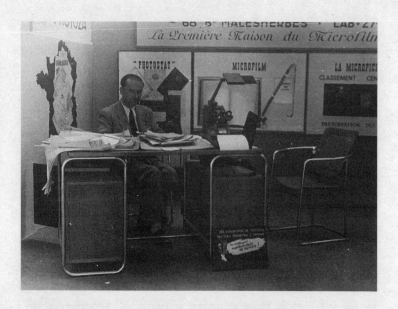

According to his American patent application, which was accepted on 12 February 1940, he made a machine 'whereby reproductions may be made on the same scale as the original or on different scales . . . The prints may be made on glass, negatives, films or sensitized papers.' In other words, he made a machine that reproduced not just documents but blueprints on microfilm and paper, and these reproductions could be to scale or – crucially – shrunk to much smaller size, making them both easy to store and illegible to anyone until Henri's machine then reproduced them again at full size. This was to become the machine's most important feature, and Henri was using technology that was then at the absolute cutting edge. No other machine in France could do this. Henri named his machine the Omniphot.

In less than a year, he sold versions of it to the Paris Observatory, the Army Geographic Service (now known as the Institut Géographique National) and the Paris Municipal School of Physics and Chemistry. Henri was so successful that in 1937 – just two years after despairing of the direction of his life to Sonia – he showed his Omniphot machine at the Paris fair, where it was spotted by a businessman called Marc Haenel. Monsieur Haenel instantly spotted the potential of Henri's invention and convinced him to go into business with him to create their own company, Photosia, where they would do specialist microfilming. Henri agreed. This was to prove an extremely fortuitous meeting, and just in time, too: Henri's machine would soon be desperately needed by the Resistance movement, and his adopted country turned out to need him at least as much as he needed it.

GLASS'
Prisonnier CAMBRAI
1940

4

JACQUES – Passivity

Paris, 1930s

JACQUES GLASS was born under a bad star. That's what his siblings always said about him, and they would say it fondly, because they really did love him but, my God, he did have a way of falling into bad luck. When he skipped school in Chrzanow, he, alone among his brother and cousins, was the one who was caught by the schoolmaster. Out of all the immigrants in the Marais who worked in somewhat grey areas of legality, it was Jacques who was repeatedly summoned to the courts to pay various fines. A year after Sonia got him and Henri off the bankruptcy charge, he was summoned to court again for, according to his court record, 'employing a woman worker outside the legal hours', for which he was fined 62 francs and 70 centimes in costs (roughly 60 euros today), plus a 5-franc fine, a sizable punishment for a poor immigrant. And yet no one was surprised this happened to Jacques. If there was a hole, Jacques's friends said, he would fall into it.

And he had many friends. Of all the Glass siblings, Jacques was the easiest to get along with. Henri was too shy, Alex so combative and Sara often away due to poor health. But Jacques was easy-going, always with a ready smile, so everyone liked him. Like his father, he was happiest sitting in cafés with his friends. By the mid-1930s he had – just about – his fur shop, and that was more than enough for him. Sonia occasionally bustled across the river to see Chaya, or maybe just to check on Jacques, and when she passed his shop it was, invariably, shut. She would then find him around the corner, wasting away the afternoon in a café with friends, and she would upbraid him, astonished at this unabashed show of laziness. If Sonia had ever spoken like that to Alex he would have punched her, but Jacques just smiled and nodded at her, and then moved not an inch. Nothing bothered him, and he was perfectly fine where he was. And as much as he frustrated Sonia, she also liked him enormously – it was impossible not to, really. When she talked about him, even when she was well into her eighties, she would describe him to her daughter as 'the best of all the family'. 'Jacques', Sonia would also later recall, 'was wonderful. But too passive.'

The idea of Jewish passivity is controversial, and for good reason. The stereotype of the meek Jew in the 1940s who went like a lamb to the slaughter has, for a long time, been used by the culpable to excuse their part in the Holocaust. When Israel objected to the 2018 Polish law criminalising any suggestion that Poland should be blamed for crimes committed during the Holocaust, Andrzej Zybertowicz, adviser to the Polish President, replied that Israel merely felt 'shame at the passivity of the Jews during the Holocaust'.[1] It has also been used in a more sympathetic manner by those who mean to show compassion to the Jews but actually end up fetishising their suffering. Julie Burchill certainly does this in her very weird philo-Semitic book *The Unchosen*, and Steven Spielberg has been accused of doing similarly in *Schindler's List* – unfairly, I think.[2] And for some Jews, too, the stereotype of Jewish passivity has fed into their feelings of self-loathing or, at the very least, self-ambivalence: my father's friend and one of the heroes of Operation Entebbe in 1976,[3] the late Michel Cojot-Goldberg, wrote in his auto-biography, *Namesake*, about how he felt 'ashamed' of his father, who was arrested in Lyon and killed in Auschwitz, and how relieved he later was when he learned his father had, briefly, escaped from the train to the camps. This, it seemed to Michel, proved his father was not passive after all, but had shown some gumption and not obediently walked towards his own slaughter – as if any Jews, Michel's father included, had much choice, when caught between Vichy laws and German military muscle.[4]

For all these reasons, Israel has long promoted the self-empowering narrative of Jewish defiance over passivity. But not every Jew in the war was a courageous rebel any more than every Frenchman was a member of the Resistance, no matter how much Israel and France might have claimed otherwise over the years. If for too long the stories of Jew-ish strength were overlooked, it would be equally untrue to overcorrect that mistake by denying the stories of passivity. There was no single narrative for Jews in the run-up to and during the Holocaust. Jacques, like his father, had been a passive soul since he was a child, always happy with the easiest option. And it was this passivity that led to his greatest misfortunes.

Jacques's first major misfortune looked to him like his greatest good fortune. Even more misleadingly, it came from his mother, the person to whom he was most devoted. By 1936, Jacques was thirty-four and still single, and as much as Chaya enjoyed being able to call on Jacques whenever she needed him, she also wanted him to get married, and that was because she wanted him to marry a particular woman.

Mindel Rotter, known as Mila, was the oldest daughter of Samuel Rotter, Chaya's older brother, and she lived in Zakopane, a Polish town about 100 kilometres to the south of Chrzanow. Chaya saw no reason why a cross-continental move should change anything about her children's lives, and she decreed that Jacques should marry Mila, just as she had planned for him when they all lived in Poland.

Henri sighed. That Jacques should marry his cousin from home was bad enough, given how many possibilities for new futures there were in Paris, but that it should be Mila was the real kicker. Why not Mila's sister Olga? Henri asked his mother. Olga was so pretty and smart and dynamic – quite similar to Sonia, in fact, which might explain Henri's fondness for her. Whereas Mila was, well . . .

Alex was more vocal in his feelings about Mila and for the rest of his life described her in the most derogatory terms he could come up with, usually combining references to her Polishness with farm animals. He undoubtedly shared those observations with Jacques but Jacques paid as little attention to them as he did to Alex's commands that he accompany him to museums. Jacques might have let Alex push him into skipping school when they were children, but they were adults now, and things had changed. Alex had his path, and Jacques had his, and his path was not to kowtow to his younger brother any more. Now, the person he unthinkingly obeyed was his mother, and so Mila was sent for. She arrived in Paris in 1936 and before he even talked with her Jacques knew he would marry her. Because that was what his mother told him to do.

Jacques and Mila.

Jacques and his new wife left the Pletzl and moved just across the river from the ultimate symbol of Parisian pride, the Eiffel Tower, on rue de la Tour. He had found a cramped and dark flat that had little to recommend it other than that it could just about double as a place for them to live and work, with the shop where he would restore and store furs at the front and the living quarters at the back, thus saving him some rent. But if he thought moving across the city, or marriage, would get him away from his mother, he was quickly disabused of that notion. Chaya soon moved in with Jacques and Mila at rue de la Tour.

It also turned out to be a pretty poor choice of flat. According to notes on Jacques later compiled by the Commissariat Général aux Questions Juives (CGQJ), the agency established in 1941 to carry out the Vichy government's anti-Semitic policies, the flat was 'extremely small' and 'badly located with no passing trade'. As a result, the business had 'no customers and its assets are immaterial'. Jacques had inherited not just his father's looks and passivity but also his utter inability to earn any money.

But he was happier than he'd ever been in his life. Alex was always baffled by his brothers, both so handsome (and, he repeatedly stressed, so tall, a key point for Alex who was about five foot two), and yet they chose to marry these plain eastern European women. The very few photos of Jacques from this era show a man who was undoubtedly content. In a photo in the album I found in my grandmother's closet, he is walking down a boardwalk, his hairline starting to recede but his familiar round glasses still in place. Like all the Glass siblings, Jacques loved beautiful things and in this photo he is dressed precisely in a three-piece suit, his face relaxed, and bearing a proud, happy smile, as he walks arm-in-arm with Mila, who smiles uncertainly at the camera. In another photo, taken around the same time, he is posing at what looks like a wedding with almost all the Ornstein cousins. None of the other Glasses are there, and neither is Mila, but Jacques in his round glasses stands at the back, smiling with his cousins. Within six years of that photo being taken, almost everyone in it would be dead.

Not even Jacques could stay oblivious to how difficult life was getting when he read his newspaper in the local café every day. In July 1934 a law was passed imposing a ten-year delay on naturalised foreigners taking public office or becoming lawyers. In 1935 foreigners had to wait four years to practise medicine, unless they had completed military service.

In 1936, France became the first European state to choose a Jew, the socialist Léon Blum, to be its prime minister. But any optimism Jews in France might have gleaned from this was tempered by the ominous fact that, shortly before he assumed office, Blum was nearly beaten to death by anti-Semites associated with the viciously right-wing Action Française league. Four years later he would be arrested and sent to Buchenwald, followed by Dachau and Tyrol, where he very narrowly escaped execution. When Édouard Daladier became France's Prime Minister for the third time in April 1938, just a month before the Anschluss (when Hitler succeeded in uniting Austria and Nazi Germany), he used his inaugural address to reassure French voters of his ongoing pacificity (and passivity) in the face of German aggression, promising to take harsh measures against illegal immigrants in France.[5] Fines for visa and employment infractions became more severe and it was suddenly much more difficult for foreigners to get temporary extensions on their residence permits or renew their identity cards. Laws were passed to fine and imprison illegal immigrants, to send illegal German immigrants back to Germany, to limit the voting rights of naturalised French citizens, and to monitor both foreign and naturalised individuals. Anti-Semitic newspapers in France had a huge resurgence at this point: the daily paper *Action Française* was read by 70,000 people per issue; the weekly newspaper *Gringoire*, which regularly cited Jews as the source of all France's problems, was read by 650,000 readers a week. The *Naie Press*, a Yiddish-language daily communist paper published in France, compared the life of an immigrant in 1930s France to that of a man 'bicycling in butter'.[6]

Long after the Second World War ended, and even up to the end of the twentieth century, French politicians insisted France was not to blame for its country's actions under Nazi occupation, as Vichy was an illegitimate regime that did not represent the country's values. As late as 1994 President François Mitterrand said, 'I will not apologise in the name of France. The Republic had nothing to do with this. I do not believe France is responsible.'[7] And yet, as in Poland, the anti-Semitic actions in France during the war were possible only because they reflected something deep within the country's psyche. Anti-Semitism doesn't just emerge like a passing fad, it grows from roots that were already there.

French politicians in the mid-1930s insisted all these new laws were merely for the sake of the country and the economy. Unlike most other western countries in the late 1930s, France was still suffering from the effects of the Great Depression and so politicians such as the former Prime Minister Albert Sarraut[8] could pretend that the anti-immigrant crackdown was merely a means 'to assume control over a foreign population that is becoming excessive and among whom certain elements weigh upon our general economy'. The suggestion that this was all simply about jobs and money was somewhat undermined by Sarraut's additional comment that it was necessary to go after 'immigrants of all nationalities who, by escaping all verification, successfully infiltrate and eventually constitute an unassimilable mass of often defective individuals, who possess uncertain resources and equivocal morality'.[9, 10]

After Kristallnacht in November 1938, in which a mass pogrom was carried out throughout Nazi Germany, and tens of thousands of Jews were attacked and sent to concentration camps, German and Austrian refugees fled west, even as right-wing French politicians scoffed that reports of the night had been exaggerated. 'There were no deaths,' declared Charles Maurras, organiser of the deeply anti-Semitic political movement, Action Française. (In fact, official records show ninety-one Jews were killed and modern historians suggest the number was almost certainly much higher.) 'The prestige of France is not threatened when one burns down a synagogue. One can burn them all. It's not our business and it has no impact on us whatsoever. No diplomatic intervention, no war for the Jews,' he added.[11]

Even native Parisian Jews were shocked by the French government's coldness towards the refugees, but many held their tongues to avoid risking accusations of being 'unpatriotic'.[12] Immigrants like the Glasses who had lived in France for years were in even more of a bind. They had thought of themselves as French, but their adopted country was becoming increasingly hostile towards them, and yet they had nowhere else to go. They had outrun the demons in their home country, but those demons had caught up with them. Not even the most blinkered immigrants who had lived through the Polish pogroms could fail to see the increasingly ominous signs in France as they crept ever closer to their front door. And Jacques, reading his newspaper in his café, would have been forcibly confronted with this reality every day.

So on 26 May 1940, two weeks after Hitler launched his offensive on France, Jacques joined the Foreign Legion. Almost a year earlier Alex had joined the Foreign Legion – which was the only French military service open to foreigners at this point – and, just as he did when they were children back in Chrzanow and skipping school, he nagged his older brother to join him. But Jacques probably would have done so anyway without Alex's cajoling. The Glass children still

Jacques (kneeling in front) in the Foreign Legion.

held Reuben up as their moral ideal and given that he joined the army in the First World War to fight for the Austro-Hungarian Empire, it isn't that surprising that the son who was always the most like him would do so too.

And just as Reuben had realised almost twenty-five years earlier, immigrant Jews in France knew that no matter how bad their country was now, if it lost to these enemies their lives would become much, much worse. Jacques signed up for the 23rd Régiment de Marche de Volontaires Étrangers, one of various regiments created by the French Foreign Legion to accommodate all the immigrants who wanted to fight for France, some out of loyalty towards the country, others because they saw it as a path towards naturalisation. While immigrant Jews generally accounted for 30 per cent of the soldiers in these regiments,[13] Jacques's own small unit had double that,[14] and the names are a testament to the loyalty of foreign Jews to their new country, no matter how much it legislated against them: Pinkus Rak, Moise Graf, Icek Zajdenverg. And from this unit of twenty-five men, at least five of the survivors would later be killed in concentration camps.

The 23rd Régiment de Marche de Volontaires Étrangers was a poorly equipped rag-tag troop of multiple nationalities and languages, and its life was short, brutal and eventful. After training in Le Barcarès in the Pyrénées, they were sent on 3 June 1940 to defend Soissons in the north of France, and then went to the south of Paris to try to contain the advance of German armoured divisions at Pont-sur-Yonne. From there, they were next sent back to the north to the Canal de l'Ourcq, where they managed not just to slow down the German advance but kill General Hermann Ritter von Speck, the only enemy general killed during the Battle of France. All this happened in the space of only two weeks. But the fighting had been costly, and many had been killed. The 23rd RMVE was dissolved in July 1940.

Jacques did manage to survive, but only because he was taken prisoner. When I was going through the shoebox at the back of my grandmother's closet it was the small rectangular metal plate, reading '*GLASS, Prisonnier Cambrai, 1940*' that caused me the most puzzlement: I knew Alex had fought for France, but I was pretty sure he hadn't been taken prisoner. I hadn't considered the possibility that Jacques – the mysterious great-uncle I never met – had also fought.

Cambrai, up in the north of France, was bombed by the Luftwaffe on 17 May 1940 and captured the following day. The Nazis then used it as a place to keep some of their prisoners, including Jacques, who was captured during the fighting either around Soissons or Canal de l'Ourcq. The real mystery is how he then got out, which he obviously did because he was soon back in Paris, but there is no record of prisoners being released from Cambrai. There are, however, records of them running away. A British sergeant-major, Frederick Read, was taken prisoner around this time and he describes in his memoir being held at the barracks in Cambrai in August 1940,[15] where life was monotonous and dispiriting, with the Germans bullying the prisoners with rubber truncheons and shouting orders at them. Every day they were sent out to work in the town at local flour mills, sugar factories and garages and these excursions were remarkably unsupervised. Read recounts his own failed escape attempt, which was hampered by his poor language skills. Jacques could speak French, albeit heavily accented with Yiddish, so he would have found it relatively easy to hide in the countryside. At least one other man from his regiment was captured and, according to military records, escaped, so the two might have run off together. It's hard to imagine Jacques running away from the Germans on his own, but with a friend there to encourage him and tell him what to do, the scenario becomes much more plausible. As to the metal plate – '*GLASS, Prisonnier Cambrai, 1940*' – a fellow prisoner probably made it for him as a souvenir, and perhaps Jacques then sent it to my grandmother almost as a trophy commemorating his escape. Or maybe he just wanted his sister to know where he had been, and that he was OK. Whichever it was, this would not be the last time he would send Sara mementos from prison.

Jacques was officially demobilised on 3 September 1940 and, although Paris was now under Nazi occupation, he returned to Mila on rue de la Tour, apparently never even considering that maybe they ought to go somewhere else. But why would he? Jacques was the least assimilated culturally of the Glasses, but of all of them he took his social assimilation for granted the most: he believed that because the French took him in they would therefore never hurt him.

Just three weeks after he returned home, Jacques's assumptions were looking increasingly shaky. Once France had agreed to stop fighting with Germany on 22 June 1940, it became effectively a collaborator, and Marshal Pétain, an old war hero from the First World War, was the new head of state. Under him, the French government fled to the town of Vichy in central France, and the country was chopped in half between German-occupied France and the new Vichy government: northern and western France, including Paris, was occupied by Germany (the occupied zone, *zone occupée*), while the south and what little else was left was controlled by Vichy (the unoccupied zone, *zone libre*). And Vichy did not wait long to go after the Jews.

On 27 September 1940 the first specifically anti-Jewish legislations came into effect: Jews who had fled to the unoccupied zone were prohibited from returning; Jewish shopkeepers had to post a yellow sign in their windows reading '*entreprise Juive – Jüdisches Geschäft*'. A census of Jews in the occupied zone was ordered, in which more than 150,000 Jews presented themselves for registration at local police stations and their names and addresses were then handed over to Section IV J of the Gestapo. In October 1940, all Jews had to have '*Juif*' stamped on their identity card. The following year, Jewish businesses in the occupied zone were Aryanised – in other words, they were taken away from the Jews – and Jacques was forced to sign over his fur business to Jacques Revillon, the scion of a large fur company. When he joined the Legion to risk his life for France he had little; now, after fighting for his country, he had even less.

Pétain had been celebrated for his bravery against the Germans during the First World War, so much so that he was known as the Lion of Verdun in recognition of his courage at the Battle of Verdun. But as France's chief of state during the Second World War, he dealt with the Germans by capitulation and active collaboration. Having seen the damage war exacted on France and the French people in the First World War, he was willing to do anything to prevent it happening again, even if that meant submitting to his former enemies. But he went further than mere obedience.

Vichy France was the only western European country under Nazi occupation that enacted its own measures against the Jews. Despite the claims by French politicians over the years that Vichy was compelled to do this by the Nazis, they in fact came up with anti-Semitic regulations Berlin hadn't asked for. As Pétain's chief of staff later said: 'Germany was not at the origin of the anti-Jewish legislation of Vichy. That legislation was spontaneous and autonomous.'[16] When Vichy introduced the 'Statut des Juifs' in October 1940 and discriminatory legislation aimed solely at the Jews in June 1941, Jewish people – in the unoccupied zone as well as the occupied one – were excluded from the army, press, commerce and industry and the civil service, but there was no evidence anywhere that the Germans demanded this of France. As historian Jean Edward Smith later put it, 'anti-Semitism was not new to France, but it became one of the hallmarks of the Vichy regime. The Statute on Jews illustrated the Vichy government's willingness to act on its own authority without German pressure and was an ominous sign for the future'.[17] The Vichy government even ordered the French police to participate in anti-Jewish thuggery, and the Germans later said they could never have accomplished as much as they did without the help of the French police.[18]

Vichy didn't want to exterminate all Jews like the Nazis did. Not exactly: it wanted to get rid of the foreign Jews, marginalise French Jews and eliminate Jewish culture from

French life[19] to protect the sanctity and unity of French culture. The high number of anti-Semitic fanatics in Vichy – such as Xavier Vallat, the first Vichy Commissioner General for Jewish Affairs, who would soon take a special interest in Alex Maguy – certainly didn't do anything to stop France's anti-Jewish mood. As a result France quickly proved to be very keen to introduce anti-Semitic legislation, and in some cases was even more efficient at enacting it than the Germans.

After the war, senior Vichy officials argued that the government felt it had to outpace the Germans in order to save the French Jews and – more pressingly for Vichy – to prevent the fascists from staging a coup in the government. In other words, the way to help the French Jews was by throwing the foreign Jews under a bus, and that by giving the enemy what they wanted they would, in some back-handed way, retain authority. And it is true that the majority of French Jews survived the war. But no government has ever achieved a political, or moral, victory by trying to outpace the far right, let alone actual fascists. The Germans quickly saw through Vichy's strategy and would soon exploit it in their pursuit of foreign Jews, and Vichy – especially from 1942 onwards – eagerly helped them, rushing to meet the deportation quotas set by the Germans by sending them Jews – babies, children, the sick – the Nazis hadn't even demanded.[20]

This has caused France some unpleasant reckonings ever since. Serge Klarsfeld, the French activist and Nazi hunter (and, later, a friend of Alex's), has done more than pretty much anyone in making France confront its culpability during the war, and just one instance of this occurred in 1991. While doing some research at the French Ministry of War Veterans, he happened upon a file of frayed and faded index cards. These were the remnants of the 1940 census of the French and foreign Jews, which was used to deport 75,000 people to the concentration camps.[21] For more than fifty years, historians had thought the cards had been destroyed and yet all the while some researchers within the ministry had known the cards existed and kept them hidden. Many in France were horrified by the discovery – especially, it turned out, those whose names were on it. So while historians insisted that the list be preserved for history, those named were terrified by such a prospect.

'How could French historians presume to serenely make use of a tool that in other times served a racist and criminal system?' one person wrote to Klarsfeld.

'It's clearly worrying that a listing of categories of citizens exists,' said Jean Kahn, the then head of the French Jewish community.

It didn't matter that most of the people on the census were long dead. Nor that France was no longer under Vichy and Nazi control. To the people whose family's names were on it, or who just saw names similar to their own, the past was ever present, and always at risk of returning. (Eventually, President Jacques Chirac gave the *Fichier Juif* – Jewish registration file – to the Shoah Memorial in Paris.)

That was how Alex and Henri felt in 1940, and unsurprisingly so, given what they'd already lived through. So it didn't even occur to Alex to put his name on the census, and Henri, after careful deliberation with Sonia, decided against it too. But Jacques was always different from his brothers. Despite having been politically aware enough to join the Foreign Legion, he was remarkably resistant to learning the lessons of the past. So even though he had had to flee his home town because of anti-Semitism, and he had just escaped from a Nazi war prison, he still had a submissive soul. Henri pleaded with him not to register, but Jacques, urged on by his frightened wife, who believed obedience was a form of self-protection, dutifully registered himself and Mila as Jewish, giving their home address – which Vichy had anyway, because they were still living in their shop which had been officially Aryanised. Henri and Alex were horrified when they found out but he waved their concerns away. He had just saved his life by taking action and disobeying authorities when he ran away from Cambrai, but the only lesson he seemed to have learned from that incident was that he shouldn't try to fight again. No, Jacques felt, it was always better to obey authorities. After all, if you did what they said, why would they hurt you?

Couturier Alex Maguy.

5

ALEX – Defiance

Paris, 1930s

ON A WARM NIGHT in the summer of 1936, Alex was in a nightclub in Montmartre with his friends. These friends included the artists Moïse Kisling and Jules Pascin, a jazz band leader called Ray Ventura and various other musicians and artists, several of whom he'd met through his first friend in the art world, Marc Chagall. This was his regular social circle, and tonight was a pretty typical night for him. He met his friends at the glamorous Opéra Comique theatre, where they attended the opening night of a new show. They then went to Montparnasse for the cafés there – La Coupole, Le Dôme, Le Café de la Rotonde – which were open late and attracted artistic sorts. There, they met up with Ventura's friend, a young singer called Edith Piaf, and the group went on to a small club nearby where Charles Trenet was singing. They next headed off to the Montmartre nightclubs, and after that, dancing at the Boeuf sur le Toit, a cabaret where the avant-garde artists hung out until the purple morning hours. It would be another night with no sleep for Alex – there was just too much to do and to see and to drink and to eat. Who has time in Paris to sleep more than one night a week?

In the decade and a half since Alex arrived in Paris, he had lifted himself out of poverty and put himself at the absolute centre of the city's artistic and bohemian demi-monde. Everything around him was glittering and fabulous, and for the first time in his life Alex felt like he belonged. The Galician savage, he liked to say, had become the darling of Paris. Forty years later, when writing about this brief period, he described it as 'the happiest time of my life'. But on that particular night, as he sat in that cabaret, he felt a terrible tug of sadness. Because as he looked around at all that he had, everything he had ever wanted, he knew he would have to give it up.

By 1936, Alex was running a thriving couture house, built up purely by word of mouth, that employed over sixty people and put out four collections a year. When he had turned down Nina Ricci's offer a decade earlier to work with her at Raffin he had bet everything he had that he could make it on his own. Against the most extraordinary odds, his bet had paid off.

'[Alex Maguy] was responsible for the livelihood of all of his workers. He was personally concerned with each, from the smallest of the *petites mains* [the seamstresses] to his salespeople,' reads Alex's entry in the book, *The Dressmakers of France*. Alex became known for his tailoring and his coats, and long after he switched from fashion design to art dealing, the coats he designed for my grandmother that I saw in her closet were always beautifully made, always with a clever detail like a fluted sleeve or exaggerated collar, and always still looking new even though my grandmother had been wearing them for decades.

'His own studio, his preoccupation with art, made one suspect he would prefer [to make] evening clothes. But here, too, the fine balance of what was wanted showed him to be an excellent businessman,' according to *The Dressmakers of France*.

Alex was so busy he had to hire an assistant to help him with his sketches, as drawing was never Alex's talent. 'A distinguished young man, though quite timid, came to show me his sketches,' Alex later wrote. 'I was quite impressed. He was an extraordinary draughtsman, with strong personality revealed by his drawings. His name was Christian Dior.' And Alex and Dior, two seemingly very different men, would go on to have strikingly parallel lives over the next few decades.

Like Alex, Dior had found the bohemian Parisian life a thrilling release from the cloistered, closeted world in which he'd grown up, but whereas Alex's life had been circumscribed by poverty, Dior's had been hemmed in by privilege, raised by starchy governesses and a dominating father who disapproved of his son's artistic ambitions.[1]

'I suggested to my family that I should study Fine Arts. There was an outcry! I was not allowed to join the Bohemians. To gain time and to enjoy the greatest possible liberty, I was enrolled as a student in the École des Sciences Politiques, which entailed no commitments. Such was the hypocritical way in which I contrived to carry on the life I liked,' Dior later recalled.[2]

And the life he liked was a lot like the one Alex did, too: in his autobiography, Dior describes hanging out at the bar Boeuf sur le Toit, going to the Ballets Russes, watching Jean Cocteau films, seeing Josephine Baker on the stage. 'What a hectic life! My parents were in despair at having a son who was so incapable of concerning himself with anything serious,' Dior writes, and Alex would have sympathised, having had similar arguments with Chaya.

After the Dior family fortune collapsed in the stock market crash, and the art gallery Dior had opened with a friend shut down, Dior started working as a fashion illustrator. Soon he was making sketches for designers such as Schiaparelli, Alex's old friend Nina Ricci – and Alex himself. It was inevitable the two of them would eventually meet as they mixed in the same circles, and it was through Dior that Alex befriended the aspiring designer Imre Partos, a Hungarian Jew, who would become a very important figure in Alex's life in a few years' time.

The other illustrator who provided sketches for Alex's label was René Gruau, who became one of Alex's most loyal, and most enduring, friends. He would also, in the next decade, become the most famous fashion illustrator in the world thanks to his future alliance with Dior. Gruau's fluid, languorous illustrations of Dior's famous New Look collection in 1947 helped to translate what became the most influential fashion breakthrough of the twentieth century to the masses, and he would continue to be the label's artist for more than half a century, coining modern fashion illustration as much as Dior coined modern fashion. John Galliano, head of design at Dior from 1996 to 2011, later said Gruau 'captured Dior better than any other' because of their 'enduring friendship'.[3] And both of them started with Alex in the mid-1930s.[4] Alex might have struggled at times as a designer, but his skill at talent spotting was pretty much unsurpassable, and this is a testament to his natural, and extraordinary, sense of aesthetics.

Yet even with Dior's and Gruau's help, the work was punishing. On one day alone, Alex did a fitting with a successful cabaret owner who insisted on drinking from her whisky bottle as he was draping the fabric around her, and walked through his studio completely naked between fittings, unbothered by the sixty employees working there; another fitting with the French singer Lucienne Boyer, described later in her *New York Times* obituary as 'the queen of Paris nightlife in the 1930s'; and a third one with Suzy Solidor, a bisexual cabaret singer who was so popular with artists, including Tamara Lempicka, Jean Cocteau and Francis Bacon, that she became known as 'the most painted woman in the world'. After the war she was known as something else when she was convicted of being a collaborator.

Alex was not a big name, like Chanel or Balenciaga, but he was doing well enough for his company to be valued in the early 1940s by the CGQJ at 2,233,823.30 francs, or almost 90,000 euros today – an unarguably respectable sum. (By contrast, Jacques's business was valued at less than 200,000 francs, or 8,000 euros today.) In his salon, which he moved out of its original office space and into a far more glamorous setting on Avenue Matignon, he had twenty-nine armchairs, proof of the number of clients and journalists he regularly had to seat, and the salon itself was fronted with a large window, between a pair of heavy silk curtains, looking onto the street, through which children could peer into his workplace, just as he and Sara had once looked into Lanvin's.

The two youngest Glasses were always charmed by Parisian style and as adults they recreated it enthusiastically in their own wardrobes: Alex wore formal three-piece suits and buckets of cologne, with shoes that had two-inch heels for some much-longed-for extra height, and Sara wore berets, wide belts and peasant-style blouses with tapered trousers. When you move to a new country and don't want to be seen by the natives as a foreigner, you can change your accent, or you can change your clothes, and the latter tends to be easier. It is a way of leaving who you were behind and sending a pleadingly optimistic message to those around you that says, 'I know I may not sound like you, but I am one of you.' Or maybe it's like being a besotted lover in a new relationship, copying your partner's style. Whichever, it's an expression of love.

And Alex expressed his love for France through his clothes. He built up a successful export business selling a

A friend, Sara and Alex.

fondly exaggerated image of French chic to, in particular, British and American customers. It was a style that felt a little kitsch for Parisians, but for foreigners this heavily outlined version of French style was a canny formula. It was also one that reflected Alex's status as an immigrant. Like a man who moves to Britain and immediately adopts the mannerisms of Bertie Wooster, or one who moves to the United States and becomes a hardcore baseball fan, or like Henri, for that matter, in his three-piece suits in the 7ème arrondissement, it was not enough for Alex to simply be in France. He had to embody that country. As much as he thought of himself as an outsider, there was always a part of him that wanted to prove to the French bourgeoisie that he understood them, and was better than them. So there had to be an exaggeration, an overcompensation, and he made clothes that were Frencher than French.

Alex also turned out to be excellent at selling. He had watched those obsequious couturiers carefully through the window as a kid, and he was happy to copy them, if it sold some dresses. That he did it with his rough Yiddish accent made it seem even more authentic to clients bored with the polished patter in other salons. Also, Alex really loved to sell – unlike other couturiers, he did not see it as beneath him to push his goods, to tell women that if they were buying the blue dress they really also ought to buy the red, and maybe to make up a little lie from time to time and say that the English princesses had been in the other day and ordered these skirts, so perhaps the client should, too, as they would soon be the latest fashion. As a salesman, Alex united the schmooze of French designers with the pushiness of the market traders in the Pletzl and back in Chrzanow, and it was an extremely effective combination.

One of the ironies of fashion design is that a profession ostensibly built to celebrate female beauty has, for more than a century, been dominated by gay men. The question of whether Alex was gay or bisexual was one that was raised in his lifetime by his friends and colleagues, but always behind his back. When I was starting to research Alex's life in Paris I met the now late designer Ilie Wacs, who worked as a sketcher for Alex in the 1950s. After some preliminary small talk he brought up Alex's sexuality: 'He was such a dandy, you know? Always in heels, always heavily perfumed, but he talked about his girlfriends, so we in the studio could never figure it out. Did anyone in your family know?'

No one in the family did. Alex rarely spoke about his romantic life, and no one dared to ask. It may be that Alex was neither gay nor straight but both and neither: Paris in the 1920s and 1930s was a centre for not just the sexual freedom of Josephine Baker but also the sexual fluidity of Jean Cocteau. In the artistic and fashion worlds in which Alex worked, such sexual liberation would have been, if not the openly acknowledged norm, at least a quietly accepted practice, and the idea of putting a name to such experimentation, to define yourself by who you happened to take to bed on Tuesday, would have seemed as absurd as naming yourself after the colour of the jacket you happened to wear on Wednesday. Such things were mutable, and nailing down the sexual preferences of the individuals in Alex's milieu is like trying to fix a wave to the shore.

But while Alex's friends would have been comfortable with homosexuality, his family – and more specifically, his mother – would very much not. Same-sex relationships were not accepted in the world in which she grew up, which was also the world in which Alex grew up, and Alex desperately cared about the good opinion of his siblings and his Ornstein cousins. Certainly in his memoir he takes enormous pains to stress his heterosexuality. He writes about how one of his neighbours initially refused to speak to him, 'because he believed that all couturiers were homosexuals. But he quickly discovered that I was an exception, a rare exception, to that rule. He soon saw many very pretty ladies coming up the stairs to my place.' There are multiple if vague references to various 'conquests' – all emphatically female – and dimly described remembrances of young women who desperately wanted to marry him.

These little asides are frustrating in their opacity and almost laughable in their clumsiness. My father had warned me not to take Alex's memoir too seriously, and while I'd been prepared to treat his descriptions of his achievements with some scepticism, it soon became clear to me that the more questionable elements of his story were the references to his personal life. Alex always found it easy to talk about what he did, but how he felt was a very different story. Unlike the shoebox in my grandmother's closet, he fully intended his memoir to be seen by others, so there was a limit to how honest he could, and would, be. If he wasn't willing to discuss the possible complexities of his sexuality with his family, he certainly wasn't going to do so in a book that he hoped would immortalise his reputation with the public.

Alex's sexuality, like my grandmother's sadness, was something none of us in the family talked about while he was alive, or even after he died. It can be hard to see someone you know so well clearly, to fit together the puzzle pieces when your mind can't even grasp how the image should look. But I wondered if the truth was more obvious to those who worked with him. So I asked one of Alex's assistants, who he employed in the 1980s, if she ever got any sense of her former boss's sexuality?

'When I knew him he was almost rampantly heterosexual – he was like an octopus around me sometimes,' she said.

'But I always got the impression that he was largely homosexual for the first half of his life and largely heterosexual for the latter, just from who he was hanging out with at those times. But honestly, I don't think Alex would have ever even thought about it in those terms. It was just who he was at those times.'

In the early 1930s Alex bought a home that was as luxurious as his salon had become: a duplex on the Île de la Cité, with large bay windows that looked out over Paris. To help him decorate his apartment he pulled in his friends Christian Dior and René Gruau to advise him. On the walls Alex hung paintings by his friends, such as Pascin and Kisling, and when he threw cocktail parties all his guests would stand on his terrace and watch the flashing lights of the *bateaux mouches* – tourist cruises – as they sailed up and down the Seine. Even though his working days were exhausting, his nights were relentless: if he wasn't throwing parties in his glamorous apartment, or seeing his siblings, or going out for drinks with his beloved cousins, he was running around Montmartre or Montparnasse with his friends. After all, to stay at home and do nothing – like his father did, like his brother Jacques did – was to feel nothing. To do everything was to live. And just as Alex was living exactly as he wanted, he realised he'd have to lose it all.

WHILE JACQUES'S CAREER was more typical of a Jewish immigrant and Alex's was the more exceptional, when it came to their feelings about the approach of Nazism, it was

Jacques who was the unusual one and Alex more archetypal. Jacques's blind belief in France's loyalty towards foreign Jews put him in the minority, while Alex's nervousness was far more common among their demographic. For obvious reasons, eastern European Jews recognised the dangers of Nazism far quicker than French ones, and many realised it was worse than what they had previously escaped.[5] Alex was even more pessimistic – or realistic – than most of his peers. His experience in the pogrom as a child had left him with a lifelong cynicism about anyone's loyalty towards Jews and, as much as he loved Paris and became a part of Parisian life, he never kidded himself that he was anything but a foreigner, and his lifelong retention of his Yiddish accent was a statement of that, to himself and to others. He refused to assimilate his tongue, instead defiantly remaining, as he put it, 'authentic'.

Unlike Jacques, he didn't take his safety in France for granted. So no matter how dazzled he was by his newfound popularity on nights out in Montparnasse, he never forgot the dark forces that had so blighted his childhood and now approached France. He demonstrated against Action Française and Croix-de-Feu, two nationalistic political parties that Alex rightly recognised as riddled with anti-Semitism, and he watched their rise closely and the accompanying national mood for appeasement. Being involved in the art world gave Alex particular clarity on the situation, as Jewish artists were increasingly seen in the 1930s as symbols of destruction of France's heritage. *Le Figaro*'s Camille Mauclair raged against

'The Monparno crowd'. In one article, he claimed 'the proportion of Semites is around 80%', and he insisted that Alex's friends were conspiring to destroy French art:

> One must admit that if Jews have produced
> marvellous poets, they have never excelled in plastic
> arts. How then to explain that the current art market
> is in the hands of Jewish merchants and critics,
> and that they therefore push Jewish painters to the
> forefront of 'living art', all agreeing to attack the
> Latin tradition and to obey the spirit of negating
> criticism, of dissociation, of overturning of values,
> which is the old Bolshevik base of their race.[6]

By 1935, the major art magazines refused to include even the names of these immigrant Jewish artists in their emphatically French pages. The national mood was becoming all too obvious to Alex. 'In the horror of the pogroms, I had seen the damned beast take form, seen its hideous face. It grew and grew, ever more monstrous. And now it appeared everywhere, here in France, among so-called patriots, but in reality degenerate reactionaries, all wearing the same grinning mask,' he wrote.

His first step was to deal with the one member of his family who he considered to be the easiest to manipulate and the simplest to get out of France: his sister Sara. In 1937 Alex managed to find a way for her to go to New York and, in doing so, very possibly saved her life. And yet he doesn't mention this event once in his memoir, or even that his sister left France. This initially astonished me: after all, not only was this a major event in the family, but given how much Alex liked to trumpet his successes, to ignore the fact that he, with great prescience and skill, ostensibly saved his baby sister from the camps seems inexplicable. The most sympathetic explanation would be that by the time he was writing his memoir Alex knew all too well how homesick Sara was in New York, so he couldn't bear to revisit this saga because of the guilt. And there is some evidence in the letters between them over the next few decades that he was aware to some extent of how unhappy she was. But a more likely reason, I think, is that Alex simply didn't consider it was that big a deal, not compared to what was happening to him at the time, and so he just didn't bother to write it down. He was writing his story and therefore he focused on himself – he did not want to write about what happened to his sister. And this sums up what it was like to be related to Alex: if he liked you, his generosity was immense, his heart enormous. But these qualities were too often obscured by his infuriating self-centredness, which sometimes came across as a lack of interest in other people. Alex loved his siblings very deeply, to the point that they were the only people in the world who had the ability to hurt him. They were the bruise on his arm that was too tender to touch. And so while his mother and siblings hardly make an appearance in his memoir during the 1930s, the truth is he tried to save them repeatedly.

When Alex realised he could only get Sara out of France,

he set about trying to get French citizenship for himself and his family. He was too late: on 21 September 1937 his application for naturalisation was rejected, despite his having lived in France for almost two decades and his growing celebrity. Alex refused to be beaten and so, in defiance of the unarguable odds, he tried again, and once again he was rejected. Devastated, on 20 September 1938 he wrote a furious and heartfelt letter to the government in protest:

> I was painfully surprised when I learned that my naturalisation application had been rejected. The very serious circumstances we are now going through make this refusal even more painful. I am young, brave, fit and eager to have the opportunity to defend this French soil that was welcoming to me and my family. I work with many French people and we fight heart and soul together for our work; it is my dearest desire to now continue the struggle with them – in French – in the most serious of conditions. I hope to have contributed to the renown of French taste and couture abroad. It is for me a moral obligation and an expression of gratitude for your country that make me ask you, sir, to reconsider my application.

But it was no good; for once, Alex couldn't make a sale. The noose around foreign Jews in France was already too tight. German and Austrian Jewish refugees were being rounded up and put into French internment camps; there was no chance France was going to give citizenship to a family of Polish Jews, and, Alex realised, even less chance the country would protect them.

HE CAME UP with another idea of how to save his family: he would sign up to fight, protecting the home he loved from becoming like the former home he hated. So once France reluctantly joined the war in September 1939, he decided to follow in the footsteps of his friend Kiki Kisling, who had fought in the French Foreign Legion in the First World War, and join up. 'I'm ready to sacrifice a limb of my body to win this fight against the Germans, my enemies,' he told his friends.

But it turned out that France wasn't so keen for his limbs. The Legion was already becoming oversubscribed, largely with Spanish Republicans[7] but also because the German and Austrian Jews who had been interned by France were told they would be released if they joined the Legion. So Alex required some help convincing the Foreign Legion that they needed a five-foot-two-inch Polish-born fashion designer, and he turned to someone who would become a very important part of his life, a man called Colonel Jean Perré.

Alex happened to be the colonel's daughter's couturier and when she introduced him to her father in the mid-1930s, his eyes must have lit with the same kind of excitement as when he met Chagall or Piaf: here was someone whom he respected, certainly, but who could also be useful to him in his ongoing project to establish himself in France. A large, barrel-chested man, Colonel Perré was an old-fashioned French military man, the kind who believed in France's sovereignty above all. He was anti-Semitic in the way a lot of his demographic was: it wasn't that he specifically hated the Jews, but he didn't want France's innate French character to be altered by a load of suspicious outsiders. But a Jew like Alex, who wrote letters to the government begging to be allowed to defend 'French soil'? Well, that was the kind of Jew a military patriot like Colonel Perré could support.

Back in the First World War the colonel was widely seen as the equal and rival of Charles de Gaulle, and the two competed for command of the same regiment. De Gaulle won that contest, but Perré made a name for himself as a skilful tactician with tanks, and in 1919 he went to Poland to command a tank battalion of the first Polish armoured units against the Russians. He had a further connection with the Poles: he was in the command staff of the 1st Armoured Polish Brigade and was one of the French advisers introduced in the Polish high command. He was a tough man who respected other tough men, and when he met Alex, an almost aggressively masculine Polish fashion designer, the two formed an immediate bond. Colonel Perré, who was by this point in the high command of the French Army, wrote a letter endorsing this young Jew's bid to join the Legion. Doors were swiftly opened and, at last, one of Alex's applications was successful. Just as Alex had always suspected, what mattered in life wasn't what you knew but who.

On 2 October 1939 Alex assigned a manager to look after his salon and he said goodbye to his workers, his mother, his brothers, his cousins and his friends. 'Courage,' he said to his cousin Josek. 'I will see you after the war.' He took his favourite pieces of art by two of his oldest Parisian friends off the wall in his living room – a small drawing by Pascin of a young woman and a painting by Kisling of a little boy – and he packaged them up and sent them to the Tel Aviv Museum, in what was then still Palestine. He wrote in his memoir:

> I felt I was doing my duty as an Israeli soldier, as
> a member of the Resistance, as a pioneer, donating
> to Tel Aviv. I added my brick to the building. I was
> certain that we would emerge victorious from this
> struggle. And I was confident that Israel would be
> born. No one – other than Helena Rubenstein –
> had ever before made a gift of two paintings to the
> Tel Aviv museum.

This story certainly fitted in with Alex's character, but when I read it in his memoir I wondered how much self-mythology was going on here. Could he really have owned museum-worthy art as early as 1939? I called up the museum to ask if Alex and Helena Rubenstein were the first people to donate paintings to the museum and the museum's archivist firmly denied it. I sighed, and was about to cross out the paragraph in his memoir. Typical Alex, I thought, trying to make himself sound like a bigshot and celebrity by proxy. But the archivist then casually added, 'But Monsieur Maguy did send those paintings to us in 1939.'

'Those particular paintings? In 1939?'

'Oh yes, absolutely. In 1939. Other people donated several paintings before him, but those two he sent are still in our permanent collection.'

This was to be the first of many instances when I learned not to underestimate Alex and his claims. Because the story was correct, and he had indeed left his stamp behind him before going off to war. He had just given the tale a brush of showman's pizzazz.

UNSURPRISINGLY, a short, heavily perfumed couturier with a taste for the finer things in life found the Foreign Legion a bit of an adjustment. The French Foreign Legion was and is notoriously tough, even by military standards, and because it, uniquely in the French military, allowed in foreigners, it was filled with the dispossessed from around the world – refugees, vagabonds and flat-out criminals. German intelligence gleefully exploited the Legion's rackety admissions practice by stuffing it full of Nazi spies during the 1930s, hoping to destroy the Legion by infiltrating it. Once their ruse was discovered the German legionnaires were shipped out, but the French authorities retained long-held suspicions about the Legion, and therefore wouldn't let it fight in Europe when France finally entered the war.

Alex had always prided himself on being a tough foreigner, but even he was taken aback by how tough and foreign

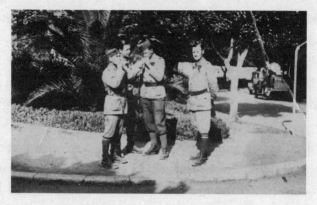

Alex, far left, in the Foreign Legion, 1941.

his fellow soldiers in the Legion were. Largely made up of Spanish Republicans who fled Franco and Jewish refugees from central and eastern Europe, the Legion was regarded by officers as an unpromising mix of communists and intellectuals.[8] Alex described them as 'a mob of rough and tough guys' and, in a rare moment of vulnerability in his memoir, admits he was bullied relentlessly.

'I found it hard to break with Parisian life,' Alex wrote. And initially, he barely broke with it at all. Stationed in Barcarès in the southern corner of France, Alex would train during the day and then sneak out to the local nightclubs when the rest of the men were in bed, enjoying a social life that wasn't all that different from his life back home. Alex took lifelong pride in getting the better of authority figures around him, but he was remarkably bad at doing so. Just as Nina Ricci had caught him re-selling designs, and his mother had caught him stealing meatballs in Chrzanow,

Alex's night-time excursions were quickly exposed when he failed to make it back to the camp in time for reveille, and he turned up reeking of booze at the start of inspection. He was promptly put in the stockade and in his memoir he describes his humiliation at length: 'The Legion getting too much for you, Glass? Sorry you enlisted?' his fellow soldiers jeered at him, walking past.

Others would have been cowed into obedience. But Alex felt only defiance and a determination to be tougher than ever. He never felt any embarrassment about describing his falls to others, because they were a chance to show how he rose up and fought back.

From then on, he trained more intensely than anyone else. And he still went out most nights, too – but as a concession he started wearing a watch so he always got back in time.

Eventually, even Alex had to give up the nightclubs. The training got harder and he was put on night manoeuvres as the so-called Phoney War, which lasted from September 1939 to May 1940, neared its end. 'We are being toughened up for war,' he later recalled writing to Kisling, who was too old to join the French Army this time so was whiling away the war by painting in his studio in Marseille.

'I hope you'll get leave to come eat a good bouillabaisse here with me in the south,' Kisling wrote back. 'But for now, forget about Paris. After the victory, knowing you as I do, you'll restart [your business] in no time. For the moment, make war.'

On 17 April 1940 Alex had no choice: he and his fellow soldiers were sent to Cherbourg where they were armed with equipment and packed onto ships. None of them knew where they were going, but they knew it wouldn't be Europe, because French authorities still weren't allowing the Legion to fight on the Continent. The dropping temperature told them that they weren't heading southwards either: they were going towards the Arctic Circle.

Alex was part of the 13th Demi-Brigade of the Foreign Legion, a unit that had been set up only the month before and would soon gain legendary status. It still has a reputation as 'one of [the French Army's] most honoured units'[9] and it was later described by de Gaulle as being 'at the heart from the very beginning of the forces of Free France for the liberation of our homeland honourably and victoriously'.[10] Formed initially to help the Allies in Finland and Norway, it was put under the command of Lieutenant Colonel Raoul Magrin-Vernerey, a tough military eccentric who personified the Foreign Legion itself: battle-scarred from the First World War and saddled with disabilities that should have disqualified him from military service. Various head wounds, and crude attempts to operate on them, had left him with a notorious temper and, either because of or despite that, he was a formidable fighter. Alex worshipped him.

According to Alex's memoir, one night in early May he was keeping watch on the bridge of the ship, the *Ville d'Alger*, when he saw Magrin-Vernerey walking towards him.

Above them, they could hear enemy planes circling, and Magrin-Vernerey thought he saw fear in the inexperienced soldier's face.

'Don't worry. The planes can't see you. And even if they could, what would they do? Make a big hole in you and you would be dead. Your friends and family would mourn you but for you it would be over,' he said with a smile.

But Alex was not one to be teased, even by a lieutenant colonel. 'I don't agree. I came here to fight for my country!' he replied.

Magrin-Vernerey grew serious then, his moods always changing as swiftly as the Nordic sky. 'Don't worry. You'll fight. We'll win.'

When his troops asked him why they were there anyway, Magrin-Vernerey treated the question with the same nonchalance with which he first spoke to Alex: 'Why? Because my orders are to take Narvik. Why Narvik? For the anchovies, for the Norwegians – I haven't the faintest idea.'

In fact, it was for the iron ore. The Germans and Allies were both determined to seize Norway, because both sides realised it was the way to gain control of the iron ore, which was transported out of Sweden and through the Norwegian port, and was so important to the German war machinery. Hitler also saw Norway as a potential naval base, while British forces saw it as a way to open up the Baltic for the Allies. The French saw it as a possible second fighting front a safe distance from France, thus allowing the Legion to battle the Germans without risking harm to France itself or its civilians. The Narvik campaign would turn out to be one of the biggest battles since the invasion of Poland.

On 13 May the 13th Demi-Brigade landed on the Bjerkvik beaches, close to Narvik. As the British battleships and destroyers started firing on the German defenders, and the Luftwaffe fought back, bombing and strafing the beaches, the French Foreign Legion soldiers were ordered to jump overboard, in the middle of the battle, and swim through the freezing North Sea to shore. Weighted down by his artillery, Alex swam in water so cold it felt as if it were burning him, and he watched many of his fellow soldiers drown around him, either shot by the Germans or sunk by their own equipment, their terrified faces illuminated by the house fires fringing the coast as civilians' homes were bombed. It was like dying at the edge of the world.

'*À moi, la Légion!*' Magrin-Vernerey cried, the Legion's version of 'Follow me!', and the soldiers who survived the frightening landing pressed onwards up the beach.

The Norwegian Army was an allied troop but Magrin-Vernerey never really trusted them: 'The Norwegian Army is nothing more than a bunch of dull farmers. They are useless. Half of them are paid German spies anyway,' he was reported to have said.[11] The Norwegians weren't entirely sure about the legionnaires either. In one book my father bought in Narvik, when retracing Alex's steps, the historian describes them as 'not like other soldiers. Many of them were pure bandits, feared and hated by the inhabitants of Bjerkvik and Narvik.'[12] Their terror was understandable: thirteen adult civilians and a five-year-old boy were killed during the fighting on the beach, and afterwards the legionnaires tore through the few houses still standing near the beach to see if they could find any German soldiers hiding inside, shooting down doors and breaking windows to gain entry, heaping fear on top of trauma for the inhabitants. The French Foreign Legion was not known for its manners.

Fighting alongside them for Narvik was a scrappy patchwork of other international allied troops, and together they became known as the 1st Light Infantry Division, which was put under the command of the extremely formidable General Émile Béthouart. This included the 5th Demi-Brigade of Chasseurs Alpins, the 27th Demi-Brigade of Chasseurs Alpins, a mountain troop made up of Polish refugees called the Polish 1st Carpathian Demi-Brigade and various Norwegian units. Also fighting with them was the now legendary Captain Marie-Pierre Koenig, a man who had acted with enormous bravery in the First World War and would become an essential part of the allied resistance in this war, too. Between them all, they managed to take Bjerkvik, overcoming the Germans and their firepower. But the 13th Demi-Brigade's battle against the Nazis, and the elements, had only just begun.

Alex and his men were ordered to pursue the retreating Germans up into the barren hills north of Bjerkvik. Even though it was spring, the temperatures were freezing and the mountains covered in snow, making it even harder to spot the Germans, who were wearing white uniforms. Alex was still determined to prove himself and show that he was not the precious couturier the legionnaires initially thought. And so, one night when the men were all resting around a frozen lake in the half-light of the midnight moon, Alex got up, stripped in front of his commanding officers, got a sharp rock, broke through the thick ice on the lake, and dived in, to show these old legionnaire war dogs he was as tough as them. It worked: several of these legionnaire officers would become Alex's lifelong friends.

Lake dives aside, the fighting continued. The battles in the hills against the Austrian mountain infantrymen were hard and savage. After enormous loss of life, the legionnaires eventually triumphed and when they stood victorious on top of their mountain, they were able to wave to the Chasseurs Alpins on top of the neighbouring mountain that the Chasseurs Alpins themselves had just seized.[13]

Fighting continued over the Narvik port, and the Germans were retreating. But just as the Legion was nearing Sweden, pushing the Germans over the border and into Swedish internment, they were summoned back home: Germany had broken through French lines and all troops and equipment were needed for defence. Magrin-Vernerey refused: 'My legionnaires and I won't leave until we've taken Narvik,' he declared. After a few more days of hostilities, in which Alex fought in hand-to-hand combat, they accomplished their mission. But any joy they felt was tempered by their frustration at not being able to stay and secure the port, and the German forces would ultimately recapture Narvik. As the 13th Demi-Brigade sailed away from Norway, Alex looked back at the port he and his fellow legionnaires had won, at the cost of ninety-three legionnaires and so much suffering in the cold. Dozens of German ships were burning in the harbour, like a giant Viking funeral pyre.

It had been a brutal battle, and Alex had been exceptionally brave. His lake diving turned out to have been unnecessary because his fighting had convinced his superiors that he was a true soldier. Along with the rest of the brigade, he was awarded the Croix de Guerre 1939–1940, but Alex alone was awarded a Bronze Star, specifically for him, and he was later cited for his courage in the military dispatches of General Béthouart. Alex, at last, had proven himself.

The port of Narvik is still there, compact and picturesque, fringed with houses in shades of mustard, pink and red, built on top of the ashes of those destroyed in the battle. At one end is a large, bright-red brick building, the iron export terminal, the object of the battle eighty years earlier. All day, trains run along the coast towards it, carrying iron ore. Life continued and continues. Outside the new Narvik War Museum, which opened in 2018 to preserve and tell the stories of the 1940 battle for the port, is a children's playground, where sweet blond Norwegian children play happily on a climbing frame while their parents learn what their grandparents endured. A few kilometres away from the port are the cemeteries for the fallen French and German soldiers, with lists of names of the dead, and there you can also see a simple stone memorial thanking the French soldiers, surrounded by a rainbow of small flowers: *'La France, à ses fils et à leurs frères d'armes tombés glorieusement en Norvège. Narvik 1940*'. Whatever anxieties the locals felt about the legionnaires are long gone, buried with the dead in the ground and in the sea.

The 13th Demi-Brigade sailed back to France, docking at Brest on 13 June 1940, the day before the Nazis marched into Paris. Magrin-Vernerey joined the fight, but it was too late, and Paris fell. So Magrin-Vernerey decided to take his men to Britain and fight from there, alongside Charles de Gaulle and the Free French. Alex and his fellow soldiers went to Trentham Park to be part of the Resistance. Alex would lie awake at night, listening to the BBC radio for news from home, learning English from the newscasters' clipped diction. For the rest of his life, when Alex talked about the BBC he would get a dreamy look in his eyes and say it was his 'one source of hope' during that bewildering time. But it also caused him enormous anxiety to hear how Paris was now like a garrison, with the Jews at the mercy of the Vichy laws and German soldiers. So when Magrin-Vernerey asked Alex to stay in the Demi-Brigade, which became the main unit of the 1st Free French Division in de Gaulle's Free French forces, Alex refused. He had to return to Paris, he said, where he was responsible for his mother, brothers and cousin. He couldn't stay in England, he added, because he wanted 'to defend French soil and fight my hereditary enemies, the Nazis'.

'I know you will do good work,' Magrin-Vernerey replied. 'We will win this war and meet again, Glass.'

Alex was not the only member of his troop to feel that he had to return to France, despite his loyalty to de Gaulle – General Béthouart also said he had to go. De Gaulle took Béthouart to the Rubens Hotel in Victoria for lunch in an attempt to convince him otherwise. Just a week earlier, de Gaulle made his famous radio appeal from London, in which he told the French people the war was not over for them, despite the fall of France, and he asked for anyone who could to join the French Resistance. He asked Béthouart what he thought of the appeal.

'I think that you are right. Someone has to stay and fight with the Allies, but personally I have 7,000 men to repatriate and can't in good conscience abandon them before they are safely home,' Béthouart replied.[14]

So General Béthouart, Alex and the rest of the demobilising soldiers sailed first to Casablanca, where they stayed for a few weeks, and then to Marseille. Among the other returning soldiers was a young man called Jean Seytour. It was a sad return for the soldiers to their homeland, a now humiliated France. But Alex was full of defiance, because he and Seytour had a plan.

'In Grenoble, under the patronage of Béthouart, my friends, including Seytour, swore to form a "*sizaine*" [six-pack], a resistance group of men acting under the rule of secrecy,' Alex wrote. 'Because the Armistice had been signed and defeat accepted. But for us, the resistance had just begun.'

6

SARA – Emigration

Paris and New York, late 1930s

THE DAY SARA'S LIFE changed for ever did not seem portentous to her until it was too late. As usual, she woke up in the flat she shared with her mother on rue des Rosiers, early because she had to get to work, but not so early that her mother hadn't already cooked her breakfast. Sara had never been a good eater, and she never would be, so she picked at the food Chaya had made. And then after kissing her mother goodbye, she walked out of their two-room apartment, down the hall past the communal telephone that had recently been installed for all the residents, out the door and onto the streets of the Pletzl. It was February 1937 and she was twenty-six years old.

WHEN I STARTED working on this book, I'd planned to focus on my grandmother, but it quickly became clear that was impossible – partly because her and her siblings' lives were so entwined but also because she turned out to be the hardest to research. Whereas her brothers led lives of masculine adventure, which were then recorded in official archives, my grandmother represented the quiet feminine: domestic, private – what George Eliot describes in *Middlemarch* as 'a hidden life', and she made sure to hide as much of it as possible. And so, as Eliot says, my grandmother's was a life of 'unrecorded acts', which is not an easy proposition for a memoirist. I'd always preferred domestic stories to action ones, but when I started my research I felt myself doing what I'd done to her in life: I avoided her. Investigating Alex Maguy's adventures was both practically and emotionally easier than prying into my grandmother's melancholia.

When I at last turned my attention to her, I initially did a kind of displacement activity, searching through archival records for her life, those bureaucratic background cameras ticking off the key moments: here's a marriage, here's a house move, here's a death. But I eventually realised that the reason I wanted to tell my grandmother's story was not because of things that happened to her, as was the case with her brothers, but because of the inner emotional drama that she thought she hid away but never could, not really. We all picked it up from her, but no one ever talked about it, or explained it. My father and uncle didn't ask her about it because they feared exacerbating it, and I didn't ask them about it because I could see how much it pained them. But if I'd pushed her away because of it in life, I could at least try to understand her after she died. And that was a story I was not going to find in archives.

So I had to talk to those who knew her best, and that meant her sons: Ronald and Richard, my father and uncle. I dreaded hurting them by asking difficult questions, but it turned out that what had hurt them most was feeling like they had to keep these stories to themselves. At first they, like me, found it easier to talk about action than emotions, and my father sent me near daily emails with attached photos he had of his mother doing things: dancing with her husband in Long Island, visiting him in Paris when he was an adult, sitting with me in New York when I was a child. After several dozen of these, I went to see him and said that I had enough photos – what I needed was details of her life, and by that I meant her emotional life. He went silent and looked down, withdrawing inside his own thoughts. When I went home later that evening I expected little to come of that conversation. But the next day he sent a long email detailing exactly what I'd asked for, and then several more over the next few weeks. Slowly, Sara's life, which she'd always kept in the shadows, came into focus.

IN THE WINTER OF 1937, all the Glass siblings were happy – happier than they'd ever been, happier than they'd ever imagined they could be. Henri and Jacques were married to women who loved them, Alex was successful in his career. But of them all, Sara was the most surprised by her happiness because, during her long years in the sanatoriums, she'd had the best cause to assume it would always elude her.

When she finally returned to Paris for good in the early 1930s, Alex frequently took her to the galleries and while he loved the Monets, the Cézannes and, most of all, the Picassos, she preferred the Renoirs. At home she painted pictures of Renoir-esque young women, with their soft eyes, chestnut-coloured pompadours and gentle smiles. When at last she was well enough to start working, she decided to follow a career that allowed her to use the only talents she had confidence in: drawing and painting. She didn't have Alex's manic drive to achieve the impossible, but nor did she have Jacques's quiet acceptance of the least life had to offer, so she enrolled as a non-matriculated student at the École des Beaux-Arts to study fine art. Every day she would leave the Pletzl and cross the Pont Neuf, walk through the school's grand gates, and study in the elegant nineteenth-century building, the chic Boulevard Saint-Germain on one side and the Louvre on the other, Parisian style to her left and classical art to her right. After she finished her course Sara decided to follow Alex and Jacques into the garment trade, not in couture or as a tailor in the Pletzl, but rather something in between. She got a job at a wholesale clothing supplier making patterns for fabrics sold to the mass market. Decades later, she would show her sons some of the designs she had made: patterns full of colour and swirling lines, often with paisley shapes – a psychedelic rejection of the brown drabness of her childhood and the antiseptic, linear whiteness of the sanatoriums. Like Alex, she knew life had more to offer than what she had known, and she was seizing it through her designs. Like Henri, she set out to be as Parisian as possible, not because she thought about assimilation, but because Paris fitted her as naturally as a silk dress fits a doe-eyed woman in a Renoir painting.

Some people will move to a foreign country and it will still feel foreign after thirty years, their home country always being their baseline for normality. Others will feel naturally at home after a matter of weeks. The relationship one has with a place is as deeply felt as one's relationship with a person. Sometimes the place that fits you best is what was once unimaginably far afield, and other times it will be the street where you grew up; you might find true love with a holiday romance or you might find it with the boy next door. But no matter how much you love your adopted country, it's harder than people think to bury your origins, especially if you move after puberty, as Sara did. The cadences of our thoughts, never mind our speech, tend to be set by then. Most of us still dream of our childhood home, and when we read scenes in novels set in a home, a school, a park, it's the ones we knew from our youth that we picture, no matter how long ago we left them behind. The mind's eye has a way of snapping us back to the past. So do our parents. I moved from New York to London when I was three years younger than Sara, and, like her, I quickly felt at ease in my new home. Yet I still have my American accent, thirty years after moving to London, and this is largely because my parents still have theirs. To speak differently from my parents would require a strength of will and lack of self-consciousness I apparently do not have, and, as a result, English people still see me as American.

Sara, however, had no such difficulties. Maybe she did dream of Chrzanow, and maybe she thought of her home on Kostalista when she read books, but she never mentioned it. None of the Glass siblings did. They never pointed to a building and said, 'Oh, that reminds me of our school back in Chrzanow', never compared a street in Paris to Aleja Henryka. Chaya never spoke French, and with her heavily accented Polish and Yiddish she reminded her children of their origins with every syllable. Perhaps because Sara lived with her until she was twenty-six, her crisp French was occasionally sprinkled with the odd Polish or Yiddish expression; when she was tired she would say, '*Je suis feshluffen*', and when she had to carry something she '*schlepped*' it. But in the main, her identity was wholly rooted in France. I was amazed to discover Sara was as Polish as I am American, because while I come across like a nationality mongrel, she never seemed anything other than French to me.

But while I will always have happy associations with the city of my childhood, Sara did not have that luxury. Her memories of her home town were terrible: the poverty, the pogroms, her father's protracted death. She left it physically and she also left it mentally. There was no home behind her that she even had the option of returning to; it had disappeared behind her like the ground crumbling away beneath the feet of a cartoon character frantically running for safety. So when she made herself over as French, it was partly because she wanted to, but also because she had to.

And France was good to her in return. By her early twenties she was working in a job she loved and living near the brothers she adored, in a city that made her heart expand just by looking at it. Her beloved cousin whom she played with in childhood, Rose Ornstein, had married a doctor called Herman Brenner, a close friend of Rose's brother Alex. Dr Brenner was very kind to Sara, helping her manage her pleurisy when she was back in Paris, and Sara often went to visit them in their apartment nearby. She would look around at their happy home and dream of a time she, too, might have her own apartment, away from her mother. And just then, she met a man.

His name has long since vanished in history, because Sara never spoke about him later in life, and her brothers avoided the subject. But he was, Sonia later told Sara's sons, a dental student, Jewish, a socialist and she loved him. Soon after they met they were engaged. There are glimpses of him in the photo album I found in my grandmother's closet, or at least of a man who looks like he probably was him: dark-haired and young, and in the one photo that survives of them together, handsome and smartly dressed, on a picnic with a group of friends, her arm looped casually through his. As Sara walked to work on that cold morning in February 1937, hours away from when her life would change, perhaps she thought about their imminent wedding, and especially about her life after the wedding. She would move out of her mother's apartment, at last, and her life would truly begin. Henri and Jacques were happy in 1937 because they were happily married; Alex was happy because he loved his work. Sara was about to have both professional and marital contentment. She was at that wonderful point in a young person's life when it feels like everything is about to begin and the world seems fringed with joy. And then that evening, when she came home from work, her mother told her that Alex was coming over for supper, and he was bringing some colleagues.

The week before in Berlin, Adolf Hitler had given a two-hour-long speech to mark the fourth anniversary of the Nazis' seizure of power in Germany. In a typically rambling and demented speech he promised that 'the National Social-ist Movement will prevent the Jewish people from intruding themselves among all the other nations as elements of inter-nal disruption, under the mask of honest world-citizens, and thus gaining power over these nations.'[1] In France, the ostensibly liberal Popular Front government was adopting a hardline stance towards refugees, as it knew Hitler's rise would mean more Jews would come to France seeking asylum, and this, it concluded, would be problematic. 'The problem of German refugees has far more serious demographic ramifi-cations than any other refugee problem has ever had, and it must therefore incline us toward prudence,' read one internal foreign ministry memorandum from a few months earlier.[2]

The French art world, as Alex knew, had already shut out the Jewish artists in the country.

Sara would not have been thinking about any of that. Alex, however, very much was, as he climbed the stairs to his mother and sister's apartment on that February evening in 1937. And following behind him was a couple, and a thirty-five-year-old man.

When Sara later described this meeting to her children and grandchildren, she would tell it quietly, shyly, self-deprecatingly, focusing on the practicalities of how she ended up in the United States. Alex and the second man told it with more enthusiasm and bluster, proud of their active roles in this tale. Sonia had a more wry take on the proceedings. But this is probably the only story in the entirety of my family's existence about which there has never been any disagreement. Everyone agreed about who was there, what they said, what they thought and what happened next. But at the time, only one person in the room understood what was actually going on, and how this story would likely play out. And that person was definitely not Sara.

The three guests were American: Oscar and Rosa Kellerman,[3] and Bill Freiman, and he was tall – taller even than Henri. None of the Americans spoke French, and none of the Glasses spoke English but Bill spoke Yiddish, so he acted as translator. They all sat around Chaya's kitchen table – Alex, Sara, the Kellermans, Bill. The Kellermans, Bill explained, were in Paris to do business with Alex, and he was going to travel around the Alps once the Kellermans didn't need

him any more – had Sara ever visited the Alps? Sara had no wish to talk about the sanatoriums, so she shook her head. Anyway, there wasn't much room to talk because Alex, as usual, filled the room with his words, saying he'd brought his guests here because he promised them the best kosher food in the whole of Paris, and he talked about which famous person had worn his coat this week and what magazine he'd been in last week. Sara couldn't figure out the relationship between the Kellermans and Mr Freiman: the Kellermans were obviously married, but, as she would tell her children years later, Mrs Kellerman seemed to be flirting with Mr Freiman, plucking at his sleeve, batting her lashes at him, trying to get something from him – attention, acknowledgement – which he clearly had no wish to give. Instead, confusingly, he stared only at her as he told jokes about the things he'd seen in Paris. He said how happy he was to be getting some good Jewish food at last because the French food was intolerable, and he made jokes about that, too. But Sara never really liked jokes, at least not the kind he was making. He was handsome, but his Yiddish was coarse, rough, working class and he made no attempt to hide that. Anyway, she'd always preferred men who looked more like her father and Jacques, dark and delicate. With those bright blue eyes and a big handlebar moustache, he was like a cowboy in a Hollywood movie. Sara had never liked cowboy movies: she liked French actors like Maurice Chevalier and Charles Boyer, so chic and elegant. This American, with his jokes and his broad chest, was more like John Wayne.

'Dinner is ready,' said Chaya, bringing out the food and taking her seat.

Mr Kellerman ate hungrily, apparently unaware of or unbothered by his wife's increasingly obvious flirtations with Bill. Sara, as usual, picked at her food, and when Bill asked if she worked Alex answered for her.

'She's an artist, I told you – really nice paintings, and such a beauty herself all the famous artists want to paint her,' he said, to Sara's confusion. Not only was that not true but Alex never spoke that way about her.

Sara mostly kept her head down but every time she looked up she noticed Bill was staring at her and it unnerved her, so she quickly looked down again. Then, just as Alex was about to launch into another story about his great fashion successes, Bill interrupted him.

'You are the most beautiful woman I have ever seen and I am completely in love with you,' he said, looking straight at Sara.

The room went silent.

'Come to America with me next month. I'll get you a return ticket so you can go back if you want. But come with me. I'm an honest, hard-working man and I'll take care of you,' he continued, reaching his arm across the table.

Sara did not reach back to take his hand. Instead, she made a forced laugh. 'Is this the famous American sense of humour?' she asked.

But he shook his head, shaking off her hint. 'I am not joking. I fell in love with you the minute I saw you. Come with me. I will look after you. I promise,' he said.

Sara looked to Alex for help, but for once he said nothing. Her mother also sat there silently. Mrs Kellerman couldn't understand what was happening but she had a good idea, and she looked like she was about to burst with fury. Only Mr Kellerman kept eating, utterly unfazed by the scene in front of him. Sara realised no one was going to help her here, so she told Bill that he was clearly drunk and if he didn't stop it she would have to ask him to leave.

Dinner continued, awkwardly, with Bill pointedly staring at her and Sara pointedly staring down at her plate. At least, she thought, after this dinner she wouldn't have to see him again. It would be over.

It was not over. Alex brought the American over twice more that week for dinner – without the Kellermans, at least – and both times the scene replayed itself, with him telling Sara that he loved her. If she thought she would be free of him once he finally sailed back to America on 2 March, she had once again underestimated him. As soon as he was back home a week later the phone calls began. Every few days he called her on her building's shared phone, begging her to come and join him, telling her he loved her, promising to treat her well. Just one transatlantic phone call in those days would have been a big deal; a dozen was akin to him sending her diamonds.

Initially she scoffed at his proposals, but Alex started to push her to accept them (it had been Alex, of course, who gave Bill Sara's building's phone number). He told her the Nazis were coming and were going to kill them all. This invitation to America was a gift from God and if she turned it down she was as stupid as Mila. If she went to America she would be able to get the rest of them out of Europe – and if she didn't, she was condemning them to death.

'You're going to kill us, is that what you want? You marrying this guy is our last chance,' Alex would tell her, while she cried in a chair.

Other times, he would try a different tactic, one covered more in sugar than vinegar: 'He's a millionaire on Park Avenue, he works in the fashion business – what more could you want? He's a handsome guy, and so tall! Taller even than Henri! I've known him for years, he's a great guy,' he would say, smiling at her, stroking her pale hand. One man was pulling her to America and the other pushing her, and between them she started to break.

Eventually she went to Henri for help. What should she do? She didn't want to leave her home, her fiancé, her family. But if she didn't, would they all be killed by the Germans? Henri sighed. While he didn't follow the news quite as closely as Alex, he certainly knew about what was happening in Europe, mainly because of Sonia. She read newspapers every day, in multiple languages, and she had been warning Henri about Hitler for years. Henri also had kept some friends from his time in Danzig, and so he knew very well how that city had been taken over by the Nazis in 1933, and how the Jews had had to flee. Meanwhile Sonia heard frequently from her family scattered around Poland about the rise of fascist groups there. So when Henri had mentioned Alex's plan to Sonia the week before, after having heard about it from his mother, Sonia said, unhesitatingly, 'She should go.' They'd all lived through pogroms and terror before. The prospect of any of these things returning was not an abstract concept to them.

'You should go,' Henri told Sara.

'And that's when your grandmother knew she was going,' Sonia later told me.

Sara went to Rose and Herman Brenner's apartment and cried, and they told her she should listen to Henri; maybe Rose and Herman would come and live in America, too, one day. Who knew what might happen with the world's politics going the way they were? In what must have been a state close to shock, Sara began to accept that she was going to America to marry a man she didn't know and liked less. She would never have done it just to save herself. But for her whole family? Of course she went.

Alex and Jacques had tried to save their family by going to war. Henri would do his part through his work. The only option open to Sara was the one that countless women had been forced to take before her: marry someone she did not love. It is the traditional form of female sacrifice, so common that it was considered at the time expected and unremarkable. What would have been extraordinary, in the eyes of those around her then, was if she'd refused to do it.

But how did she explain any of this to her fiancé? Did she say goodbye at all, or just disappear for good? How do you tell the love of your life, with whom you're planning a life, that you're leaving him to marry someone you've barely met? Her photo album, of her life in France in the 1930s, is a wordless yet eloquent testimony of not what she said, but how she felt about leaving behind her love and her life. At some point, she diligently went through it and either tore out whole photos and ripped them up or, with her thumbnail, scored out the faces of the people in the pictures so she wouldn't have to remember them (she carefully left photos of Henri, Sonia, Jacques and Alex alone – she didn't have to forget them). Someone picked up some of the pieces, glued them back together and stuck them in the album. Initially I assumed it was Sara, having remorsefully mended her photos after destroying them in a fit of high emotion. But my father said it was most likely his father, 'walking behind her and picking up the pieces of the photos and taping them together as quickly as she could destroy them'. Her husband always thought she was so beautiful, it pained him to see any photos of her destroyed. And then, after her rage had passed and she saw her photos restored, she saved them in her shoebox, where they were safe but she didn't have to look at them. But whoever did the repairing couldn't – or didn't – replace the faces she had gouged out, so in several photos my grandmother is standing in Paris, smiling happily, holding the arm of a man with no face – a ghost, a vanished past.

On 3 June 1937 she sailed on the SS *Manhattan* from Le Havre to New York, on a ticket Bill sent over for her. 'Sara Rykfa Glass, draftsman' was how she was described on the passenger list, and in the box for nationality someone wrote 'Polish' only to cross that out and write 'Heb' – 'Hebrew'. As in Poland, her Jewishness was now seen as more relevant than her born nationality. As she sailed off, she watched France fade away, the only place she'd ever been happy. She had nothing to think about over the week-long journey but what she had left behind.

Bill met Sara at the dock. He had a big smile on his face; she did not, but she was relieved that at least the Kellermans weren't with him. They got in his car and as they drove she focused on the sights around her, trying to familiarise herself with this new land she was expected to call home: the cars, the clothes, the advertisements on billboards in a language she did not understand. Next to her, Bill chattered away in Yiddish over the noise of the engine, and when she finally focused on what he was saying, she realised a couple of things pretty quickly: he was not a millionaire, he did not live on Park Avenue and he did not work in the fashion industry. It turned out he barely knew Alex at all. He lived in Farmingdale, Long Island, where he ran a Texaco gas station. Alex had completely lied to her, and the few sketchy images she'd had of her life in the States – living in the city, sharing a life with someone as interested in fashion as her – dissolved into nothing. Instead, she would be living in the middle of what was essentially nowhere, with a man whose life had no connection to her interests and passions at all. But it was too late to go back, because as soon as she accepted Bill's ticket and got on the ship her fate was fixed. Two weeks to the day after her ship docked in New York, she became Mrs William Freiman.

IN PARIS, Sara had found a city that encouraged her aspirations and inspired her every day with its beauty. Farmingdale, Long Island, was not Paris. Back in 1937 most of the town's businesses were located on Main Street: the pharmacy, the hardware store, the bank. Kids rode their bicycles up and down it all day in the summer, swerving around cars parked diagonally in front of glass-fronted stores. People lived on side streets and dead-ends in identical two-storey houses, most of which had an American flag either affixed to the roof or on a pole in the front lawn. There was a cinema in

the town but that was mainly for the kids. When the adults wanted entertainment, they would go to one another's houses for supper and gossip about their neighbours. It was called Farmingdale, Long Island, but it was really Small Town, America.

Farmingdale was formed by a series of early twentieth-century American phenomena. New York, uniquely in the United States back then, had excellent train lines and, as a result, the city was one of the earliest examples of urban flight, with people increasingly moving out of the city and commuting in to work. The American suburbs started to emerge, as immigrants who had arrived in New York in the late nineteenth century realised in the early twentieth century that instead of living in dirty and diseased tenements on the Lower East Side of Manhattan they could instead move to comparatively bright and spacious houses outside the city.

Suburbia is often depicted as quintessential Americana but in many cases it was least partly moulded by immigrants, and Farmingdale was, by the time Sara arrived, largely populated by second-generation working-class German and Italian immigrants, who might not have spoken English at home, but firmly considered themselves to be American. Just as the suburbs were starting to boom in eastern Long Island, the American aviation industry arrived. Long Island was a natural airfield: situated on the west of the Atlantic, close but not too close to one of America's biggest cities, with large flat plains for take-offs and landings. When Charles Lindbergh made his famous transatlantic flight in 1927, he took off from Roosevelt Field, 13 miles from Farmingdale. This was the golden age of the American aviation industry and thriving aircraft companies, such as Liberty, Grumman, Republic, Ranger and Fairchild, needed a huge number of workers. This coaxed yet more people out of the city and into the Long Island suburbs. By the mid-1930s, Farmingdale's population had doubled in twenty years to 3,500.

So Farmingdale looked very American and was shaped by American social shifts. But Sara would also have found it in some ways grimly reminiscent of Chrzanow. Whereas Chrzanow's name came from the Polish word for horse-radish, Farmingdale's original name was the similarly prosaic Hardscrabble. By the 1930s, it was populated by working-class Catholics and Jews and when Sara arrived it was, despite the nearby aircraft manufacturers, still a largely rural community; many of her neighbours were potato farmers. And while there obviously weren't pogroms in Farmingdale, there were other problems.

'There was also a lot of racism in the town,' William Rappaport, who ran Farmingdale's pharmacy back then, told me. 'White supremacist groups had a big presence in Farmingdale, especially during the war. There were marches, meetings and open anti-Semitism. And that made the Jewish community especially tight-knit.'

Alongside the racism, there was, Rappaport said, a suspicion of 'difference': 'Aspirations, cultural interests, all these were seen as weird, and anything that made you different was weird. So even though the city was just a train ride away, no one would think of going there to see a museum or play. You might go to Brooklyn to see relatives, but that was it. Even reading the *New York Times* was a sign of over-intellectualism,' he smiled. Instead, people were expected to read the local paper, the *Farmingdale Post*.

As in Chrzanow, another small town, there was a feeling that what Farmingdale had to offer should suffice, and anyone who wanted more was getting above themselves, and nothing was worse than that. There were few places less suited to a young Francophile with a love of culture and beauty, and with ambitions for a glamorous, fulfilled life than Farmingdale, 1937.

When I visited Farmingdale on a hot spring day, I was struck by how similar it felt to Chrzanow still. Both are pleasant and clean, with pretty streets and friendly people. But it has not been easy for small towns to adjust to the twenty-first century, and on the day I was there Farming-dale felt as silent as an abandoned ranch in an old Western, even on a weekday afternoon. There were vacant shop fronts, and the family-run stores had been crushed by the big chains and out-of-town shopping centres. While there are still some aviation companies in Long Island, many such as Grumman have long since closed down. With big cities just down the road (Krakow for Chrzanow, Manhattan for Farmingdale), how do you stop the young people leaving as soon as pos-sible, desperate for something to do other than hang out on the same streets they've been hanging out on since they were kids? When I left and returned to the nearby cities where I was staying, it was like slipping from a faded sepia photo into a three-dimensional film. And that's how it must've felt, in reverse, for Sara, arriving in Farmingdale from Paris eighty years earlier.

Farmingdale was waiting for her when she arrived, and not especially warmly.

'Everyone knew about Bill's French bride long before she turned up,' said William Rappaport.

Given how little Bill himself knew about her, their knowledge of Sara was presumably limited to the fact that she was French and she was to be his bride. This was more than enough for them.

'What's wrong with American girls? They not good enough for you, Bill?' people asked him.

'If you didn't find anything you wanted in Farmingdale, couldn't you have just gone to New York?' others asked.

Some were simply so stumped as to why handsome Bill would marry a Frenchwoman they assumed he must have got her pregnant while he was in Paris. She was probably one of those kinds of Frenchwomen.

And these questions did not stop once Sara arrived in this strange, unfamiliar small town. People asked them of Bill in front of Sara, taking it for granted she wouldn't understand, and not really caring if she did. And soon enough she did understand, because she was good at languages. She heard them muttering about how her husband had had many lady friends, and maybe he still did, maybe that's why he went into the city so much, and she heard them talking about how unfriendly she seemed, how snooty, how superior.

And she probably was snooty or, more accurately, aloof. She realised that none of these people were interested in art, or fashion, or culture – all the things that represented to her high-mindedness, sophistication. These people, it seemed to her, were little different from the Polish peasants. Like her brothers Henri and Alex, she felt that a lack of aspiration was an admission of a lack of soul. Only those who are dead inside fail to want more than the little half-inch of life they've been given.

But Sara was also shy and sad, and these are often mistaken for snobbishness. Talking about her snobbishness was a convenient smokescreen for the simple fact that none of her neighbours wanted to be friends with Sara, because she was a foreigner, even though most of them had immigrant parents themselves. But then, they wanted to be American and she did not. She would never be one of them, because she didn't want to be.

'She was a French lady in a rough Long Island town,' my father's cousin Ann Horowitz, who grew up in Farmingdale, told me. 'She wasn't ever really going to be accepted.'

She tried to make a life there: she decorated her and Bill's home as beautifully as she could in Farmingdale, and breakfast and dinner were always on the table on time for him. She would go for walks and get to know the town. But days would go by when she wouldn't speak to anyone but her husband. And on days when he didn't come home, she spoke to no one.

Bill's family were the only people who talked to Sara, as they could talk to her in Yiddish. They all lived close by: his mother Rose, who lived with them part of the time, his older brothers Jack and Mike, and his younger sisters, Rita and Sadie. The few surviving children of Bill's siblings, all of whom are at least in their seventies now, stressed to me how much their parents liked Sara: how pretty they all thought she was, how kind they thought she was, and how protective they were of her when they felt Bill wasn't treating her right.

This may all be true, but it wasn't how it seemed to Sara. When my parents got engaged in 1974, Sara arranged to meet up with my mother, her daughter-in-law-to-be, for the first time. As soon as they were sitting down she spoke, in a terrible emotional rush, of how Bill's family had bullied her when she arrived in the States: they made fun of her accent, she said, of her love of art, and of her interest in clothes. 'Why are you interested in *that*?!' she recalled them sneering at her. For almost forty years she'd been waiting for a female relative in whom she could confide the pain she'd felt on her arrival in America, and it had festered inside her for decades.

Maybe Bill's siblings did like her, but just didn't know how to reach out to her, or were bewildered by how different she was from them. And maybe she was just too homesick to understand them. But if she felt alienated from her in-laws that was nothing compared with how she felt about her husband.

Bill was kind – Alex hadn't lied about that, at least – and he really did love her. That turned out to be true, too. He loved to show off his French bride – so beautiful, so classy – but as far as he was concerned, he'd brought her over, provided her with a little house on Cornelia Street, and she could figure out the rest. He'd done her this incredible favour, rescuing her from Europe – what on earth did she have to complain about? But she did complain. She wasn't nearly as grateful to him as he thought she would be.

In another world their marriage could have worked because, in many ways, they were well matched: they both had religious parents but weren't religious themselves, and they both had dreams of a better life than the ones they were born into. But theirs was a match that was forged in lies and impulse, and forced into being by politics and circumstance. It would have been a miracle if it had worked, and neither of their families dealt in miracles.

Sara looked at this American, with his coarse jokes and coarser Yiddish, the way assimilated Jews in Paris looked at people like Chaya and the rest of the Pletzl: didn't he understand he was supposed to hide those parts of himself? Didn't he want to improve his social standing, and not be seen as just another working-class Jew? And didn't he understand that his behaviour reflected negatively on her, by association? For Sara, Paris had been her step forward, and this American had pulled her back to a life she thought she'd left behind. Bill was smart, so he sensed how she felt, and it hurt him.

And, most of all, she wanted to be with someone else.

'Your mother left her heart in Paris with that dental student,' Sonia later told Sara's sons.

The fights started not long after they got married. They got worse when Bill revealed that he wasn't going to help bring the rest of her family over from Paris, because it would cost too much. Sara was devastated: the only reason she had married Bill was because she thought it would get her family out of France, and they would be with her in America. But from Bill's perspective, he was the wronged party here. He had certainly not been told that paying for all his in-laws to come over was part of the deal – in fact, according to Sonia, Alex had promised to support Bill for the rest of his life if he married Sara. But Bill understood sooner than Sara that the promises Alex made during this whole episode didn't amount to much. Bill was able to shrug off such things; Sara, however, was crushed. She was stuck and now she really was alone. She had given up everything for something that was worse than nothing.

Sara was desperately unhappy. Just how unhappy is apparent from looking at the passenger lists of ships between New York and France between 1937 and 1938. In November 1937, five months after she first arrived in the United States, she went back to Paris, presumably using the return ticket Bill had promised her. She returned to New York one month later, but six months later she made another return trip. Six months after that, in November 1938, she went back again. She returned to New York a month later. On none of those trips was she accompanied by Bill.

She didn't, however, forget him. More than twenty years after Bill died, and more than eighty years after it was originally sent, my uncle Rich found a photo among my grandfather's belongings. It was a studio portrait of my grandmother, and she had sent it to him from Paris on one of her trips. It is dated 8 December 1937 and at the bottom in my grandmother's handwriting is the inscription, '*Pour mon mari cheri, Paris*'. Whether distance had made Sara's heart truly grow fonder of Bill is a question only she can answer. It seems more likely to me that she felt a wifely loyalty towards him, and knew that he was a good man, and felt some gratitude towards him for that. Few relationships are all black or all white. But what is most apparent is that, just six months after marriage, a schism was growing in Sara that would exist for the rest of her life: wherever she was, she felt she should be somewhere else. When she was in France with her family, she felt she should be in America with her husband, and vice versa. More than half a century later I would see that divide in her myself.

Who was paying for all those tickets? At approximately $130 for a round-trip in tourist class, there is no way Bill would have been able to afford all these crossings to Paris, and while Alex would certainly have paid for Sara to go back to New York once she arrived in Paris, he would not have bought her a return ticket so she could then come back again a year later. Perhaps Herman Brenner, Rose Ornstein's husband, helped, but there is no record of that, and it's unlikely he could have afforded it either.

The truth is, no one knows how Sara made three round-trips between New York and France in eighteen months during 1937 and 1938 because neither she nor Bill ever spoke about it, certainly not to anyone alive now. No one even knew about these trips until I happened to spot her name recurring on the old passenger lists, and it was definitely her: Sara Freiman from Farmingdale, Long Island. But where she once had been described as a draftsman, she was now 'h'wife' – a housewife. All dreams gone. It's easy to imagine her running back to Paris, frantic to escape her marriage, and even easier to imagine Alex all but pushing her back up the gangplank to return to New York. And that cycle might have continued for ever had Sara not realised something by the time she docked back in New York on 1 December 1938: she was two months pregnant.

Ronald Michael Freiman, my father, was born on 23 July 1939. The doctor who performed the birth botched the job so badly that, eighty years later, my dad still has long, deep scars on his temples from where he was dragged out and nearly crushed by the forceps. The first time Sara saw her son, he was, terrifyingly, covered in blood.

'If my head looks like this, imagine what that butcher did to the insides of my mother,' my dad would say when asked about the marks.

Sara couldn't run to her family for comfort any more, not even after her son's traumatic birth. Once the war had started most civilian ships were used as troop carriers or freighters. She couldn't even write to her family: from 1939, transatlantic mail was being intercepted by British Imperial Censorship in Bermuda, and some was confiscated. From 1941, it was suspended entirely between America and France, but Sara could not have reached her relatives anyway, because by this point they were all in hiding. For the next three years Sara had no idea if her family was alive or dead.

The only contact she had with anyone vaguely connected to her old life was her occasional correspondence with Alex's friend Kisling, who was then living in California, but he was just as ignorant about her family's wellbeing as she was. He wrote to her from Beverly Hills on 6 December 1942:

My dear Mrs Freiman,
    I think of you often, I think of poor Alex from whom you are cut off, I think of the worries that is causing you. Really, we have no luck, my poor friend. Each of us who is born over there we are bearing a

cross but what can we do? The only weapon we have is hope for this will soon be over and that we will find them all soon again. If you have a moment send me your news, I don't dare ask you the news of Alex of which you probably have more information than me.

I hope your husband is well, as well as your charming child,

Maurice Kisling (Kiki)

Bill took hundreds of photos of her in this era: despite all their fighting, and her disappointing lack of affection, he was always so proud of his beautiful French bride, who made their home so much more stylish than those of his siblings. But few have looked more like a stranger in a strange land than my grandmother in these photos: always in her distinctly French clothing and always standing next to various forms of Americana – a flag, a diner, a supersize car – she is like an exotic explorer among the natives. In one of my favourite photos of my grandmother, taken in 1941, she is wearing a jaunty little three-cornered hat with a peaked top and a beautiful belted coat with exaggerated lapels that was made by Alex. As ever, she is in heels and her make-up and hair are perfect, and she is bending over a little boy – my father – in a snow suit. She could be a young mother in the Tuileries, or on the Champs-Élysées – except she is standing next to a gas pump because she is at my grandfather's gas station in Farmingdale. A friend of mine used to refer to this photo as 'granny at the gas station', but I think of it more as

Sara and Ronald.

Dorothy back in black and white Kansas, but in this version she never wanted to leave technicolour Oz.

In December 1943 Sara gave birth to her second child – another boy. As she lay in bed recovering from the birth she listened to the news reports about the Battle of Berlin, in which, on 17 December, the Royal Air Force nearly destroyed Berlin's railway system. The Royal Air Force – RAF. The initials kept being repeated on the report: these were the people who were trying to save Europe from the people killing her family, Sara thought. RAF. She named her baby Richard Allen Freiman, known as Rich.

Sara had longed for a girl, whom she could dress in pretty clothes and whose long hair she could style. A girl who could be her confidante, her friend. But she adored her sons, and she poured the love she couldn't give to her husband into her boys. She was a demonstratively affectionate mother, naturally gentle and loving but also desperate to justify to herself the choice she had made that resulted in them being born. If she loved them enough, if they loved her enough, maybe it would have been worth it.

The story of my grandmother confused people – particularly, I noticed, Jewish Americans who generally, and understandably, assume that any story about escaping the war by coming to America is a happy one. That narrative is a cornerstone of the Jewish American story, yet Sara's story complicated it. When I was ten, I gave a presentation about the Glasses to my Hebrew school class in New York, and although I didn't really have the words to describe my

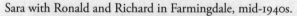

Sara with Ronald and Richard in Farmingdale, mid-1940s.

grandmother's unhappiness, I knew enough to say that she'd never wanted to leave Paris.

'But of course she was happy once she got to America, whereas her brothers were very unfortunate to be in France,' my teacher, Ms Meyers, concluded for me, thinking she was being helpful.

I thought of my grandmother, stuck in Miami at that point, still homesick after half a century. And I thought of my great-uncles, Alex and Henri, who were by then happy and wealthy in Paris. Individual lives are always more complicated than sweeps of history, but how could I explain this to Miss Meyers, in my Hebrew school classroom that, by way of interior decor, had a picture of the gates of Auschwitz on one wall? I didn't want to give the wrong answer. So I nodded and sat down at my desk.

Sara had done what she'd had to in order to survive the war. But in saving herself she lost everything that had made her life worth living. Other things took their place – her children, eventually her grandchildren – so I can't say she made the wrong choice, and she would never have said that either. But no, she wasn't happy when she got to America. She was grateful to it for the safety it provided her and the material comforts it brought her. But looking at the photos of her in Farmingdale – her make-up so perfect, her face so sad – it's clear the price she paid for survival was painfully high. 'She moved to America but, emotionally, she never really unpacked her bags there,' my father said. Sara endured a specifically female tragedy: she gave up not just her true love but her dreams and professional fulfilment in exchange for protection by marriage. Alex got a medal for going to war and Jacques could send Sara his metal prison plate. But no one was going to give her any plaudits for what she did. While her brothers performed the traditionally masculine roles of carrying out acts of extraordinary bravery, Sara endured the more feminine role of private self-erasure.

Yet as unhappy as she was, divorce was never an option for her. Americans certainly got divorced in the 1940s – in fact the divorce rate spiked after the Second World War, when couples who had rushed to marry before the war quickly regretted that decision when the men returned from fighting. But the stigma was still terrible, and, like many women of her generation and afterwards, Sara could in no way survive as the single mother of two without any kind of familial support. Anyway, that was not what Jewish women like her did. She knew what her role was now: it was to make Bill's meals and look after her boys. When she moved to America, Sara's internal life split: outwardly, she existed in the present but inside she was always thinking of what had been and what could have been, if the war hadn't happened, if she'd stayed and somehow survived, if she moved back there now, if if if. She'd only had a few years of happiness in Paris, and even fewer healthy and happy ones, a mere blink. But the ghosts from those years haunted her. After the war, she promised herself, she would go back to Paris. And thus began Sara's long wait, one that would be much longer than she realised at the time, for her life to begin again.

Bill (front and centre).

7

BILL – America

New York, 1900s–1930s

BILL HAD NEVER expected or even especially wanted to go to France, or, as he called it, 'Europe'. But when his neighbours, Oscar and Rosa Kellerman, invited him to come with them on a business trip, he thought, Hey, you only live once. So he tagged along, just for the hell of it.

Except it was possibly for more than the hell of it. Bill was an extremely handsome man, and a good-looking single guy of thirty-five in a small town will attract the eyes of the ladies, one of the ladies whose eyes he caught being Rosa Kellerman. Whether Bill and Rosa actually had an affair no one will ever know, but Sara never forgot how much Rosa flirted with him when she met them in Paris. When I asked my father about it he said that thinking about the way Rosa would still moon around his dad, years after the trip to Paris, reminded him of *The Bridges of Madison County*, 'not that I would confuse Rosa Kellerman with Meryl Streep'. Certainly the ships' passenger lists suggest something was up between them. Even though the Kellermans travelled to Europe frequently for their work in the clothing trade – three times in 1937 alone – they never travelled together. Instead, when Rosa sailed to France from New York in December 1936, her husband had sailed a month earlier. But a certain William Freiman sailed two days after her from the same dock. And when she sailed back in February 1937, she left from Cherbourg. William's ship also left from Cherbourg, a few days later, but her husband, Oscar, didn't return to Farmingdale until April, and he sailed from Southampton. Were William and Rosa staying together in New York and Cherbourg? Sara would have said yes.

If Bill went to France in 1936 to enjoy a flirtation with a married woman under her husband's nose it wouldn't have been wildly out of character. Bill was many things – funny, handsome, ambitious – but perhaps his most notable quality back then was mischievousness. He was the baby boy in his family, the fourth of five, and he always had a reputation as the cheeky one and a flirt. Among my grandmother's belongings I found a photo of him judging what is clearly a beauty competition. He is standing on stage in a suit holding a microphone, his dark hair slicked back, and on either side of him is a woman in a bathing suit, each wearing a sash that reads 1936, the year before he sailed to Paris. His pencil moustache is stretching out with his wide smile. He looks pretty pleased with himself.

He and Oscar Kellerman were not close friends – in fact, they hardly socialised at all. But Oscar had learned from his last trip to Paris that he would need to bring someone who spoke either Yiddish or French in order to talk to the fashion merchants there, and it was a lot easier to find a Yiddish speaker than a French one in Farmingdale. It was not explained to Bill that he would be acting as an unpaid translator on this trip; instead, he planned to ditch the Kellermans as soon as they docked in France so he could tour the country by motorcycle and ski in the Alps. But, they told him, if he wanted his return ticket that would have to wait until after their meeting with this Maguy fellow.

The Kellermans owned a wholesale clothing business and the reason they travelled to Paris so often was to buy patterns and fabrics on the cheap. Alex had become one of their pattern suppliers, because it was by doing jobs like this that he was able to keep his couture business afloat. He schmoozed the people who ran these companies, but he loathed selling his beautiful designs to what he described as 'those *schmatte* merchants', tacky Americans who would tell him to design a sleeve differently so that it wouldn't drag in their macaroni cheese.

But one American Alex liked right away was Bill. 'Your grandfather was a smart man,' he would tell me, even though they hardly ever saw one another due to Bill's longstanding belief that he'd been to Europe once and there was no need for him to go again. Bill couldn't have given Alex any money, and he certainly didn't have any power when Alex met him, so I often wondered at Alex's fondness for my grandfather.

After all, the number of people Alex truly liked could be counted on one hand, and Bill was very much one of them. He was smart, no question, and tall, which was always an important factor for Alex. But Alex's feelings for Bill seemed to go beyond mere facts and I suspect they lay in how they met, which was through the Kellermans.

Bill disliked Oscar Kellerman about as much as Alex, and neither of them was any good at disguising their feelings. Alex used to recall how he liked Bill so much when he met him with the Kellermans that he invited him over for dinner, and it's easy for me to imagine how that original meeting went, with Bill translating for the Kellermans and him and Alex quickly understanding their mutual loathing of these cheap clothing merchants.

'Tell that piece of dirt that he can go to hell if he thinks he's getting this pattern for less than 40 francs,' I could picture Alex saying.

'How about 30 francs if he promises his wife won't wear it?' Bill would have responded.

'Deal!'

'Mr Maguy says you can have the pattern for 70 francs.'

'Seventy! That's ridiculous!'

'He says Eleanor Roosevelt bought this pattern when she was last in Paris.'

'Wow, really? We'll take it!'

And so on.

I never saw Alex and Bill in the same room together, but I'd have liked to. In some ways they were very similar.

'And you must meet my sister,' Alex said to Bill at the end of the meeting with the Kellermans. 'She's an absolute beauty, a model. Healthy, fun and very keen on American men. She always said she wanted to marry one. You're just her type!'

A pretty French girl? Sure, why not. Just for the hell of it.

To Sara and Alex, Bill Freiman looked like the epitome of America, with his broad shoulders, blue eyes and fondness for cowboy hats. But like them, he was the product of immigration. And also like them, his name was not what he said it was.

MOSES FREIMAN was born in 1902, in a tenement on the Lower East Side of New York. Although he was American by birth, he, along with his brothers and sisters, spoke only Yiddish until he was seven years old. Like Chaya, his mother never learned the language of the country she lived in, and his father spoke only enough English to work, and in their neighbourhood back then, that was utterly typical. Like the Glasses, his parents, Sam and Rosy Freiman, came from the Austro-Hungarian Empire. They immigrated to the United States in, respectively, 1893 and 1889. Sam probably came for the reason most Jewish men emigrated to America, which was he was looking for a better life. Rosy's story was a little more complicated: she was running away from her family. According to what she told relatives later in life, her parents had arranged a marriage for her when she was a teenager, but after the wedding she realised her husband was gay – or, as she experienced it, had no interest in women. As an uneducated, sheltered, Orthodox teenager in eastern Europe, she had no way of explaining the situation to either herself or her family. So instead, she left the marriage and ran away to America to escape her parents' wrath for disgracing the family, somehow scraping the money together to come to New York. A few years later, she met Sam, the same year he arrived, and the two married. If she had run away from her husband back home, this means that when she married Sam she committed bigamy. But it is unlikely she ever thought about it that way, and it certainly didn't break her marital stride: within a decade, they had five children: Michael, Yakov, Sarah, Moses and Rivka.

Between 1880 and 1924, 2.5 million eastern European Jews emigrated to the United States. Close to 85 per cent of them came to New York City, and 75 per cent of them settled initially in the Lower East Side.[1] This was America's Pletzl. And as in France, the Americanised Jews – who were largely Reform, or not very observant – were less than thrilled by this influx of foreign, Orthodox Jews into their country: 'From a religious point of view, the Russian Jew is further from the American Jew than the American Jew is from a Christian or infidel,' one New York Jew told the *New York Times* then.[2] But American Jews felt more secure about their position in their country than their French counterparts did, so they worried less about how these immigrant Jews would reflect on them. Although they occasionally lectured them directly, urging them to leave behind what one of the

American Jews at the time described as their 'impractical, outlandish and medieval beliefs and customs',[3] they expected this would happen naturally down the generations. And in the main, they were right.

By the time Bill was born in 1902, the Lower East Side was the largest Jewish neighbourhood in the world and was known as New York's – and, by extension, America's – Jewish ghetto. But that generalising term does a disservice to the varieties of immigrants, and how they created their own tiny worlds within the crowded and noisy New York neighbourhood. Hungarian Jews lived above Houston Street, Galician Jews between Houston and Grand Streets, Romanian and Levantine Jews between Allen Street and the Bowery, and Russian Jews below Grand Street. The Freiman family – occasionally renamed Fryman by census takers – lived at 102 Allen Street, suggesting Sam and Rosy were actually Romanian, even though the US censuses from the time repeatedly described them, as they later would Sara, as Austrian. The building wasn't especially big, but according to the 1900 census, twenty-two other families lived in it, because it was a tenement.

By 1900, 90 per cent of Jews on the Lower East Side lived in tenements,[4] which were five- or six-storey homes that had been subdivided by landlords into apartments for families, most just 25 feet wide and 100 feet long, with barely any light, ventilation or fresh air, for $12 a week. There was no indoor plumbing, just a lone tap outside that would supply all the water for the building's tenants to clean, cook and wash, and only one outhouse for every twenty tenants, although rather than walking all the way downstairs and out in the freezing cold to use it, many would use a chamber pot and simply dump the waste out of the window, only occasionally checking to see if anyone was walking below. They didn't even have gas light until the early 1900s, and residents tended to cook with coal, meaning they were living in what were essentially pitch-black caves, and they would have to grope their way through the dark hallways to find the stairway and their apartment, feeling along the walls with the flat of their palms. Tenements first emerged on the Lower East Side in the 1860s as a solution to overcrowding, but as immigrants continued to move to New York, and the immigrants who were there continued to have children, the tenements themselves became emblems of overcrowding. A tenement apartment that housed four people in 1870 would, by 1900, be home to ten or twelve. They were dirty, dark and disease-ridden, but for most immigrant Jews in New York they were home, and the Freimans lived in theirs for twenty years.

When Sam Freiman moved his family into a Lower East Side tenement, he was, like most Jewish immigrants in that neighbourhood, illiterate. He worked as a pedlar, meaning he sold second-hand clothes and rags from the street, and every day he would have to dodge 'loafers' – generally Irish-Americans – who hung around on street corners and outside bars shouting anti-Semitic abuse at him[5] as he worked in the snow and the rain to earn, at best, pennies. A letter written in 1855, when one-third of Jewish wage-earners were pedlars, describes the life of a Jewish pedlar in the city:

> When the newly arrived Israelite asks what he shall do to make a living, he is most commonly advised to go and peddle. Accordingly a basket is hastily fixed up and he is hurried into the country. The country merchants receive [him] coolly and oppose him step by step. An acrimonious feeling takes hold of the pedlar's heart – he is disappointed and discouraged, and yet he goes on from day to day, changes the basket for the bundle, the bundle for the horse and wagon peddling, and finally emerges a sleek, thrifty merchant. Have the history of one of these men and you have the history of them all.[6]

Sam never became a sleek and thrifty merchant; instead, he did something else that was all too common of his demographic: he abandoned his family. Absconding fathers and husbands were so common among the Lower East Side immigrants that one of the several Yiddish daily newspapers in New York at the time had a regular column devoted to missing men. Sometimes they died in a drunken brawl. Sometimes they died of pneumonia after getting drunk and either falling in the river or falling asleep outside in the bitter New York winter. Most commonly, they simply ran off, worn down by trying to provide for their multiple children by selling rags. Bill later told his sons that his father was a drunk who died in the gutter, but none of Sam's children ever knew for certain what happened to their father, other than that he disappeared in 1911 and they never saw him again. Like Chaya when Reuben went off to war, Rosy was suddenly a single mother in a country whose language she never learned, with five children to support on her own, aged between seven and sixteen. But unlike Chaya, she did not have Henri to support her. Instead, she had Moses.

Moses was nine when his father vanished and the last of the boys still to be at school. Like almost all Jewish immigrant children in the Lower East Side, Moses' older brothers, Michael and Yakov, dropped out of school at eighth grade, because fourteen was the age when children could get work permits, and families in the Lower East Side needed money a lot more than they needed educated kids. Many of these kids worked in sweatshops, sewing garments or rolling cigars from 6 a.m. until 11 p.m. for 50 cents a day, in horrifically perilous conditions. In one single fire in a New York sweatshop in 1911, the year Sam left, 146 workers were killed, half of whom were Jewish teenage girls.[7] Because Moses was the last boy at school, this also meant he was the boy who was most at home and became the man of the house, even though he was still in single digits. Perhaps for that reason, or maybe it was just always in his nature, Moses started getting into brawls in the neighbourhood.

'Your grandfather was the wild child in the family. Always a character,' my father's cousin Herb Freiman, the son of my grandfather's oldest brother, Michael, told me.

I'd never met Herb until I started researching this book, and I then spent a day with him in Long Island where he lives, not far from Farmingdale. In fact, despite my grandfather having so many siblings, and all of them living pretty much next door to one another for most of their lives, I knew almost no members of his family. But when I walked into Herb's house and saw him waiting for me on the sofa in his living room, my breath caught in my throat: he was the spitting image of my grandfather, who by that point had been dead for twenty-five years. That same cheeky smile, those same bright blue eyes ('The Freiman eyes,' Herb said, knowing what I was thinking) and, even though he was hooked up to an oxygen tank, the same inexhaustible jokey demeanour. His cousin Ann, Rivka's daughter, also joined us. She was the only one of my father's cousins that I knew as a child and I remembered she'd always been extremely thin and careful about what she ate. That was still the case when we met at Herb's, almost thirty years since we'd last seen one another. When she casually mentioned what she weighed that morning, a low number by anyone's standards, Herb shot back, 'Well, Ann, the good news is the circus is going to hire you to be the Fat Lady!' When we then went out to lunch at Herb's club and Ann picked half-heartedly at her salad, he teased her again, saying, 'Slow down there, Ann. Eat one more grape and you won't be able to fit in the car!' This was exactly how my grandfather used to talk, and while Sara couldn't stand it and thought it tacky, my sister and I thought he was funniest guy we'd ever known.

Herb was similarly delightful. I wished I'd got to know him sooner.

'Bill was born with a stutter, so he probably got into fights about that. But he taught himself to speak elegantly, more elegantly than anyone else in the family. But he fought because he wanted to protect his family,' Herb said.

My grandfather did talk elegantly – I'd forgotten that. Eloquent and fast, with an enormous vocabulary, without a hint of Yiddish accent. He also took care to lose what he called his 'Jewish accent', by which he meant the rising inflection and nasal tone which are still vocal signifiers of Jewishness in modern pop culture, in everything from Woody Allen movies to *Curb Your Enthusiasm*. As far as Bill was concerned, it was how his family talked, and he was determined to sound different from them. But if he talked well he wrote even better, always in cursive, so florid it verged on calligraphy, and wonderful long letters full of gossip and advice and philosophical thoughts. He was actually left-handed but, through characteristic force of will, he'd taught himself to write with his right hand so as to be able to use a fountain pen without smearing the ink. You'd have never guessed that he didn't speak English until he was seven and was illiterate until he was ten. And that, of course, was entirely the point. Like Alex, Bill dreamed of a better life than the one he was born into, and the way he spoke and wrote were an expression of that. There was a reason I knew almost none of his family: he didn't want me to. They were part of a world he wanted to leave behind.

Life in the tenements was brutal. Newspaper headlines from the time give a sense of the chaos and cost: 'Three Perish in Midnight Fire! Flames Sweep Through a Big Five-Storey Tenement! Other Tenants Missing!'[8] 'Eight Dead By Fire! Awful Tragedy in Hester Street! Woman Burned to Death in Sight of Crowd! Faces of Tortured People Seen at the Windows!'[9] Being a child in the tenements was especially perilous. All the buildings had yards, but these were hemmed in by other buildings and were often where the outhouse was, so were dark and disgusting. Instead, children preferred to play in the street, but because of the lack of decent lighting cars and bicycles didn't see them. In 1911, when Moses was nine, 183 children in New York were killed by moving vehicles and a further 381 were hit but survived.[10] There were parks and playgrounds, but these were often far away, meaning a three-year-old would have to walk ten or even twenty blocks, dodging cars, just to play on swings. Some mothers in the tenements – especially those who had been abandoned by their husbands – found life so hard that they would put their children on so-called orphan trains that took poor inner-city children out of the metropolis to live with rural families and essentially work as farmhands. Rosy, fortunately, did not do that, but life would have been extremely hard for all of them. Her income was supplemented by Michael and Yakov working, probably in factories, where they would have earned a couple of dollars a week, and it's possible that Sam occasionally sent the family money from wherever he'd disappeared to, but there was no evidence of this. Ultimately, they would have largely had to depend on Rosy's paltry earnings as a seamstress while each of the children looked after one another, each one hurrying after the other in school until they, too, could leave and earn money.

Moses picked up English quickly when he went to school. But he also desperately wanted to earn money to improve his family's situation generally, and as a child he sold ribbons on the street after school. As a teenager, he gave driving lessons. He was always looking for a crack in the wall through which he could crawl and find some money. By 1920, just as the Glasses were leaving Chrzanow, Rosy decided it was time to move her family. This might have been partly because of her youngest son, who got in so many fights that, for his own safety, she needed to get him out of the Lower East Side. But also, this was the trajectory of all Jews who wanted to lift their family into the middle classes: they had to get out of the Lower East Side. Many Jews went uptown, or to Brooklyn or Harlem. A friend told Rosy she should go to 'the centre of the universe' and so, according to family legend, she closed her eyes and pointed to a place on a map of New York. She landed on Long Island.

By the time the Freimans left the city, the Lower East Side was changing irrevocably. Within a decade, it wouldn't even be largely Jewish any more but instead became an Italian neighbourhood. Cities shift and flux, and today when you walk through the Lower East Side there are pickle stores next to Italian delis next to encroaching designer boutiques. During the 1920s, the Jewish population of the Lower East

Side plummeted dramatically, from 260,000 to 100,000,[11] and this was partly because of a situation the Glass family in Paris would have found familiar.

Since the late nineteenth century, Congress had been quietly passing laws banning various groups of people from entering the United States. By the time the First World War began, these barred groups included such alleged threats to the American way of life as polygamists, lunatics and Chinese labourers. In 1916 the American lawyer and eugenicist Madison Grant published his still influential book, *The Passing of the Great Race*, in which he stressed the danger of the changing 'stock' of American immigration, with more and more people coming to America from southern and eastern Europe instead of what he deemed to be the more superior countries in the north and west of the Continent. The Nordic race, he wrote, was 'being literally driven off the streets of New York City by swarms of Polish Jews' and he urged tighter immigration laws 'if the higher races are to be maintained'.[12] Almost exactly one hundred years later, the President of the United States, Donald Trump, would echo Grant when he told members of Congress in January 2018 that America needed more immigrants from Norway and fewer from 'shithole countries', by which he meant El Salvador, Haiti and certain African nations. Trump was widely condemned for it at the time, but his poll numbers did not suffer. Like Grant's in 1916, it felt like his words were prising open a box of ghouls that America seems to re-open every century. In the first two years of Trump's presidency, the FBI reported a rise in hate crimes motivated by race in America[13] and attacks against Muslim, South Asian and Middle Eastern communities rose by 45 per cent.[14]

After the First World War, national feelings of patriotism made their familiar transition into expressions of racism and anti-Semitism. Just like in France, Jews were associated with radicals, Bolsheviks and European revolution, and anti-Semitism became not just acceptable but, in many circles in the United States, respectable. The *Dearborn Independent*, a weekly newspaper established by the notoriously anti-Semitic Henry Ford, had, in 1925, a circulation of 900,000, making it then the second most popular newspaper in the United States, because it was distributed in all Ford's car dealerships. At that time, it launched a vicious campaign against so-called Jewish influence in the United States, spurred on by Ford's certainty that Jews started wars in order to profit from them. 'I know who started [the First World War]: German-Jewish bankers,' he was widely quoted as saying. Throughout the 1920s, the *Dearborn Independent* ran articles with headlines such as 'The International Jew: The World's Foremost Problem' and 'Jewish Power and America's Money Famine'. In case readers hadn't grasped Ford's point, the *Dearborn Independent* reprinted and distributed the *Protocols of the Elders of Zion*, the already discredited forgery that claimed to show Jewish plans for world domination. Ford eventually closed down the paper and issued an apology, written for him by the then chairman of the American Jewish Committee, Louis Marshall. But even though his views had been criticised at the time, by Jews and non-Jews alike, he was capturing elements of the national mood. F. Scott Fitzgerald acknowledged as much in *The Great Gatsby*, when the oafish character Tom Buchanan talks airily about how 'if we don't look out the white race will be – will be utterly submerged.' Through Tom, Fitzgerald captured – as journalist Pankaj Mishra put it – 'a deepening panic among America's Anglophile ruling class'.[15]

Madison Grant's book was hugely popular and had enormous political influence. He was close friends with Presidents Theodore Roosevelt and Herbert Hoover, and the former publicly praised his book. He also knew the American politician Albert Johnson, who sponsored the Immigration Restriction Act of 1921, which set a limit of 350,000 immigrants allowed in each year. This, Johnson wrote, would help prevent America from being polluted by hordes of 'abnormally twisted', 'unassimilable' Jews, 'filthy, un-American and often dangerous in their habits'.[16] The bill passed easily, but it did not go as far as its supporters had hoped. So in 1924 Johnson, along with Senator David A. Reed of Pennsylvania, turned to Grant as a self-appointed expert on world racial data for statistics that would support tightening quotas on immigrants from southern and eastern European countries. The Immigration Act of 1924, or the Johnson-Reed Act, as well as targeting Jewish immigrants, effectively banned all Arabs, East Indians and Asians from entering the country. Jewish politicians from across the country, alongside many Catholic ones, tried to fight the bill, defending immigrants' contributions to the country. But it wasn't enough, and the bill passed overwhelmingly in both the House and the Senate.

Grant's influence wasn't limited to 1920s America. It is not a surprise that a book that advocated segregating races with 'undesirable' and 'inferior' traits, described Jews as 'social discards' and endorsed the 'one drop rule'[17] to prevent mixing between the races would be welcomed in 1930s Germany. Grant's book was the first non-German book the Nazis ordered to be reprinted when they came to power, and Adolf Hitler told Grant, 'This book is my Bible.' The same book President Theodore Roosevelt described in 1917 as 'a capital book; in purpose, in vision, in grasp of the facts our people most need to realize'[18] would, less than twenty years later, become inspiration for the Nazis. Hitler also praised America's restrictions on naturalisation as proof that America endorsed the Nazi project, and ultimately the Immigration Act helped to facilitate the Holocaust because it prevented thousands of European Jews from escaping to America, including Anne Frank and her family.[19] Sometimes America isn't quite as far away from fascism as it thinks.

Grant set out to change New York's racial mix and, in that regard, he partially succeeded. Reed's immigration laws had an enormous effect on immigration in general, Jewish immigration in particular, and on the Lower East Side specifically. In 1920, the year before the first of Johnson's laws was passed, there were 800,000 new arrivals into the country, among them 120,000 Jews. By 1925, the numbers had fallen to 295,000 and 10,000 respectively.

When President Trump arrived in office in 2017 and issued an executive order that he himself referred to on Twitter as a 'Muslim ban', barring the citizens of seven Muslim countries from entering the United States for a period of ninety days. (He had previously, in 2015, during the presidential campaign, called for 'a complete and total shutdown' of the country's borders to Muslims, and suggested establishing a government database of all American Muslims, not unlike the 1940 French census of Jews.) Many people – politicians, journalists, Nobel laureates, leaders of Jewish organisations – described the so-called ban as 'un-American'. But it was only un-American in as much as what America should be; in regard to what America actually is, it was all too American, and Trump comes from a long line of white men who have set out to make America racist again. President Trump was not the first or even most successful American politician to set out to ban Muslims from the country, and this is a shameful truth about a country that was founded by immigrants for immigrants. But one of the wonderful things about America is there are always people who resist, and people in the 1920s made many of the same points about Johnson that people in 2017 made about President Trump. Dr I. Mortimer Bloom, rabbi of the Hebrew Tabernacle of West 116th Street, said this at the time:

> The immigration restriction bills are a denial and
> a reversal of long-cherished American ideals and
> traditions, an affront to the memory of the founders

of the Republic, a dagger thrust into the hearts of
thousands of human beings who yearn for an
opportunity to lead the normal decent life which
their own lands deny them and a staggering blow
to humanitarians everywhere . . . Not as a Jew, not
as one whose co-religionists happen to be seriously
affected by the proposed legislation, but as an
American steeped in the best traditions of his land,
an American who craves for his country to be true to
the high and holy mission for which she was called
into being, do I cry against these discriminatory,
heartless, un-American bills.

With hardly any alterations, Rabbi Bloom's words could
have run as an editorial in the *New York Times* or *Washington
Post* almost a hundred years later, and would have looked
completely in tune with the times.

Throughout the 1920s, families like the Freimans were
moving out of the Lower East Side, and fewer and fewer
Jewish immigrants were coming in to replace them.
Although the neighbourhood would remain the centre
of Yiddish-speaking life in America, the Jews themselves
were being absorbed across the city. Grant might have succeeded in restricting Jews coming into the United States, but
he resoundingly failed to make New York any less racially
mixed, let alone less Jewish. Any politician who thinks he
can ethnically cleanse America would do themselves a favour
by learning their history.

As Annie Pollard and Daniel Soyer wrote in their book about New York's immigrant Jews, *Emerging Metropolis*:

> New York had already become in some senses a
> 'Jewish city'. At nearly a third of the population, Jews
> were New York's largest single ethnic group, and they
> profoundly influenced the city's culture, politics and
> economy. Of course, the city shaped them as well.
> This was especially true of the second generation,
> those born and raised in New York, who in the 1920s
> came into their own as the dominant segment of the
> community. Jewish immigrants laid the foundation
> for the Jewish metropolis. Their American-born
> children and grandchildren built on that groundwork
> for the remainder of the 20th century.[20]

But this assimilation wasn't entirely straightforward. Ritzier neighbourhoods across America barred Jews and in the 1920s prestigious universities, such as Harvard and Yale, introduced stiflingly restrictive quotas on the number of Jewish students.[21] As in France, in the United States the Great Depression then led to a rise in open anti-Semitism; in the 1930s it was the norm in the country's private school systems to have a quota on the number of Jewish students admitted, and the same went for medical and law schools. Meanwhile Christian applicants were specified in advertisements for white-collar jobs.[22] It was a blatant attempt by America's elite to stop the assimilation of Jews of Bill's generation, the

Sara, Bill and Ronald.

children of immigrants who arrived at the beginning of the twentieth century, and further proof of how close America and France were in their attitudes towards Jewish immigrants between the two world wars, and how differently things could have gone in both countries, had they simply had different leaders.[23]

By the time the Freimans had moved out to Farmingdale, most of the children had, like the Glasses, tweaked their names: Michael, Yakov, Sarah, Moses and Rivka became Mike, Jack, Sadie, Bill and Rita. Bill, more than the rest of his siblings, was ambitious to make his mark and rise, not just stay for the rest of his life in the Jewish community within Farmingdale.

'Bill always liked to show off, to impress, whereas the others didn't want to draw attention to themselves so much,' Herb, Mike's son, told me. 'And in the end, he would be the only one to make a relative success of himself, and to get out.'

Throughout the day I spent with Herb, who was in his eighties by then, and Ann, who was in her seventies, both of them were checking their phones constantly, watching the stock market. Ann had once been a trader on Wall Street, which is where my father worked, too, and that's probably why he remained in touch with her; of his other many cousins, including Herb, I never heard anything.

'How much did you make, Ann? You selling?' Herb would occasionally shout out. He loved it; over his lifetime, he had made an impressive amount of money on the stock market, as proven by his large and stylish house. Ann, too, had done well.

But their parents did not have Bill's drive to get out, and get away. Of that generation, only Bill aimed for the golden ring. In 1937 when he went to Paris, he owned a Texaco petrol station in what was then a plum location in Farmingdale, opposite the Republic Aviation manufacturing plant. But he was always cooking up more plans, and his various careers would eventually include making glassware, working as a subcontractor for the military, selling industrial fabrics, working as a stockbroker and a real estate agent. He was indefatigable, because he knew he didn't want to just sit on the porch every night, gossiping about the Farmingdale neighbours, and that was why he was still single at thirty-five: he didn't want another Long Island girl. He wanted something different, someone who would show him another kind of life.

When Bill saw Sara in her apartment on that winter's night in 1937, he thought he'd found what he was looking for. She was unlike all the girls he knew at home – she talked about art, and clothes, and style. With her by his side, he wouldn't live the kind of life his siblings did. She would lift him up. Even better, she was a woman who needed rescuing, and ever since he was a child he had been rescuing women, most obviously his mother. So this was a dynamic that felt very familiar to him. But to his shock, it turned out she didn't want to be rescued. Worse, she saw him as a coarse American who dragged her down. Deeply hurt, he would occasionally

Going clockwise from the top: Bill, Alex, Richard and Ronald in the US, mid-1940s.

be cruel to her, telling her he'd been tricked into marrying 'damaged goods' because of her weak lungs. Sara withdrew from him even further. In many ways, they were similar, in terms of their backgrounds and their aspirations. But Sara didn't want someone who was like her – she wanted someone different. For the rest of Bill's life, he would only want her. In his eyes, she would always be the beautiful French girl he saw in that dark apartment. But there wasn't anything he could do to make her love him like he loved her.

Whereas Sara was changed irrevocably by her unhappy marriage, Bill was made of tougher stuff. Even when he was ninety, he would joke around with people and call up my father to talk about the stock exchange, always looking for good business opportunities. He never stopped fighting for a better life. Whatever sadness he felt about Sara not reciprocating his love, he proudly hid it from those around him with good humour and inexhaustible energy.

Herb was the same. As the day I spent with him wore on, I realised certain things in his life were more complicated than they looked – a divorce here, serious health problems there – but he never let any of it dampen his mood. As it got later in the afternoon, one of his daughters quietly told me that her brother, Herb's youngest son, had died in 9/11. As it happened, a friend of mine had also died in 9/11, and I was staying with her parents on this trip to the US, so I went over and told Herb how very sorry I was for the loss of his son, and about my friend. His face collapsed, like a tarpaulin that had its pole removed, and those bright blue eyes looked dull for a second. I felt like I'd reached into his chest, put my finger on the softest part of his heart, and stopped it.

'Yeah, well . . .' he began, his repartee stilled. 'Yeah. Thank you.'

As well as having the Freiman eyes, Herb had inherited the Freiman way of dealing with tragedy, which was to plough ever onwards, distracting himself instead of dwelling. The Glass tendency, by contrast, was to obsess privately about the past for ever.

Bill and Sara would eventually leave Farmingdale. His siblings always thought it was Sara who pushed them away, but in truth it was Bill. He wanted to move forward. In Sara, he thought he saw someone who wanted to move forward with him, and he was half right about that: she did want to move forward, she just hadn't wanted it to be with him. And as much as he was able to hide it, that was his tragedy.

ménage juif Glass qui demeurait
Victor Cousin et qui était recherché par vos
services demeure actuellement 60 Avenue
des Minimes 3ème étage. Leurs fausses cartes
d'identité est établies au nom de Classe.
Ce ménage juif continue ses occupation.

8

HENRI AND SONIA –
Denounced

Paris, 1940–1943

WHEN THE NAZIS marched into Paris on 14 June 1940, a beautiful bright sunny day, Henri and Sonia were in their flat on rue Victor-Cousin with the shutters tightly closed. Their neighbourhood was so quiet Sonia was sure she could hear the marching all the way over on the Champs-Élysées. The few Parisians who were still in town had, like Henri and Sonia, closed their shutters too, so they wouldn't have to see the German uniforms swarming through their beautiful streets. But for Henri and Sonia, it was also because they didn't want to be seen.

The Nazis' arrival was not a surprise. The French had been waiting for the Germans to attack Paris for weeks, and the reason Henri and Sonia's neighbourhood was so quiet was that most of their neighbours had fled the city. Henri and Sonia refused to leave, partly because they couldn't abandon Chaya and Mila, neither of whom was willing to go anywhere, and partly because they didn't believe there was anywhere else for them to go. The road to the south was already clogged with people trying to get out, and there was no way Chaya could make that journey on foot. So they decided to stay where they were, in their beloved apartment. But as Sonia heard the jackboots, she knew they'd have to go into hiding.

Up until that point, they had been cheerful about their life in Paris – or at least they pretended to be so for their relatives. One of Sonia's cousins in Poland wrote to her in 1939.

Hello dear Zosia,

    Do not hold a grudge against me that I do not write so often, although I think of you all the time. You must know the times we live in are not peaceful. Nothing happens here and if something bad happens nobody intervenes. I am sad when I realise that everything we believed in does not matter any more. It is only a symbol now . . . You are full of optimism, that should make me forget about my problems that stop me from sleeping. But all the news we hear suggests everything is worse than it was during the Great War.

On 25 May 1940 Henri wrote what was probably his last letter to his sister before Paris fell, and he spent most of it telling her that everything was fine.

My dear little sister,

Just a word to reassure you that all is well with us. Don't be frightened by what you read in the newspapers. Life in Paris proceeds calmly with full awareness of the gravity of the situation. We are calm and confident. I am showing my machines at a fair in Paris. There are not many visitors, of course, but the ones who are there are potential buyers.

Mother is very well. I am not evacuating her. She will simply move to Mila's house. This way she won't be alone, Mila neither. And at Mila's, being on the ground floor, she won't be in any danger. Jacques and Alex are in the army and fine, the Ornsteins are all well, too. Write to us and don't worry, I kiss you often as well as your Ronny. Hello Bill!

Henri

By the time Sara received the letter, Nazis were on the Champs-Élysées and a swastika flag was hanging from the Arc de Triomphe.

How does a Polish Jewish couple live in Paris for the whole of the war and survive? And how could a woman as naturally attention-grabbing as Sonia live under the radar for four years, running away from her natural place in the sun to live in the shadows? Henri never spoke about their years in hiding. Sonia did, but she only ever told half the story. The other part of their story she kept to herself.

Of the 200,000 Jews who lived in Paris when war started,

more than half of whom were foreigners, it is estimated that, at most, only 10 per cent refused to register.[1] It is, for obvious reasons, impossible to know how many of those hidden Jews survived. But given they were Polish Jews, who stayed in Paris for the entire war and survived, there is no question that Henri and Sonia were exceptional.

Once the Nazis arrived, Henri and Sonia's relatively calm life ended. Most of the anti-Jewish legislation was passed during the first year of occupation, and Jews were banned from public places, travelling in certain cars on the metro, owning a bicycle, telephone or radio, and working in particular professions. They had to be home at specified hours and were allowed to shop only between three and four in the afternoon. Anti-Semitic posters appeared all around the city: '*Il faut aussi balayer les JUIFS pour que notre maison soit propre*,' read a popular one (We must sweep away the Jews in order to keep our home clean). Between October 1940, when the anti-Jewish legislation kicked in, and December 1941, the number of known Jews in Paris fell by 18,000: 8,000 had been arrested and were interned as enemy aliens in French camps and 10,000 had vanished.[2] From June 1942, Jews had to wear a yellow star at all times so as to make it easier for the authorities to identify them and, imminently, deport them.

Henri and Sonia never registered as Jews. Both of them foresaw the dangers ahead and Sonia, as usual, took charge. She figured out how to buy false identity cards on the black market which claimed they were a Christian German couple, called Classe. She also spoke German so fluently she could pass as a native, even to German officers, and Henri could get by. They then rented a tiny apartment on the Avenue des Minimes, under the name of Classe, and left almost everything back in their home on rue Victor-Cousin, so it would look to the police who came looking for the Jewish Glasses like they'd simply abandoned it.

Henri and Sonia's lives were saved by their identity cards but life in Paris under Nazi occupation was still crushingly difficult. The French had an easier time under occupation than the Polish, because the Nazis didn't consider the French to be *Untermenschen*. But their beloved capital city soon became almost unrecognisable. Familiar buildings were now covered with Nazi flags; cinemas – which the French had always loved – were handed over to the Germans and, for example, the Rex Cinema on one of the Grands Boulevards was renamed Deutschen Soldatenkino (cinema for German soldiers). Swastikas decked all the great Parisian monuments and propaganda posters were everywhere, warning Parisians to fight against '*le cancer du terrorisme communiste*' (the cancer of communist terrorism). With petrol almost impossible to come by, the only vehicles in the streets were German military ones, while the French made do with bicycles, the metro and their feet. French brasseries were renamed in German and the street signs were similarly redubbed. France's humiliation was total. On the newsstands only papers approved by Joseph Goebbels, Hitler's minister of propaganda, were on sale, such as the established far-right paper *Le Matin* which had eagerly become pro-Nazi, *La Gerbe* (the Sheaf) a pro-Nazi weekly rooted in racism, and *Aujourd'hui*, a once independent daily that became pro-Vichy and pro-Nazi.[3] After the war, the editors of some of these papers would be charged with treason, but during the occupation they were almost all that Parisians had to bring them news. While Parisians could see the Germans dining and living it up in the brasseries and the Ritz Hotel in Place Vendôme, they endured near-crippling rationing. The city, one inhabitant wrote at the time, was defined by 'silence and misery', and the rations were 'barely sufficient to keep people alive provided they remain lying down and don't work'.[4]

Henri and Sonia fared better than many of their fellow Parisians. As well as feeding herself and Henri, Sonia looked after Mila and Chaya, and also managed to get enough food on the black market to send to her relatives back home, who then sent her thanks in return.

5 April 1942

My dearest Zosia,

Yesterday I received parcel No5 containing 1 box of melted butter – nothing missing. Today I received 3 parcels together No1, No2 and No3 – there was between 80 and 100 grams missing in each of them.

Sweet fruit cakes were all in bits and there were only 9 pieces of butter in a box.

As the post office is not working I am sending this postcard by First Class. Last week they took lots of people from here. My cousin Azyasza H. (76 years old) was one of them. In November they took mum, grandmother and aunt. We are terrified every single day and nobody knows what happens in a couple of days. It is still a little bit cold here so we burn the fire every other day and we make wholemeal bread as there is lack of it.

I am looking forward to hearing from you.
I hope you are healthy.

Lots of love,

Lille Lemberg

Some of her relatives spent as much time in their letters griping to Sonia about family spats as they did thanking her for her bravery and generosity. Not even living in fear of their lives can alter the nature of families.

4 July 1942

My dear Zosia,

I received the olive oil and marmalade, thank you. I think some fruitcakes got damaged in the parcel and 200g of chocolate was missing.

I am worried about mum and on top of that my son and his wife do not respect me. Zenek shouts a lot since he got married. He does not care about his parents any more. I do not speak to him any more and I speak with his wife only when I need something when she goes shopping etc. This is how thankful he is for the fact I have been supporting him financially all his life.

If you have any socks size 8 you do not need, please send me 3 or 4 pairs but no underwear please. Also 20 laxative tablets as I cannot take any liquids and the herbs you sent before are not helpful for constipation. Also shaving cream and lime tea, please. Thank you for looking after me.

Lots of love,

David Lemberg

But Henri and Sonia couldn't look after everyone. One by one, the Ornstein cousins were killed off. And as they were murdered, in scenarios that were both horrific and by then unexceptional, the Glass siblings started to fall apart emotionally.

Soon after the war started Josek Ornstein joined the Resistance network, Alliance, run by Marie-Madeleine Fourcade, an extremely impressive young woman who wasn't even thirty when she created a web of spies across France. Josek was one of those spies. In Fourcade's book, *Noah's Ark: The Secret Underground*, she refers to him as 'little "Gigot"', Gigot being his spy name, and the 'little' confirming that he had the same build as Alex. Josek was arrested by the French police in 1942 when he was caught trying to cross the demarcation line to get to Paris, and the documents in his pocket confirmed that he was not only Jewish but a member of the Resistance. The police handed him directly over to the

Abwehr, or German military intelligence service, who put him in the notoriously brutal Fresnes prison, just south of Paris, where prisoners were starved, threatened and, in some cases, tortured.[5] Josek somehow – almost certainly through the Alliance network – managed to get word to Alex, who was now down in Cannes, that he had been arrested and asked for his help.

'I loved Josek,' Alex wrote. 'As kids we played together and were very close. Immediately, I went to Vichy to see Perré. Could Perré intercede to free Josek?'

The answer, unsurprisingly, was no. Colonel Perré – who had helped Alex get into the Foreign Legion – was by this point a high-ranking official in Vichy. Since 1940 he had been head of the military tribunal in Clermont-Ferrand in the Auvergne in central France, which not only specifically cracked down on resisters but had already targeted and imprisoned several members of Josek's own Resistance network,[6] meaning Perré had personally overseen the incarceration of various Alliance spies like Josek. Moreover, while Perré himself was more interested in the sovereignty of France than Nazism, he was close friends with some of the most deranged anti-Semites in Vichy. One of these friends was René Bousquet, who was then working as secretary-general to the Vichy regime police, and decades later would be indicted for the deportation of 194 Jewish children from France to the death camps.[7]

So as fond as Perré was of Alex, and as much as he considered him to be '*le bon Juif*' – an exceptional Jew who deserved saving, unlike the others – there was no way he was going to save his Jewish, Resistance spy cousin. That Alex thought he might says a lot about their friendship.

'I tried all my contacts. Nothing could be done,' Alex wrote. On 30 November 1942, at 14.36, Josek was executed at Mont-Valérien,[8] a fortress to the west of Paris, alongside eight other men in his Resistance network.[9] One of these fellow Alliance resisters, a handsome young man called Lucien Vallat, left behind a letter he wrote while in prison with Josek. It said: 'I think I have done my duty to my country and my comrades, you will never need to blush on my account. That is a great comfort to me. Be courageous. Be courageous, all of you. Farewell, everybody. Farewell, Mother.'[10] The Germans killed more than a thousand Frenchmen at Mont-Valérien during the war, almost all because they were Resistance fighters.

Alex was devastated by the loss of his favourite cousin, the person who he considered as close as a brother, and with whom he enjoyed a much less complicated relationship than he had with Henri and Jacques. 'To say I was sad would be a huge understatement. I was completely crushed, eaten by remorse not to have been able to save Josek,' he wrote.

Alex had always thought that if he befriended as many famous and high-ranking French people as possible, he would be safe and he could save his family. But for perhaps the first time, Alex realised the truth of the current situation. It didn't matter how many French people he knew, and on what side, because the majority of French people didn't care, and if Alex couldn't keep his cousin safe then he couldn't keep himself safe either.

Around the same time as Josek's arrest, Josek's older brother, Maurice Ornstein, and his wife Giselle paid a boatman to take them across the river in the town of Chalon-sur-Saône, which would take them into the unoccupied zone. They had two children, an especially cherubic little boy called Armand, who was three and a half, and a one-year-old daughter, Rosette. Before they made the crossing they left the children with a family friend in the countryside, arranging to send for them when they got across. They never made it. During the crossing they were shot, possibly by the boatman who had pocketed the money and decided they weren't

worth the risk, possibly by a soldier who had spotted them from the shore. Their children Armand and Rosette lived with a woman who Armand today remembers only as 'a woman in a white dress' – a nun? A nurse? – who miraculously didn't turn them in but instead cared for them for almost a year. However, little Armand told some of the neighbours that he was Jewish and the children had to be moved again, fast, this time to another family whose name has long since been lost in history. Armand was even put in an orphanage for a period of time, to try to keep him safe. (Armand, now eighty and still living in Paris, remembers only fragments about this time; the memories have been buried so deeply inside him for so long it's like they never existed at all.) Eventually, Giselle's sister Monique walked all the way from Paris out to the countryside where the children were – possibly dozens of miles away, possibly hundreds – took them into her custody and hid them for the rest of the war.

Not long after Maurice's murder, his sister Rose, Sara's beloved almost sister, was on a bus, also trying to cross the demarcation line. Her husband, Herman Brenner, had managed to get to the United States in June 1941, and the plan was that Rose would join him once he had sorted out a place for them to live. Dr Brenner found a lovely home for them in Queens, not too far from Sara and Bill, much to Sara's ecstatic delight. But by the time Rose set out from Paris it was too late. America had entered the war and it was no longer possible to get visas. As she couldn't get to America from France, she decided to take a bus to Switzerland and

Rose Ornstein and Herman Brenner.

somehow get to the United States from there. She hoped that the border police would be too busy to check everyone's passports, because all she had left to cling to were impossible odds. The bus stopped at the border and when the Vichy police got on and walked down the aisle towards her Rose quickly scribbled on a postcard, gave it to the person sitting next to her and asked them to send it. No one knew what happened to Rose until Sara finally received the postcard years later, after it had been held up during the war. It was addressed to her in America and it read simply, 'They are coming for me. I love you. Goodbye.' She was killed in

Auschwitz. When Sara finally received that postcard after the war, years after Rose sent it, she screamed and collapsed in her hallway, watched by her toddler son Ronald, my father.

Also killed in Auschwitz were Rose's sister, Anna, and Anna's husband, Samuel Goldberg, my relative Anne-Laurence Goldberg's grandparents. By the end of the war, of the seven Ornstein siblings only three survived: Alex Ornstein, who eventually raised his nephew Armand and niece Rosette after getting them from Monique; Arnold Ornstein, who died shortly after the war ended from health problems; and Sarah Ornstein, who went to Israel.

Anna Goldberg, an Ornstein cousin who was killed in Auschwitz, with her husband (who was also killed) and their children. Their son, Roger Goldberg, is in the middle.

The Ornsteins had come to Paris for safety, and France decimated the family. The only reason the Glasses had come to Paris was because of the Ornsteins – the gentle, sweet, funny and fun Ornstein cousins, some of them as close as siblings to the Glasses – and the Glasses never really recovered from the devastating loss. They were the roots back to the past, part of the Glasses' childhood, and when they were killed, the ties that held the family together began to loosen. Alex never forgave himself for, as he put it, 'failing my brother Josek'. But as Alex wept in Cannes over Josek, he didn't know what danger the rest of his family was in.

They tried to stay alive as best they could, the ones who somehow were living in the shadows. Roger Goldberg was the son of Anna Ornstein and her husband Samuel Goldberg. Roger and his wife, Renée, were both younger than the Glasses, but they became extremely close to their older relatives during the war. Roger and Renée were often separated as they, incredibly, both managed to travel around France while evading capture and their letters to one another are some of the best sources I found for learning what life was like for the Glasses during the war. However, they are written in an extremely stilted, halting tone, nothing like how Roger and Renée talked, and occasionally make no sense. This is because the couple had to make up a code in order to evade the censors, and despite some of the code remaining uncrackable, as the only people who could break it have long since died, it is clear that Roger and Renée were part of a Resistance network.

Roger and Renée Goldberg during the war.

'At Sonia's I learned that the doctor was in the north and that he called one evening. Which surprised me because we would have known but everyone confirms it,' Renée writes in 1943. It's possible 'the doctor' was simply a doctor, but Renée never wrote in this tone – vague, banal, pointed – in letters before or after the war. So it seems much more likely that 'the doctor' and 'everyone' referred to particular people in their Resistance network.

'Alex is on the coast where he eats a lot of oranges, but he is going to go elsewhere without a doubt,' she writes in 1943. In fact, Alex Maguy was nowhere near the coast at this point – he was hiding in the centre of the country in the Auvergne. So while he may well have been eating oranges this sentence was also almost certainly code.

And this, also from 1944: 'Henri had a serious illness, so the apartment is not very healthy. Odette and I would very much like to leave until it is disinfected,' Renée writes to Roger. Nowhere does Henri mention being ill during the war, so it is far more likely that Renée was telling Roger that Henri had been nearly captured and they now needed to stay away from the apartment for a while.

Whether Henri and Sonia were also part of a Resistance network or not, Henri was certainly part of the Resistance effort and they were both nearly caught multiple times. After the Nazis arrived Henri continued to work covertly at his microfilming company, Photosia, with Marc Haenel. The German Army moved into Haenel's building, where Henri frequently came to meet him. 'We worked under very dangerous conditions. Nevertheless, we built our machines right by the enemy,' Henri later wrote in his records.

Henri's machine, the Omniphot-Microfilm, was so good at photocopying and shrinking blueprints that when the Banque de France contacted Kodak before the Nazis arrived in Paris to ask them to copy their most important documents, Kodak recommended they go instead to Omniphot-Microfilm. Haenel, who was not Jewish, quickly grasped the value of this machine in wartime: industrial plans and public archives could be copied, miniaturised and stored, protecting them from the Nazis. So he and Henri decided to make this the focus of their business.

'For racial reasons, I was not allowed to be the owner, and Paris being occupied, I was forbidden any activities. But day and night we microfilmed public and private archives.

I threw myself into the fight,' Henri wrote in a letter shortly after the war ended. 'Everything was forbidden to me, of course; yet I built more machines.'

French politicians and companies quietly contacted Photosia to ask for help, and Henri microfilmed the archives of businesses, museums and small towns, saving countless records – of architecture, people's life savings, their homes – from decimation. He could shrink thousands of records down to the size of a thumbnail, which made them both easy to store and unrecognisable to any potential enemies wishing to destroy them. The port authority at Le Havre became one of his clients so that after the war, when the port was destroyed, Henri was able to return to them the microfilms he'd made of their designs. 'Thanks to our help – though modesty should prevent me from saying it – the port of Le Havre was rebuilt in record time,' Henri later wrote.

Because Henri was the only person who knew how to work the machine, he had to transport it around the country and do all the microfilming himself whenever the machine was hired for a job. In 1941 he went to the town of Valenciennes in the north of France, which French troops had looted and was now occupied by the Germans. He spent nine months living in the basement of the museum microfilming the local archives that the mayor had managed to save, plus another two years of repeated visits, according to Henri's meticulous records. Directly across from the museum was the local Gestapo office, in the Valenciennes park. Only once did a policeman come to the museum to see what was happening there. He looked at Henri's identity card – 'a total counterfeit', Henri later recalled – and walked away. Henri went right back to microfilming. 'It was a very close call. It really could have been the end for me,' Henri wrote in a letter.

While Henri was travelling around the country, Sonia was all on her own in Paris, tasked with looking after both Mila and Chaya, the latter of whom insisted on only eating kosher and did not give a damn how hard that was to find in Nazi-controlled, strictly rationed Paris. Every so often Sonia would go back to their apartment on rue Victor-Cousin to look through their post and pick up the letters from her family, who still used her old address. One day as she approached the building she just happened to look up at their apartment window. She saw a hand sticking out, waving frantically. Sonia recognised it as belonging to the concierge of the building, with whom she'd always been friendly, and she knew what her friend was telling her: 'The police are searching the apartment for you. Stay away and run away.' Sonia ran. Another time a French policeman did catch her and arrested her for having false papers. Sonia refused to cry, but she pleaded with him, as a Frenchman, to have mercy. He refused. On the steps of the police station, as he was just about to turn her over, Sonia desperately offered him all the jewellery she was wearing – all costume, of course, but it looked real enough for the policeman. He could have pocketed the jewels and still turned her over, but he was kind enough – or dumb enough – to let her go. Another time she was seized by a German officer and, gathering all her self-control so as not to show the slightest hint of fear, she imperiously told him she was the wife of a high-ranking German politician and if he mistreated her in any way her husband would hear about it. Terrified, the officer let her go. Henri had always known Sonia was an extraordinary woman, but it wasn't until the war that she herself realised how extraordinary she could be.

But the biggest danger for Sonia turned out to be her neighbours. Several times, when she came to rue Victor-Cousin to look through the post, she would find letters of denunciation from her former neighbours taped to the front door, telling the Vichy police that Henri and Sonia were still in Paris. Even though it was always extremely dangerous for her to return to rue Victor-Cousin, Sonia started coming back more often, just to tear the denunciation letters off the door.

Sonia had told me about these letters, and it was a story I assumed I'd have to take on good faith. How do you prove someone tore a denunciation note off a door eighty years ago? On a sunny afternoon, a decade after Sonia died, looking through the shoebox in my grandmother's closet, I found out how. Because there, among the photos, was a photocopy of one of the denunciation letters. One read:

The Jewish family, Glass, who lives in Rue Victor-Cousin, and who the police are looking for, are currently living at 60 Avenue des Minimes on the

> 5th floor. Their fake identity cards are issued in the name of Classe. This Jewish household continues to live in the city.

It was written in the distinctive curlicue cursive all French children are taught. Every French exchange student I'd had at school wrote like that, as do all my French relatives, for that matter. As much as I know about France's culpability and collaboration during the war, it felt genuinely devastating to see such cruelty written in the familiar French handwriting, like hearing your father shout racist obscenities. Writing about a country behaving badly can feel abstract, clinical, even; undeniable evidence of the wickedness of the individuals within is piercingly personal. Later, Henri microfilmed the denunciation letters for Sonia, and they sent some copies to Sara. Even if they rarely talked about this, they wanted to remember it for ever, and for others to know.

It is estimated that up to a million French people denounced others to the authorities during the occupation, sending between 3 and 5 million letters to local and national politicians and law enforcement bureaus[11] although it is an impossible number to confirm, given that few saved the letters and many denunciations were made in whispers.[12] '[Denunciation] was a fundamental characteristic of Vichy France. In a sense it was the only way people could express themselves in a country where there were no demonstrations, no rights, no vote: it was the voice of the people, although a mean and petty voice, a way of swearing allegiance to the powers that be,' historian Laurent Joly said in 2008 at the world's first international conference on French denunciation in the Second World War.[13] The Vichy government didn't officially encourage denunciations, unlike Italy and Germany, but it certainly didn't discourage them either. The problem for the government was that French people got a little too enthusiastic about them, once they realised that denouncing people was an easy way to get rid of someone who was in their way, whether Jewish or not: if you wanted someone's job, or apartment, or wife, denouncing them was a good way to get closer to your goal. And given how tight rations were, there was an extra impetus to denounce one's long-hated neighbour. After all, you might not get their house, but you might at least get their food. False denunciations became such a problem that the Germans started punishing people who made them – in one reported case, sending a woman and her lover to Germany after they falsely denounced her husband[14] – and on 1 January 1942, in his New Year's message to the country, Marshal Pétain announced that anyone who made false denunciations was an 'adversary to French unity' and an 'enemy of the National Revolution'. Real denunciations, however, were a different story. Anyone who denounced Jews living illegally was helping the Vichy regime, and writers in the pro-Nazi French newspapers regularly urged their readers to denounce any foreign Jews they knew, saying it was part of their national duty. But in fact, far from 'strengthening national unity', as pro-Vichy propaganda suggested, the culture of denunciations harmed it, with neighbours informing on one another to enrich themselves personally.

In French, there are two words for denunciation: '*dénon-ciation*' refers to uncovering something, like discovering a fact, and is a neutral term. '*Délation*' suggests something more malevolent, something more rooted in self-interest with a negative impact on others. 'Vichy attempted to uphold the distinction between the two words, but to little avail,' historian Shannon Fogg writes in her 2003 essay, 'Denunci-ations, Community Outsiders and Material Shortages in Vichy France'.

But of course, not all denunciations were false or stem-ming from petty feuds. Plenty of French people considered turning in Jews to be their patriotic and civic duty, even if they had once been their friends. According to Holocaust historian Serge Klarsfeld, 75,721 Jews from France were deported to the death camps.[15] Not all of those were caught because of denunciations, but these mass arrests and mur-ders would have been a lot more difficult for Vichy to pull off without the complicity of people whom the Jews had once thought were their friends. Henri and Sonia survived the war, despite the best efforts of their neighbours, and unlike so many Polish Jews in Paris. They were blessed with an enormous amount of ingenuity and even more luck, but not everyone in their family had both or even either of those advantages. So for Jacques there was no need for any French people to denounce him, because he denounced himself.

Jacques, as drawn by Arthur Weisz, 1942.

9

JACQUES – Captured

France and Poland, 1940s

IN MAY 1941 Jacques was at home with Mila on rue de la Tour when he received a green postcard, slipped under his door. It was not from a friend.

> Préfecture de Police, Paris, le 10 Mai, 1941
> Mr Glass is requested to present himself, in person, accompanied by a member of his family or a friend, on 14 May at 7 a.m. at the Caserne Napoléon to discuss his situation. Please bring ID. Anyone who does not come at the specified day and time risks the most severe punishment.
> The Police Commissioner

Mila was in the early stages of pregnancy and not feeling well so Jacques asked his older brother to go with him. Henri not only refused but begged Jacques not to go either.

'You're going to end up like one of those poor Jews in prison camps!' Sonia later recalled Henri telling him, referring to the thousands of foreign Jews from 'enemy territories' whom France had already incarcerated in internment camps.

Jacques laughed off his brother's concerns. 'It is only an administrative matter,' he insisted. 'I'll be home for dinner.'

Early on Wednesday, 14 May 1941, Mila and Jacques left their home on rue de la Tour. It was already a sunny day and as they walked together along the Seine, past the Tuileries and towards the Marais, they would have looked to casual onlookers like the image of a happy couple taking a romantic stroll through some of Paris's prettiest places. Just before 7 a.m. they reached the Caserne Napoléon, an old barracks, just a few streets away from where Jacques's mother used to live with Sara. Photos of that day from contemporary newspapers show a small crowd of Jewish men, waiting for what they thought was a meeting with the police, milling about in the road, looking serious but relaxed, clutching pitifully small bags, containing, at most, lunch. When they arrived, the police immediately told their wives, sisters, mothers and children who accompanied them to go back home and pack suitcases for their male relatives, and then return to the Caserne as quickly as possible. This was why the men had been told to bring someone with them: so they could be sent back to fetch their belongings. This was not specified on the *billet vert* because it would have raised suspicions, and fewer men would have come.

After the women and children handed over the suitcases, they were each given a card telling them when and where they could visit the men, and then their names and addresses were taken down by the French policemen who would use them in later round-ups. (As well as being right about what would happen to Jacques, Henri was proven correct in his refusal to accompany his brother.)[1] Meanwhile the men were herded onto Parisian buses – the same buses that once took them to work – and driven to Austerlitz train station. They were then put on specially requisitioned trains and sent to either Pithiviers or Beaune-la-Rolande, or what the French newspapers openly described as 'concentration camps'.

This was the 'rafle du billet vert' (green card round-up), the first official round-up of Jews in France under the Vichy regime. Jacques's bad star was certainly blighting him now, because not only did he get summoned in the very first round-up, but he fell victim to it: of the 6,694 foreign Jewish men who had received a summons on a green postcard, 40 per cent refused to obey, either ignoring the instructions or running away. Jacques, obedient to the end, was among the more than 3,700 Jewish and primarily Polish men who believed France could never harm them, and so he did as he was told.[2]

The Glass family took no photos, but I know exactly what Jacques was wearing, carrying and how he looked. One day I was in a library in Paris, leafing through a book about the rafle du billet vert and there, in a photo of men walking along the Austerlitz train station platform, was the unmistakable figure of my great-uncle Jacques. It was the spectacles that caught my eye first: those round wire spectacles that he wore in every single photograph I have of him. But it was his clothes that proved this was Jacques. While most of the other Jews around him are, like him, poor immigrants, and so wearing workman's clothes, Jacques is so smart he looks fresh from the tailor's. He's wearing a neat white button-down shirt, its collar so starched it's almost pointing ahead, dark trousers and shoes, and a trench coat with only its middle button done up, the way fashion followers today still wear it. The only item that gives away his social class is his luggage, and that's because it was gathered together by Mila, who did not share the Glass siblings' fastidious aesthetics: he is carrying a battered suitcase, a dirty cloth bag and some rolled-up sheets, clearly gathered together in a frantic hurry. He is walking alongside the parked train, already filled with men peering through the windows; he looks focused, not even glancing at the photographer, and he looks scared.

The process that led to Jacques's arrest began eight months earlier, on 4 October 1940, when Vichy passed a law ordering the internment of all foreign Jews in what they called 'special camps'. More than 40,000 Jews were interned and the French papers covered the arrests, including the *rafle du billet vert*, enthusiastically. 'These arrests have been carried out in the most correct way,' *La Dépêche du Monde* reported the day after the *rafle du billet vert*. *L'Écho de Pithiviers*, the only local newspaper in its area, was less restrained in its joy. In a front-page editorial headlined '*Israël dans le Loiret!*', colum-nist Jean de Nibelle crowed that Jews would now be:

> behind barbed wire, rather than at the head of
> our city halls and our great places, as they were
> previously under the regime of Blume, of Zay, of the
> Levys and the flea-ridden Semites they brought with
> them . . . Today the rule of the Jews is over. France,
> finally, is protecting herself from them. Thus, the
> wheel turns! And the Jews, yesterday, all-powerful,
> are today merely miserable animals of concentration
> camps! After having betrayed and ruined us, here
> they are reduced themselves, impotent and almost
> deserving of pity![3]

Few people had lived lives with less power than the Jews who were arrested in the *rafle du billet vert*. Along with the 3,430 Polish Jews and 157 Czech Jews there were 123 Jewish men officially classified as 'stateless'. These were poor immi-grants who had come to France for a better life than the terrible ones they'd had at home, and whom the Vichy government had gone after because they were easy targets. Jacques was typical of the men who were caught: foreign, ostensibly unemployed and basically broke thanks to Vichy's increasingly impossible regulations regarding foreign Jew-ish employment. Jean de Nibelle, in his *Écho de Pithiviers* column, makes the still popular anti-Semitic reference to Rothschild, as though the men coming to the camps were fat bankers as opposed to men who lived in basements and often went without breakfast and lunch in order to give their children supper.[4]

A police report made soon after the *rafle du billet vert* read that 'among certain French Aryan circles, it does not seem that the new rules receive full approval.'[5] But these particular French circles were less concerned about anti-Semitism than about the drain on French resources: 'It is estimated that these measures all too often reach married men and fathers with families who will be left destitute, and consequently, the children and women will be left in the care of the French government,' the report continued.

This reaction to the mass deportation of thousands of men was heartless, but prescient. Without their husbands and sons working, the women struggled. Jacques Biélinky was a Jewish journalist who had come to France in 1909 as a political refugee after surviving the pogroms in Russia. Between 1940 and 1942 he kept a diary, but it wasn't until the *rafle du billet vert* that Biélinky really started to notice – or at least write about – Jewish persecution in France. Two days after the round-up he writes about the plight of the women left behind: 'Huge emotion among the Jewish community because of the mass arrests. Thousands of women with children left without support are worried about starvation. Many women have gone to the police commissioners to beg for food.'

Terrified, Jews in Paris went into hiding. Many left the homes in which they were registered, and synagogues, especially those that had been the centre of Polish Jewish life, were now almost empty out of fear the police would arrest anyone they found there. Jewish aid organisations relied on donations to feed the families of the prisoners.[6]

Despite all he had been through, and everything he saw in front of him, Biélinky remained optimistic. On 20 May he writes: 'Among Jewish circles, it is thought there will be no more arrests and mass internments in camps. A social worker has gone to visit the camps and plead for the sick.'

Whatever the social worker did, it wasn't enough for the Jews in France, including Biélinky: in 1943 he was arrested, deported and killed in Sobibor.

Mila was luckier. She was able to stay in her apartment for another year and a half, largely thanks to Jacques Revillon. Revillon was Jacques's *administrateur provisoire*, who had been put in charge of Jacques's business affairs when it became illegal for Jews to run a business, and he was extraordinarily kind to Mila. He wrote numerous letters to the Commissariat Général aux Questions Juives (CGQJ), urging them to let her stay in the flat, describing the situation as '*plus critique*'. Given the atmosphere in occupied Paris at the time, Revillon's kindness to Mila, a very Polish, very Jewish woman, and not an especially easy-going one at that, seems remarkable. And Revillon, it quickly turned out, was an admirable man, in that even though he earned money from looking after Jacques's business, either his conscience or his business sense could not allow him to continue. Eight months after Jacques's arrest, in January 1942 – still relatively early in the war – Revillon wrote to the CGQJ saying he could no longer look after '*les affaires Israélites*' (Jewish businesses) because doing this work risked 'discrediting my company and causing problems with our American customers . . . This is a very serious imminent threat.' Revillon made it sound like the problem was working with Jews, so he was officially relieved of his duties. But the truth was he didn't want to be associated with Vichy. He continued to help Mila throughout the war, writing letters on her behalf to the government about Jacques and allowing her to stay in the apartment for as long as it was safe.

The other person who helped Mila was Sonia. She looked after her throughout her pregnancy and made sure she had plenty of food, holding her hand when she was crying with fear. She also helped Mila make sense of the card she'd been given telling her when she could visit Jacques, and how to get there. Sonia's role was to protect Mila and, between her and Revillon, they did an amazingly good job.

Once Jacques rejected Henri's advice and was on the train at Austerlitz, no one could look after him. The journey to the Loiret in north-central France from Paris is a pretty easy one, taking only a few hours, and Pithiviers is less than 100 kilometres from Paris. But it was not a pleasant trip for Jacques. Thousands of men all crammed together on the train, confused and fidgety because no one was giving them any answers, all they could do was try to squeeze into a place by a window and watch the countryside roll by.

Eventually they were told that half of them would go to the camp at Beaune-la-Rolande and half to Pithiviers. Jacques was assigned to the latter, and when they finally reached the train station he got off among 1,700 rag-tag men,[7] and marched through the little town with the police. The men all carried their rolled-up bags for what they thought would be a mere few nights' stay while the townspeople watched them silently, uncertain if they were watching a funny parade or a mournful spectacle.

When the men reached the camp, they walked in through the gates and, as ordered, quietly queued up. They registered their names with the black-booted French guards who were sitting at a small wooden table, recording everyone's information in notebooks. Each prisoner was given a number – Jacques was 470 – and assigned to one of eleven barracks. After that, they walked towards what was now their new house.

I went to Pithiviers on a hot July day in 2012 with a group of about thirty other people, on a trip marking the seventieth anniversary of when our ancestors had been deported from the camp. We met in the Marais, near the Shoah museum, and boarded a bus, in a pale and presumably unintentional echo of the *rafle du billet vert*. It was a lovely drive from Paris to Pithiviers, past fields of wildflowers and sunflowers, home-made roadside advertisements for *foie gras* and colourful houses with red slate roofs. The views became lovelier the closer we got to the camp. There was almost a sense of excitement among the group, as if we were making an important pilgrimage. But it turned out we were making a pilgrimage to nowhere: if it weren't for a stone memorial, its former location would look like just another French suburban street. All signs of the French concentration camp had vanished, hastily erased after the war when France tried to pretend that what had happened had not. We milled around pointlessly on the side of the road and then, with much less excitement, reboarded the bus. I shouldn't have been surprised that Pithiviers had vanished off the earth, but I was, and I felt a vague sense of pointless anger on the drive back to Paris, like I'd been duped by France's post-war subterfuge here, setting aside a day to pay my respects to something that no longer existed. (Five years after I visited, in 2017, it was announced that the long-abandoned Pithiviers train station, where the Jews arrived before being taken to the camp, would be turned into a museum about the French deportations. France's attitude towards its past is, at last, starting to evolve.)[8]

But even if Pithiviers itself no longer exists, the records, carefully compiled by the black-booted guards, remain. So while it might not be possible to walk among the original barracks with tour groups taking photos, as you can at Auschwitz, it's very easy to get a clear picture of what Jacques's daily life there was like.

Pithiviers had originally been built for German prisoners of war, but when France became occupied there wasn't any demand for German prisons any more, only Jewish ones – foreign Jews, that is: no French Jews ever stayed in Pithiviers.

The entrance was on a normal pedestrian road – no need to hide the fact that France was interning Jewish immigrants simply for being Jewish immigrants – and conveniently near the railway station so that more prisoners could be brought in with efficient speed. After signing in on that first day in May, Jacques and the other men were directed to the right, towards a row of narrow, regularly spaced barracks; Jacques was originally assigned to barrack 7, then, after more barracks were built to accommodate the growing numbers of incarcerated men, 11 and then 18. He slept in his barrack, washed there, watched the time go by there. Three times a day he'd walk a short distance to the dining hall, which was next to the infirmary. Management offices were also close by, as was a large vegetable garden. Menus were posted weekly telling the men what they would eat every day. 'Monday,' read the menu of 22–29 December 1941, 'Breakfast – coffee; Lunch – vegetable soup, glazed carrots and cheese; Supper – vegetable soup, mashed potatoes and cheese.' Never any meat or fish, just vegetables from the garden mashed, puréed or sugared.

But as prisons went, Pithiviers was not so bad. Family members came to visit twice a month and there was even a place where the Jews could worship on Shabbos and the High Holy Days. Many of the men there already knew one another from home or through the Foreign Legion – Jacques knew several men in the camp from his regiment. Most important, the French guards didn't beat the inhabitants, and while that was a pretty low bar for describing a place as not bad, it was a crucial one. That the guards were not cruel to them, sometimes even friendly, confirmed to Jacques and the other inhabitants of the camp that they didn't need to be scared. Nothing bad would happen to them in Pithiviers – they were only there because they didn't have the right identity papers, and they needed to be kept there during the war for the sake of the economy. They were safe. It was all OK. Everything was fine.

Most of the men spent their days working on local farms, but Pithiviers itself was not a labour camp. No one had to work, and they did so for free, purely to relieve their boredom. There was also cultural life in the camp: many of the men played chess and there was even a Yiddish theatre troupe. Guards encouraged all this because they considered it important to maintaining morale. Decades later, I found a remnant of this cultural life inside the shoebox in my grandmother's closet: on a yellowed piece of paper, mounted on a slab of cardboard, someone by the name of Arthur Weisz had made a pencil portrait of Jacques, round glasses on his face. It is dated 22 June 1941, and above the date Weisz wrote '*Camp de Pithiviers*'.

Weisz was another prisoner in Pithiviers and he made many portraits of the inhabitants, who would then send them back to their families as keepsakes. When I made the trip to Pithiviers with other descendants, two of the people on the bus said they had their own Weisz drawings. For one of them, Weisz's portrait was the only likeness they'd ever seen of their father. Jacques, on the other hand, was well photographed, so I know for certain how accurate Weisz's portrait is, and it is amazingly close. He gave Jacques an air of gravitas that he often lacked in photos, due to his shyness and occasional nervous giggle in front of a camera's lens. Weisz captures his calmness, which Alex and Henri saw as passivity, and his gentleness, which too often came across as weakness. Jacques's arms are thin, a sign of wartime deprivation, but his face is handsome. It is, in truth, the kindest likeness that exists of Jacques and a testament both to Jacques's likeability and to Weisz's generosity. (Weisz was later killed by the Nazis in an unlisted concentration camp, but probably Auschwitz.)

This is not the only image I have of Jacques in Pithiviers. Also in my grandmother's shoebox were two black and white photos, both stamped on the back: '*12 Avril 1942, Camp d'Hérbergement de Pithivier LE GESTIONNAIRE*'. One photo shows eight men and the other shows nine, and many of the same men, including Jacques, appear in both photos. Both pictures are rather oddly posed: in one, a man is sitting in a bucket and his friends are either holding him in it or pretending to pour water on his head from watering cans. In the other, they are all arranged awkwardly on a ladder in one of the barracks. Photos like these, showing the men larking around and having a merry old time, were often staged by the camp guards and sent home to the prisoners' families for propaganda purposes: see, everything's fine here! It's basically a holiday camp! But the forced larking was unnecessary because the men are their own propaganda. They look strikingly healthy after almost a year of living at Pithiviers, and they look happy, making smiles too genuine to be forced. The former is proof of how relatively well they were treated in the camp, and the latter a sign of their complete lack of anxiety about the very near future.

These men all worked in the management (*gestionnaire*) office, a more suitable place for weedy, unathletic Jacques than the fields. Arthur Weisz stressed in his portrait of him that that's where Jacques worked in Pithiviers, taking particular care over his armband on which he drew a little circle and wrote: '*Pithiviers Camp d'Internement LE GESTION*'. Jacques was probably quite good at helping in administrative affairs, keeping track of which prisoner was in which barrack, punching holes in paper as his time drifted away, drawing up the records I would later use to write his story. But it might have also cost him his life.

When he was in Cambrai in 1940, Jacques went out every day to work on nearby farms, and this is almost certainly how he escaped from that POW camp. Dozens of people from Pithiviers took advantage of the camp's similar lack of security, running away in their early months of incarceration when they went out to work as farmhands. The local police soon put a stop to that and tightened security, but it's entirely possible that, had Jacques been going out to work instead of staying in the camp, he would have run away too. Maybe his success in escaping from Cambrai would have emboldened him to try again. Maybe he would have sneaked back to Paris, met up with Mila and gone into hiding with

Jacques is at the back, partially obscured by a
bucket handle (above) and on the far left (below).

her, with Sonia and Henri's assistance. Or maybe this could never have happened, even if he'd spent all day hoeing potatoes instead of filing papers. Maybe he always would have gone back to the camp instead of grabbing his chance. After all, he chose to stay in the camp, sitting at a desk and following orders, instead of working outside and then running towards the sunset. Stay where you are, don't question things, put your life in the hands of others, just trust – those were Jacques's natural tendencies, and they were how he always felt, whereas his brothers never felt like that. One brother in particular.

According to Alex's memoir, one day in 1941 he went to Pithiviers, determined to get his older brother out. Alex describes a dramatic encounter with a guard who, on realising he was Jacques's brother, threatened to put him in Pithiviers, too.

'I put my hand in my jacket pocket. It was a bluff. I was completely unarmed, not even a pocket knife. But I had my hands and I could strangle him. I was ready to take action and that was obvious,' Alex writes.

Having scared off the guard, Alex finds Jacques and tells him he's come to save him.

But Jacques won't leave. He's French, he says. He has nothing to fear. He's here under the protection of French policemen. He has confidence in them.

'"I'm a French soldier." These were his only thoughts. French, blind patriot. One could weep with rage to see him thus, submissive, obedient, confident,' Alex writes.

Whether this scene ever actually happened is impossible to prove. Certainly there's no record of Alex going to Pithiviers, although if he broke in and scared off a guard there wouldn't be. It's possible that Alex was giving a little showman's pizzazz to a slightly different story that instead Henri and Sonia told their daughter, their nephews and me, and Alex also corroborated.

When Jacques was arrested, Mila was two months pregnant. In late December 1941 she gave birth to their daughter, Lily. Jacques was granted leave on 30 December in order to see his wife and daughter. This was the story my family always told and yet the more I thought about it, the less likely it seemed. Why would Jacques be given leave from the camp? I suspected this to be some souped-up lore. Until one day I was in the Shoah Memorial in Paris, looking up Jacques's records in Pithiviers, and there it was, in unarguable black and white: '*Permis à deux jours du 30 au 31 [Décembre] inclus, rentre 1ère Janvier 1942.*' He really had left the camp.

'But Glass,' the guards said to him before he got on the train to Paris, according to what Jacques then told his family, 'if you don't return, we will kill all your friends here, and we will track you down, and we will find you, and we will kill you, too.'

The birth of a child was, according to Pithiviers' rules, insufficient reason for a prisoner to be granted home leave. So according to Jacques's records he had to go home because '*femme gravement malade*'. But he'd have had to produce medical notes proving Mila was at death's door, and even then he probably wouldn't have been allowed to go. So quite how Jacques pulled off this home visit is a mystery. Perhaps Alex really did bully a guard into letting him out. Perhaps – and this strikes me as the most likely scenario – the guards just liked Jacques and knew him well enough to trust him to come back. However it happened, Nathalie Grenon, the director of CERCIL (Le Centre d'Étude et de Recherche sur les camps d'Internement dans le Loiret et la Déportation Juive), who helped me with my research into Pithiviers, described Jacques's two-day excursion from the camp as '*plus exceptionnelle*'. It was to be Jacques's greatest piece of luck, and his last.

Jacques arrived at Mila's bedside to find Henri, Sonia and Alex all waiting for him, along with his newborn daughter. According to Sonia and Alex, this is what happened and what was said.

Run, they told him. This is the chance of a lifetime! You've never had any good luck, Jacques, but this is the luckiest break a man like you could have. We can help you. We will hide you. You will never get another chance like this. We are your family. They will kill you. We know what we are talking about. Listen to us. Run.

Jacques held his tiny daughter and looked at his brothers – his brothers, with whom he'd run through the forests of Chrzanow, with whom he'd lain beside while listening to the pogroms, who had always helped him fight off bullies in school and then fight off bailiffs who nearly destroyed his business before he had even started. He had relied on his brothers all his life. But Jacques had always relied on someone else more. First it was his mother, to whom he invariably deferred, and then it was his wife. He had registered his name and address in 1940 when she told him to do so, which was how Vichy knew where to send the *billet vert* condemning him to Pithiviers, and he would do what she advised now. They all looked at Mila. She was lying in bed, listening, her eyes shut.

'Mila?' Jacques asked.

She opened her eyes and looked around, like a queen preparing to make a regal pronouncement.

'*Mon Jacques a donné sa parole,*' she said.

My Jacques gave his word. He must go back.

Alex started shouting at her: 'You stupid woman! You're going to kill my brother and I'm going to kill you!' For once, Henri and Sonia didn't try to hold him back. Instead, they just looked at her aghast.

'Mila, please, see sense, if he goes back they will kill him!' Sonia said.

Even Henri, quiet measured Henri, joined in: 'For God's sake, they're killing Jews. We can help all three of you. Think of your daughter!'

But Mila was implacable, as certain of her decision as a cow is sure that life on the farm will always be good. Realising that there was no point reasoning with her, Henri, Sonia and Alex turned to Jacques.

'If you go back they will kill you, your stupid wife and your baby daughter. What kind of man are you? Stay and protect your family, for God's sake!'

'Jacques, please, we can help you. I will get you fake ID, you'll be safe here.'

'If you go back on the train, Jacques, you'll never see your daughter again.'

But they knew it was no use. Jacques never listened to them when Chaya or Mila was around, and he'd never had their drive, their determination to make it, to succeed, or even just to survive. He was already looking out the window, holding Lily, planning his departure.

And so, on New Year's Day 1942, Jacques got the train back to Pithiviers. He walked back into the freezing camp, his footprints in the snow the only part of him left outside in the free world. He was checked off by the guards who either laughed at his passivity or simply took it for granted, and the gates closed behind him. They would never open for him again. His brothers were right: he had missed his chance.

Mila and Lily.

Was Jacques simply a fool for returning? For so long I thought so. On the bus ride back from Pithiviers I talked with the other descendants, some of whom remembered going to the camp as a child to visit their relatives. One woman spoke to me about how all the children of the prisoners knew each other, and all the men knew one another's children.

I told her about Jacques going back to the camp after his home leave to visit Mila and I rolled my eyes – wasn't that just absurd? What an unforgivable waste of an opportunity. Surely her father would never have done that. But she reprimanded me for my callousness.

'There was a real sense of camaraderie at the camp after all that time,' she told me. 'It's hard for you to believe now, I know, but there was. And that's why he returned. He would never have abandoned his friends.'

Jacques always had bad timing, but his decision to return to Pithiviers could not have been timed worse. Less than three weeks after he walked back to the camp the Wannsee Conference was held in Germany, at which plans were formalised for the implementation of the Final Solution: the killing of all the Jews in Nazi-occupied Europe. As early as March 1942 more than 1,000 Jews were shipped out on one train from France to Auschwitz. In early summer, German and French officials met to plan more mass deportations.

The men in Pithiviers heard the rumours from home. But on 14 July, Bastille Day, they were reassured, again, by the Préfecture of Orléans that they would be protected, because they were French, and they were told not to listen to rumours. Less than twenty-four hours later they were told to pack their bags. The next day women and children prisoners suddenly arrived at the camp, and that's when the men really started to worry, but it was too late.

On 17 July 1942 Jacques was ordered onto a cattle train by the French police, along with 928 other prisoners from Pithiviers and Beaune-la-Rolande. This was Convoi 6 and among Jacques's fellow prisoners on the train were ninety-six women and twenty-four children.[9] One of the women was Irène Némirovsky, author of *Suite Française*, a series of novels about life in occupied France that was finally published in 2004, having been saved and preserved by her daughter during the war and in the decades afterwards. Némirovsky had planned to write five novels in her series, but she had only finished two when she was arrested. When the police arrived to take her to Pithiviers, she told her young daughters, 'I am going on a journey now.' It was one from which neither she nor Jacques would ever return. They were both thirty-nine years old.

There were a hundred prisoners in each wagon, standing pressed up against one another in the airless train.

'They won't eat us, they're just taking us somewhere to work,' the prisoners muttered to one another reassuringly.

'Maybe to Drancy?' another suggested, as they'd heard about another French internment camp that had recently been opened.

In fact, the reason Jacques and the rest of the prisoners were shipped out so suddenly was that Vichy was now going after the Jews so relentlessly that they needed the space in the French camps for the new arrests. The day before Jacques's train left for Auschwitz, French police completed the now infamous Vel d'Hiv round-up, in which more than 13,000 Jews, including 4,000 children, were arrested, with most held at an indoor cycle track in Paris before being sent to the camps. French police had tracked them down using the 1940 Jewish census, and the man who helped to plan the round-up was René Bousquet, secretary-general of the police and close associate of Colonel Perré, Alex's friend. According to US diplomatic papers, Pierre Laval – by now the head of government – met with a group of American Quakers at this time and told them that 'these foreign Jews had always been a problem in France, and the French government was glad that a change in the German attitude towards them gave France an opportunity to get rid of them.' Laval, the papers add, 'made no mention of any German pressure'.[10] By the end of 1942, the French government deported almost 40,000 Jews.[11]

For three days and nights, in the stifling July heat, Jacques and his fellow prisoners travelled in the train. There was only a tiny window, no room to sit – certainly none to lie down – no food and no water. The only toilet was a small scrap of hay in the corner of the wagon. The smell quickly became so bad people were throwing up where they stood, worsening the stench and the misery. There was hardly even any air. Some people literally dropped dead where they stood for lack of water. At a certain point – the French/German border, it turned out – the French guards and drivers got off and were replaced with Germans. Seeing they were at a station the prisoners cried out the window, 'Water, please water!'

'None for you, Jews!' came the response, in German, from the civilians nearby. 'This is hell,' the prisoners wept, but it was not, because hell was still to come.

They knew now they were in Germany. And Germany, they said anxiously to one another, was a civilised country, right? Surely they were just here to work.

They arrived at Auschwitz-Birkenau in the evening. '*Raus! Schnell! Schnell!*' yelled the guards, hurrying them off the train, beating them with truncheons.

A LOT IS KNOWN ABOUT Convoi 6, more than most deportation trains because a relatively high number of people who travelled on it were still alive when the war ended – 91 out of 928, and many of the details I've given above come from the survivors' testimonies kept at the Shoah Memorial in Paris. It was still so early in the war that the Nazis needed the prisoners to help construct Auschwitz-Birkenau, so there was no selection process when the prisoners arrived in Poland – everyone entered the camp and none were sent to the gas chambers, at least not immediately. As a result, there are only two associations for descendants and relatives of victims of a specific deportation train, and one of them is that for Convoi 6. It was with this association that I visited Pithiviers in 2012. The year before, 928 trees were planted in Israel in the name of Convoi 6, one for every adult and child who travelled on that train.

The tree feels like an apt memorial for Jacques, the boy who once ran through Chrzanow's silver birch tree forest and was then sent as a man to Birkenau, a camp whose name derives from the German for 'birch tree'. Did Jacques realise, as he walked into the death camp, he was only 18 kilometres from where he was born? Had he spotted the thin Galician birch trees through the tiny window in the train, and did they look familiar to him? Did they make him think of his brothers and the Ornstein cousins and how they used to hide in the forests? And of his father, buried in the shadow of birch trees only kilometres away from where he was now? Did he wonder why he, alone among his siblings, hadn't risked anything to stay alive? Why he was the passive one among them and how this was the conclusion to that story? Did he think about the weird irony of his life, how he had always wanted to stay still, but was forced to travel so far, and yet ended up right back where he began? Perhaps he thought, No matter how hard a Jewish man tries, even if he fights for another country, he will still get sent back to the place of his father's grave instead of enjoying his daughter in her cot – always the past for the Jew, never the future. Never forget who you are and where you're from, because no one else around you will, and they will send you back. During all that deprivation and degradation on the train, it had felt like the world was ending. Instead, Jakob Glahs walked out to find he was simply back home. Like waking from a bad dream, but the nightmare continues in real life. It had always been thus, the threat just beneath the surface. He simply hadn't wanted to see it. He had crossed a continent and he hadn't seen it. But now he was back to where he started and he could see it. At last, he saw it. Once again, his brothers had been right.

Or maybe Jacques thought none of those things. Maybe he was already too sick and too tired and too naturally unself-reflective to think like that at all. And who could blame him? He was always Jacques, only Jacques, why ask more of him than he was? Anyone who expected him to be other than he had been is the foolish one – Alex had learned that, and so had Henri. He had always been utterly true to himself: gentle, popular, caring, weak, trusting, loyal, unlucky, kind. So Jacques was not sent directly to the gas chambers, as so many Jews arriving at Birkenau soon would be. But according to Auschwitz's records, he lasted fewer than three months building his own tomb, so close to the place of his birth. He was killed on 6 October.

ON 5 OCTOBER, the day before Jacques was murdered, Revillon wrote another letter to the CQJD on Mila's behalf, asking for her to be allowed to stay in the apartment and stressing that she did not know where her husband was and was very anxious. Sara, too, was worried, and wrote to the Red Cross for help. She would have to wait for two years to get a reply. Henri, Sonia and Alex did not make enquiries. They might not have known where Jacques was, but they had a pretty good idea.

Mila and Lily eventually went into hiding, almost certainly with help from Sonia as there was no way Mila could have evaded the Vichy police on her own with a newborn baby. Miraculously, they managed to survive the war, but this was to be the one miracle in poor Mila's dumb, cursed life. After the war was over, she returned to rue de la Tour, living in that dark little basement beneath the fur storage business, because it never occurred to her that she might want to do something different. Sara finally received definitive proof that Jacques was dead in November 1944 from the Red Cross, who wrote to her confirming his death in Auschwitz. For the rest of her life, whenever someone asked her about her brother Jacques, Sara would answer quietly, 'They sent him home.'

After the war, Mila was very isolated in Paris. Photos of her from that period show her with her beloved toddler daughter, holding her baby almost vampirically close to her, the only thing she had left in the world. There is never

anyone else in the photo. She didn't marry again, she barely made a living trying to run Jacques's old business on her own, and in the letters she wrote throughout 1945 to the Service de Restitution des Biens des Victimes des Lois et Mesures de Spoliation, which was set up to provide some compensation to the Jews whose money and property was taken from them by Vichy, she frequently mentions being '*dénuée de tout*' (completely bankrupt). Alex refused to see or speak to her and whenever he heard her name he would spit and say, '*Elle a tué mon frère!*' Henri, uncharacteristically unforgiving, also refused to speak to her, furious that her stupidity had condemned his closest brother to his death. Worse, she remained unrepentant about it: Mila lived for another thirty years after Jacques died, and not for a moment did she ever think she made a mistake in telling Jacques to go back to the camp. She never asked herself if maybe she had listened to her brothers-in-law then perhaps Jacques might still be alive and she wouldn't be living in penury on her own with her daughter in this dank old basement. After all, she would say, he gave his word.

Her sister Olga, who now lived in the United States, helped a little. But she found Mila such a drag, always complaining about her life and never taking any responsibility for her actions, that they hardly spoke, let alone saw one another.

The only people who helped Mila were Sonia and Sara. Both of them felt sorry for her, and even more sorry for Lily. They, unlike Henri and Alex, were able to look at the truth about what happened to Jacques square in the face; they knew what he was like – had always been like – and they also knew he was a grown man who had made his own choices. Unlike his brothers, they didn't blame a foolish woman for his death. Whereas Alex in particular had always tried to make Jacques into something he wasn't by denying his true nature, and continued to do so after he died, the women accepted him as he really was. So after the war Sara sent Mila provisions, and Sonia secretly visited her, bringing money and food, and listening silently to Mila's endless list of grievances against the world. Sonia was known in the family as a chatterbox, because she said what she thought. But Sonia was also very kind and knew when to say nothing and let others speak, and she let Mila speak.

The only other person in the family who helped her was my father, who moved to Paris in the 1960s and happened to live around the corner from Mila. He occasionally went round to her apartment for dinner – Mila was an excellent cook, and loved to make heavy Polish dishes, but my father often had to pay for the ingredients. At other times, she would come to his apartment, ringing his doorbell at odd hours of the day.

'I need to use your bath!' she would call up to his window.

There was no bathtub in her apartment and so, at the age of fifty-something, she would go to see her twenty-five-year-old nephew, and beg to use his.

Lily grew up to be a sweet, quiet gentle girl, a lot like her father in many ways. But because of the consanguinity of her parents, she was born with a hole in her heart and she was known back then as a 'blue baby', because her lips purpled from oxygen deprivation, the consequence of her weak heart. When Lily was fourteen, Sonia heard about a doctor in Denver who specialised in helping such children, and she talked her neighbour, who happened to be a radio producer, into putting on a telethon to raise money for Lily to go there. Incredibly, this worked, and Lily flew to Denver to have her heart repaired. The operation was a success. When I was going through Sonia's belongings, two decades after she died, I found a publicity shot of Lily leaving the hospital that the radio station took. It's a very staged photo,

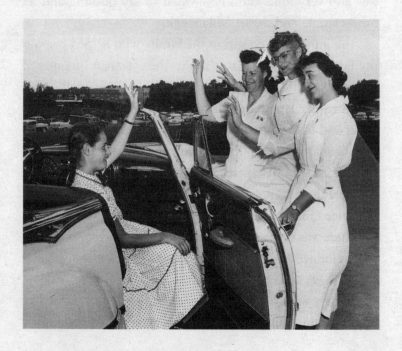

Lily as a teenager.

almost comically so, with Lily sitting in a car, stiffly waving to a trio of nurses who wave back to her. But it's also an extremely sweet photo, because of Lily: she looks so happy, a typical fourteen-year-old, her tidy plaits swinging gently as she waves to her nurses, a little girl about to enjoy health and happiness the likes of which she'd never previously known. Before she left the hospital, her doctor told her she should be fine, as long as she never got pregnant, because her heart was not strong enough to support two lives.

A few years later, when Lily was in her very early twenties, she was walking in Paris near the Luxembourg Gardens when she spotted a man sitting in a café and fell in love at first sight. His name was Victor, he came from Bolivia and they married almost immediately. She moved with him to South America, and, too in love to remember or care about any medical edicts, she quickly became pregnant. About five months into her pregnancy, my father got a call at his office in New York. It was Sonia, and she had just spoken to Victor who had called her in a panic: Lily was dying.

'Should I tell Mila? She's just getting over pneumonia and I worry that she wouldn't survive the trip,' Sonia asked my dad.

'Sonia, I can't tell you what to do – you know her better than me,' he replied.

'Fine, never mind!' Sonia said, slamming down the phone.

Sonia decided not to tell Mila, believing, maybe correctly, that travelling to Bolivia and seeing Lily die would kill her. But not knowing pretty much killed her, too. After Lily died in Bolivia, Mila found out that Sonia had known before-hand and hadn't told her, thereby preventing her from saying goodbye to her daughter. Understandably, she flew into a desperate rage and refused to speak to Sonia ever again. But this meant that for the last ten years of her life she hardly spoke to anyone. Instead, she sat in the same basement flat Jacques had bought for them thirty years earlier, crying on her own, surrounded by tear-soaked photos of Lily. She her-self died in the early 1970s, a sad and lonely life that finally came to an end. And when she went, Jacques's branch of

the family tree – blighted by bad luck and bad circumstances, both of which were made infinitely worse by bad
choices, from father to mother to daughter – withered away
to ashes.

Alex with the Aymards
in Saint-Gervais-d'Auvergne, 1943.

10

ALEX – Myth-making

France, 1940s

IN THE AUTUMN OF 1940, Alex, fresh from demobilisation, was in Grenoble with his fellow resistance fighters, the Sizaines, talking about how to save their now humiliated country. Alex was keen to sneak back into Paris to see his family, to save his mother, to check on his business. But his close friend and fellow Sizaine, Jean Baptiste Seytour, who – unsurprisingly, given his name – was not Jewish, convinced him they would do better establishing a base in the unoccupied southern zone before making Resistance runs to Paris. Alex agreed, but where should they live? Alex's money was in Paris. Seytour had the answer for that too.

Seytour, an aspiring actor, had grown up in Nice, and, luckily for him and his fellow legionnaire, his father still lived there. So he and Alex moved in with Pierre Seytour, and for the next few years, they lived a pretty fabulous life down on *le Midi*. Alex's friend Kiki Kisling lived nearby, and they often went to his place for dinners and drinks. Alex's former draftsman, Christian Dior, was also down in the south of France, after being demobilised from the army, and he was staying with his father and beloved youngest sister Catherine in the pretty village of Callian near Grasse, about 40 kilometres from Cannes. According to Alex's memoir, when loyal friends in his salon in Paris sent him a supply of civilian clothes, he shared them with Dior because the two of them were the same size (short, in other words). Alex's other illustrator, René Gruau, was there too, and it was in this period that he became friends with Dior, establishing a lifelong working relationship. It was through Gruau that Dior learned he could resume his draftsman work down in the south. He was soon even busier than he'd been in Paris because several designers had outlets in Nice, Cannes and Monte Carlo, and they desperately needed an illustrator as there were no photographers – or film – to take pictures of the dresses.[1] Among these designers were Chanel, Hermès – and Alex Maguy. Although Alex's salon in Paris, like Jacques' fur business, had been taken from him by the CGQJ under 'Aryanisation' laws, he was, in recognition of his war record, given permission in 1941 to open up a salon in Cannes. He chose an elegant little building at the plum address of Place Mérimée, on the promenade next to the seafront.

'Cannes was a refuge for Parisians in exile,' Dior's biographer, Marie-France Pochna, wrote, describing how the Bohemians would spend their days sunbathing on the beach and their nights throwing costume parties so wild the police threatened to shut these 'bacchanalian orgies' down. It was a world that would have felt cheeringly familiar to Alex.

As well as height, work and social life preferences, another connection between him and Dior was a proximity to Resistance activity. Alex was working with the Sizaines and Dior's sister, Catherine, was about to become an important figure in the 'Massif Central' network. Gitta Sereny later described the Massif Central as 'one of the most dynamic intelligence [Resistance] movements in Europe,'[2] and it had similar ambitions to the Sizaines, as it focused on gathering information about German train and troop movements for purposes of sabotage. It was also one of the most brutalised Resistance networks: most of its leaders were killed by 1942 and Catherine Dior herself was arrested in June 1944 and deported to Ravensbrück.

For almost a year, Christian Dior had no idea whether his sister was alive or dead, until he got a phone call in May 1945 saying that she would be arriving in Paris the next day by train. When she came home, she had been so starved that it was several months until she could eat solid food. But no family's story was simple in occupied France, and the Diors are a neat illustration of that: whereas Catherine was in the Resistance, her niece, Françoise, became a full-throated Nazi, promoting Hitler and burning down synagogues.

Dior himself would spend much of the war working as a designer for Lucien Lelong alongside another aspiring couturier, Pierre Balmain. Lelong – who would play an important part in Alex's life after the war – managed to keep his label open during the war. The few other designers who were able to do this – Jacques Fath, Marcel Rochas, Maggy Rouff – did so by selling to wealthy French collaborators and visiting German officers. In fact, according to fashion historian Dominique Veillon, this proved to be such a lucrative market that the French fashion industry made 463 million francs in the year, up from 67 million francs only two years earlier.[3] As much as Dior loved Catherine, he also had to eat, and so he spent the later part of the war selling clothes to the wives of men who enabled the torture of his sister. It was very hard to avoid working for collaborators if you worked in the luxury sector and lived in France during the war.

For the first few years of the war, Alex's life in the south of France was comfortable and glamorous. He was living in the Seytour family's flat and his life was as sociable as it had been in Paris, hanging around with, as he puts it, 'my friend Seytour'.

An obvious question about this period of Alex's life is whether he and Seytour were lovers. Certainly Alex writes about him in his memoir more warmly than he does his own family, and it's not a completely outlandish conclusion to draw about a fashion designer and an actor living together so closely for so long. According to Seytour's records he was married the whole time he was with Alex, to a woman named Caroline Antoine, but there is no mention of her in any of Alex's records, and that marriage ended in divorce in 1944, without any children. As far as I know, Alex never told anyone in his family about Seytour, and after he left Nice he never saw him again.

Alex's salon became so busy he had to employ twelve people to help meet the demand. But as well as being a working salon, the shop became a hangout for Resistance fighters. The Sizaines would meet there often and, in the absence of any weapons, as the British hadn't yet started parachuting in supplies, they plotted how to derail German trains coming into France. Other Resistance fighters who came to Alex's salon included the French novelists Joseph Kessel, who worked as an aide to Charles de Gaulle during the war and later wrote *Belle de Jour*, and his nephew, Maurice Druon. Kessel's lover, Germaine Sablon, a singer and actress and just the kind of person Alex would know from Paris, was another frequent presence.

The mystery of what Alex actually did during the war only became more puzzling the more you asked him directly about it. It wasn't that Alex didn't talk about his war years; it's just that the few stories he told were disjointed, non-chronological and utterly improbable, anecdotes so worn down with re-telling they were like sea-tossed pebbles, smoothed from years of repetition, the grit long since washed away. I – and many others – suspected they were a smokescreen for something else, distractions, jimmied-up anecdotes rendered into self-mythologies. The question was: what he was distracting people from?

Almost everyone who thrived and survived in France during the war later engaged in some kind of self-mythology. Once the country was liberated and the shame of France's collaboration was exposed to the world, the reality of the recent past, for many people, needed to be obscured, black covered in white. For some the motivations were obvious, for others the story was more grey.

When Alex's memoir arrived in the post, I flipped through the stories of early 1930s Paris to get to what I hoped would be the long-awaited answer of what Alex did to survive the war. There were some stories, ones my father and I had heard dozens of times from Alex himself: barely sketched allusions to arrests and brave standoffs against collaborators, more fully sketched stories about his glamorous life as a couturier in Cannes. On page 118 it looked as if he was about to start detailing what life was actually like during the war. I turned the page eagerly – but there was no page 119. Nor a page 120, 121 or 122. Instead, the memoir blithely skipped from 1943 to 1945 with the story resuming on page 131.

Was this just a fluke? Did twelve pages merely get lost over the years, and did those twelve pages just happen to be the ones on which Alex described his war years? Or did Alex write those sections up and then decide he didn't want anyone to read them and so threw them away? Had he, in fact, been a collaborator?

Plenty of big-name fashion designers collaborated or at least worked with the Nazi occupiers, including Coco Chanel, Louis Vuitton and Jeanne Lanvin. Cristóbal Balenciaga designed for Franco's wife, Jean Patou made dresses for Hermann Göring's wife, and Hugo Boss – who was German and based in Germany – not only joined the Nazi party but made the Nazi Youth uniforms.[4] Marcel Rochas refused even to say hello to former customers and friends if they were Jewish, pointedly crossing the road to avoid them.[5] Pretty much the only people in France at that time who could afford high fashion were Nazis and collaborators, so the few designers who continued to work in Paris during the war would have worked with them. It wasn't impossible that Alex might have done too, and if so, that would have explained how he, a Polish Jew, didn't just survive the war but flourished.

Alex himself might have been opaque about what he had to do to survive the war, but the records were not. During the war he became such a person of interest that the files on him at the CGQJ could barely contain all the letters and records of his various comings and goings. Repeatedly investigations were conducted into his business affairs, and repeatedly nothing happened. This was remarkable, given how blatantly Alex was hosting Resistance meetings in his salon, but it turns out there was a simple reason: in his CGQJ file there are letters from his old friend and protector, now known as General Perré, defending Alex's right to own a shop. Even more remarkably, Xavier Vallat, the Commissioner General for Jewish Affairs (head of the CGQJ), personally wrote a letter on 13 February 1942, ordering that Alex's case should be looked at favourably and he be left alone:

J'ai l'honneur de vous faire connaître que les
renseignements sur l'intéressé étant favorables,
il conviendrait de lui faire savoir que je ne vois
pas d'inconvénient à ce qu'il exerce la profession
de couturier créateur modeliste . . .

When I initially found this letter in a file about Alex in a French archive, my stomach sank into my shoes. Vallat was a vicious anti-Semite who looked like a movie villain straight from central casting, having lost an eye and a leg in the First World War. He was also the most important person in the CGQJ – in other words, the man in charge of all anti-Semitic activity in France. He was the man charged with the Aryanisation of the French economy – conducted entirely by the Vichy government with no pressure from the Germans – and his passion was the elimination of Jewish culture from French life. All of this made his defence of Alex's shop seem especially bizarre, and the first time I read it I was sure that I'd found, at long last, confirmation of my worst suspicions: Alex was a collaborator, a spy for the enemy, and this is why he was so protected.

But the morality of French politics during the war was far too blurred to be confined by simplistic black-and-white outlines, and, as various war historians later explained to me, what this letter reveals has, in fact, little to do with Alex. Instead, it shows the changing and conflicting loyalties in the Vichy government. Yet whereas most Jews in France suffered – to say the least – from these political shifts, Alex benefitted from them.

Like Perré and Pétain, Vallat was another old military vet, and while he was a massive anti-Semite, he was, above all, a Catholic nationalist, almost as anti-German as he was anti-Semitic, one who saw the sanctity of France as his first priority.[6] So anyone who fought for France was, for him, a

Frenchman of honour, even if that man was a Polish Jew. Thus, because Alex was a decorated veteran of the Narvik campaign, Vallat intervened on his behalf, which was almost like the British Home Secretary stepping in to adjudicate on a small local matter, but that was how much he cared about those who fought for France, whatever their religion. Vallat's priorities would soon prove to be his undoing. Within weeks of writing in defence of Alex, the German ambassador to Vichy, Otto Abetz, ordered Pétain to dismiss him, which he did. Vallat was all for the Aryanisation of France, but not at the cost of turning it into Germany, and his uncooperativeness became too much for Nazi Germany. They replaced him with Louis Darquier de Pellepoix, a pro-Nazi French politician who was in Germany's pay before the war, and it was Darquier de Pellepoix who ensured the deportation of France's Jews, including Jacques, to Auschwitz. Darquier de Pellepoix definitely did not care about Jacques's war record, or that of any Jew, so for the Jews he was worse than Vallat, but in Vichy it was all relative. Vallat remained an unrepentant anti-Semite for the rest of his life, and there is no evidence he ever met Alex or that Alex ever knew he owed his wartime livelihood to him.

Even though Alex's connection to Vallat turned out to be innocent, a fog of suspicion started to form around Alex in the eyes of both Vichy and his fellow Resistance fighters. He didn't especially help himself: when General Perré came to visit the shop, Alex made a big show of presenting him with a military cap. Alex didn't care that Perré was on the other side:

he saw him as an old friend and, more importantly, a useful connection. And when Alex went to Perré for help when he heard that his cousin Josek Ornstein had been arrested, the rumours really began.

'My Cannes branch was busy, too busy for some. People saw military officers and beautiful women there, which created doubts. Was I even kosher?' Alex wrote.

As deeply as Alex loved France and believed in defending the Jews, there was always one cause that Alex believed in above all, and that was Alex. He would do whatever it took to survive, and if that meant being friendly with some people in Vichy during the war, well, he would say, that wasn't the worst thing in the world. He was still, and would always be, the hungry little boy in Chrzanow, determined to scrape his way from the bottom of the sewer to reach the stars. He grew up thinking, 'No one will help you except you.' And that was the lesson he lived by for the rest of his life.

During 1941 and 1942, Alex and the Sizaines ran Resistance missions to Paris. Alex was one of the few Jewish members of the group, and thus he risked more than most, as it was forbidden for a Jew to go into the occupied zone. For Alex, the danger was the appeal.

'I crossed the line of demarcation several times with a guide,' he writes. 'I was always in front to open the way. Nothing could frighten me. A rage to live burned within me. I felt invincible.'

What Alex was actually doing on these missions remains somewhat mysterious. According to letters from his cousins

Renée and Roger, he was meeting up with them and his siblings, and his memoir corroborates this. Given that Renée and Roger Goldberg were in the Resistance, it looks like they were his main points of contact for passing information back and forth. He was, according to Sonia and Henri, at Mila's bedside when Lily was born in 1942, and he repeatedly appears at Sonia's lunches in Renée's letters of that year. He also, at some point, managed to smuggle Chaya out of Paris and down to Cannes, where she stayed with one of his fashion clients, a Madame Armande. Alex achieved an enormous amount in his life, escaping the depths of the Polish pogroms to climb to the top of the French art world, all thanks to his cunning and determination. But that he managed to sneak his truculent, strictly kosher, non-French-speaking mother across the demarcation line was possibly his most extraordinary feat.

He also wanted to check on his business, because it was no longer his. A man called Joseph Paquin took it over in 1941, when businesses in the occupied zone were Aryanised, and Alex is as vicious about Paquin in his memoir as he is about the Nazis who killed so many members of his family, describing him alternately as 'a rat', 'a bastard' and 'the little shit'. Alex would have hated anyone taking over his business, but the story of Paquin reveals something more about the world of French collaboration than Alex's ego.

Born in 1873 in the small north-eastern village of Mont-Bonvillers, Joseph Nicolas Paquin also worked in fashion. He married his wife, Hélène, on 23 December 1894, and on the morning of his wedding, every newspaper had the same front page: a photo of Colonel Alfred Dreyfus who, the day before, had been unanimously found guilty by seven judges of passing on French military secrets to the Germans. As the newly wedded Monsieur and Madame Paquin began their married life, they did so against the backdrop of what remains a universal symbol of anti-Semitism.

Paquin was a less successful Paris couturier than Alex. As well as Alex's business, he was given the businesses of three other Jewish designers – at least one of whom was then killed in Auschwitz – and he was paid 2,000 francs a month for each. Madame Paquin certainly enjoyed the financial benefits of seizing control of Jewish businesses: during the war she enthusiastically redecorated their apartment with expensive furniture and what one fellow designer described as '*bibelots anciens*' (antique trinkets). Paquin protected his freebies: when Alex was given permission to open an Alex Maguy salon in Cannes, he wrote a cross letter to the CGQJ, saying this would create 'confusion' for customers and should not be allowed. (Thanks to Alex's high-ranking friends, this letter was ignored.) Paquin drove the CGQJ somewhat mad during the war, constantly writing letters demanding more money, more help and more effective measures taken against Alex's business in the south. As I read his letters, I understood better why Alex called him 'a worm': his tone was whiny and weasely. It infuriated Alex that such a man had his hands on his beloved business in Paris, and he vowed he would have his revenge. He would not have to wait long to get it.

Back in Cannes, Alex's life continued peacefully, building his business, finding kosher food for his mother. In November 1942 the Italian army invaded Nice and because the Italians weren't especially interested in Germany's anti-Semitic focus, the only way Alex's life changed was that he started to pick up some Italian vocabulary. But on 9 September 1943, the Germans took over the Italian zones and Alex's life changed in the worst possible ways.

According to Alex's official testimonies given after the war, he was arrested three times in the south of France. Twice his powerful friends were able to help him, despite his being a foreign Jew. The third time he pushed his luck too far.

The evening of 18 September 1943 was warm, and after a long day of working in the salon Alex decided to relax in the way he'd been relaxing for two decades, which was by going to a nightclub. This time he chose the Pam Pam in Nice and, as usual, Alex had his own table and was drinking with his friends, talking with the few remaining Italians left in the city.

'Suddenly, I heard a German song being played by the orchestra. My blood rose. Disgusted and furious, I summoned the headwaiter. "Please ask the bandleader to come speak with me. I have something to say to him," Alex writes in his memoir.

When the bandleader came to Alex's table, he loudly ordered him to 'stop playing these goddamn Kraut songs'. Instead, they should play French and British military songs, starting with *Le Boudin,* the official song of the French Foreign Legion, followed by *La Marseillaise.*

The headwaiter begged Alex to leave, saying there were senior members of the Gestapo in the room. The Nazis had arrived in the city just over a week earlier. Alois Brunner, the notorious Jew hunter, came to Nice on 10 September and his police had already started conducting raids. The Germans seized control of the roads and train stations, and the Jews were now in what Serge Klarsfeld, then a child in Nice, described as 'a kind of trap'.[7] Even French Jews, who had previously been able to take their safety for granted, knew that the leniency they'd enjoyed under the Italians was over. What had been happening to their friends and families in the north was about to happen to them, and every Jew in the region was terrified. But Alex refused to back down.

'I'm a French soldier – I am not leaving,' he replied.

'They're giving you five minutes to go,' the waiter pleaded.

'Like hell will a Kraut give me orders! I'm a Legionnaire and nothing scares me,' Alex replied.

He looked at the table where the waiter had run over from, and saw three members of the Gestapo sitting with a woman. One of the men took his pistol out of its holster and pointed it straight at Alex.

'Look at this coward! With a woman at his table he pulls a revolver,' Alex crowed to the now silent room, all staring at what was going on.

The Nazi got out from behind his table and walked towards Alex, keeping his gun pointed at Alex's head. When he got to Alex's table, Alex stood up.

'I am Alex Maguy,' Alex shouted.

'We know who you are, Maguy. You're a Jew.'

'That's right, I'm a Jew and you can go fuck yourself,' he replied.

Somehow Alex managed to escape out the back of the club without being shot or arrested, but he knew he was on borrowed time now. After checking that he wasn't being followed, he went back to Cannes and to the house of Madame Armande, who was hiding Chaya for him. He left enough money for his mother to be looked after for the next year, and then hurried away before he led the Nazis to his mother. He didn't even try to hide himself, perhaps out of a sense of arrogance that he would always, ultimately, be protected. Instead, the next day he went to work as usual, and waited to see what would happen. He did not have to wait long. Within an hour, the Gestapo burst into his salon on Place Mérimée, arrested him and brought him to the Hotel Excelsior in Nice, Alois Brunner's headquarters.

BY THE TIME Brunner arrived in France, he was only thirty years old but was already known for being especially efficient at deporting Jews. He had worked as Adolf Eichmann's assistant and overseen the deportations in Austria, Berlin and Greece; in Austria alone he was personally responsible for the deportation of 47,000 Jews. By the time the war ended, he'd sent over 128,000 Jews to the death camps. From the moment he arrived in the south of France he terrorised the Jews, and the raids he ordered in Nice were, according to Klarsfeld, the most brutal that the Nazis carried out in the whole of western Europe.[8, 9] They largely took place at night: men, women and children, dragged out of their beds, shivering in their nightclothes, terrorised and arrested. Brunner renamed the Excelsior '*camp de recensement des juifs arrêtés, dépendant du camp de Drancy*' (camp for arrested Jews going to Drancy). He ostensibly turned it into a prison where he dumped the Jews rounded up during the raids. He then tortured them, beat them, ordered them to give the names and addresses of their families under pain of death and then put them on a train to Drancy, the French concentration camp that had taken over from Pithiviers. Brunner himself would, in a few months' time, be in charge of Drancy, and it is estimated that he sent 23,500 Jews to Auschwitz from there.

Alex was kept under arrest for four days, and he was beaten savagely and near continuously by the guards. When he asked why he was being singled out for so many beatings, one of the guards showed him the file they had on him. 'It was thick like a block. The spies had done their work well. I had no illusions now. I knew I would be executed like Josek was,' he wrote, referring to his cousin. But when Alex was pushed onto the train to Drancy on 24 September, he realised he would not have a fate like Josek's; he would have one like Jacques's.

The story Alex always told about how he survived the war was that he was arrested but he escaped from the train. 'Escaped from the train': I heard this so many times, and imagined it even more, that it became more than a story and more like a myth in my head. My brave great-uncle, bursting out of the train like a hero, running away from the big bad Nazis! But as I grew older I learned that fairy tales aren't true and there were whispers in the family that maybe none of this had happened. Maybe he was never put on a train at all. Who knows? Only Alex, and no point asking him, you know what he's like – you'll never get a straight answer out of him. And anyway, how on earth can you prove that someone once jumped off a train?

It was easy to find the records from Drancy detailing who got off the trains from Nice in 1943, and Alex's name wasn't on any of them, which didn't prove much. But to find out who actually got on the trains, I had to go to the archives in Nice itself.

Nice is still as picturesque as it was when Alex lived there – those elegant beachside boulevards, the palm trees swaying over outdoor cafés. I came to this beautiful seaside town to search through the dead. On the first day I found the work close to unbearable, especially when I saw row after row of the same name: whole families, from grandparents to eight-month-old babies, packed off on trains that led only to death. By the third day I felt my hide getting harder, casually flicking through list after list, getting almost annoyed with the names on the list who weren't the name I wanted to see. What did I care about Gerhard Glahs? I was looking for Glass! Out of my way, Gerhard! And just as I was thinking proudly about what a tough-hearted researcher I'd become, I saw a name that undid all my efforts to stop personalising these lists: there, listed among the Poles who were put on the train to Drancy was '*Glass, Alexandre, de 7 Place Mérimée Cannes, Juif*'. Alex really had got on the train. And he hadn't got off. Because he had escaped. Just as he'd always told us.

Alex was not the only person to have escaped from the train. When Klarsfeld was researching what happened to the French Jews he noted that there were some names who got on the train to Drancy but did not then appear on the passenger lists from Drancy to Auschwitz. Some had died. Some had been released from Drancy. But in the period of September 1943–December 1943, when Brunner was at the Excelsior and sending thousands of French Jews to the camp, there were ninety-three people who got on the train to Drancy that no one could account for. One of them was Alex.

On 24 September, Alex – by now bruised and almost broken from all the beatings – was dragged out of his cell in the Excelsior along with his cellmates and pushed by the guards towards the train station. A train was waiting for them there. But they could barely see it because their senses were so overwhelmed by the noise: the whole station was filled with the sound of men, women, children and babies screaming, crying and begging, and officers mercilessly shouting at them in French and German. The sound was so terrifying it could stop a man's heart. But Alex marched towards the train the way a legionnaire always should, unbowed and unafraid. Alongside him was the cellmate he had become closest to during his imprisonment, a lanky Frenchman called Jacques Schwob Héricourt, and the two of them got into the same train carriage together, along with eighty other men.

'Can we escape? They can't treat us like sheep. We have to do something,' Alex whispered to Héricourt. But neither of them could think of anything they could do.

As the train travelled north towards Drancy and night fell, Alex thought of Jacques. At this point he didn't know exactly what had become of Jacques, but he had a strong suspicion, and after having worked so hard not to be like his older brother, were they to have the same fate after all? Had it all been for nothing? Passivity and defiance, both paths led to the same destination when chased by these persecutors. There were some demons you could not outrun. And just as Alex was thinking this, he noticed a patch of moonlight on the floor of the train and looked up to see where it was coming from. Up in the top corner of the back of the train there was a hole where two planks of wood had rotted away. He stared at it. He knew that Jacques would not have thought about the hole, and that was what had always broken his heart about his brother: so many times he had rejected chances, offers laid out to him on a plate, often by Alex. But he always said no. Once he'd been put on the train, Alex knew, Jacques would have stood there passively and accepted his fate. Well, he was not Jacques.

He tapped Héricourt on the arm and pointed up to the hole. Héricourt looked at it, then back down to his friend and nodded, understanding. While everyone else in the carriage stared, he picked up Alex, all five feet of him, and lifted him to the opening. The train was travelling fast, 90 kilometres an hour, but what difference did it make? Die trying to escape or die a passive prisoner – Alex knew which option he'd choose, every time. And so, while the whole carriage watched, Alex reached towards the small opening and punched it, making the hole a little larger. He could now fit through it, just. And then, with a helping push from Héricourt, he threw himself out of the moving train.

'The shock was terrible. I landed with such force I thought at first it would kill me. And then I thought about the times I used to fall on my head out of our apartment in Chrzanow onto the rough pavement,' Alex wrote.

He lay there on the side of the train track, his head bleeding, his ribs broken, barely able to breathe let alone move. He heard the train speed off without him, and even though he was in so much pain what he mainly felt was the extraordinary relief of no longer being a prisoner bound for Drancy. He was right to do so: almost everyone on that train, including Héricourt, would be killed in Auschwitz. But his relief turned to fear when he heard footsteps crunching towards him and he braced himself.

'What are you doing here?'

Alex cleared the blood out of his eyes and saw a railway worker peering down at him.

'I just jumped out of a train,' Alex whispered.

The man nodded slowly, looking at him. 'You're in Saint-Rambert-d'Albon. Come with me, quickly. They'll be looking for you.'

The railway worker, and his colleagues, were communists, and therefore very happy to help an escaped prisoner evade the Nazis. They took him back to their office and called a communist doctor to set his ribs and stitch up his forehead, which had torn so badly when he hit the ground that the skin flapped in front of his eyes like a veil. When the authorities came looking for Alex a few hours later, the railwaymen hid him in a large pile of manure, knowing that the Germans would be too vain about their uniforms to look for him there, and they were right. When it was safe, they brought him out of hiding, washed him and, when he was feeling up to it, taught him how to drive a train. Alex told them about how he and his cousins used to fake toothaches to take the train from Chrzanow to Trzebina, and they all laughed together. Then Alex thought more about his cousins and told his new friends his ribs hurt too much to laugh.

After a few days hiding in the railway station Alex got a message – how and from whom he never said – that he should go to Lyon where someone would meet him and take him to a safe place. The railway workers, who presumably thought he was meeting his Resistance network, gave him a lift to Lyon and wished him *bon courage*. One of them gave him his cap, small and battered and decorated with three stars. Alex kept it for the rest of his life.

At this point the story ends, at least as much as Alex ever told it, and the pages in the memoir ended here. Alex never talked about what he did after leaving Saint-Rambert-d'Albon, where he went, who helped him. He made vague references to 'fighting in the Resistance', and that was that. I had few hopes of finding any details but I contacted various Resistance enthusiasts in central France, the area between Nice and Drancy, and asked them if they knew of any stories about a Polish Jew who had escaped from a train being hidden in their area. One, Robert Picandet, wrote back:

> I am one of the heads of the Resistance Museum
> in Saint-Gervais-d'Auvergne and here is some
> information I obtained from a former resident in
> Espinasse. He remembers Alex Glass very well.
> He lived at the home of Monsieur and Madame
> Aymard, who have both died, but their daughter, a
> Madame Gustave, remembers a sporty Israelite who
> lived with them and later went to Paris. She still lives
> in the village of Espinasse and is sure this Israelite
> was your uncle Alex. Perhaps you would like to talk
> to her?

One month later, I met Robert Picandet at the Musée de la Résistance in Saint-Gervais-d'Auvergne, the town near the village of Espinasse. It was a small museum, barely two rooms large, and full of memorabilia from the Maquis, a breakaway faction that was even more loosely organised than the Resistance. The Maquis was largely made up of French men and women who had gone underground to avoid Vichy's 'Service du Travail Obligatoire', which required people to work in German factories. Some people in the Maquis were actively against the Germans, and some were simply hiding because they didn't want to be conscripted off to Germany. Picandet explained that France was full of these renegades avoiding the French and German authorities, but the Auvergne was especially good for hiding because it was – and is still – so agricultural. This meant that there were lots of places to hide and, just as important, there was a special feeling of solidarity between the farmers and the resisters in the Auvergne. There had always been a cooperative tradition among the Auvergne peasants, and during the war they eagerly helped their undercover countrymen. Without the assistance of the agricultural workers, the resisters could not have survived: farmers and shopkeepers gave them food, local officials gave them false papers, the villagers would put them in touch with other resisters, the local gendarmerie gave them warnings if there was danger coming, and that danger usually came more from the Vichy police than the Germans.

Many Jews hid around the Auvergne, so Alex certainly wasn't unusual in coming here, Picandet told us. Several of the people hidden in the area were sent by a Vichy official.

'Who was that?' I asked.

'General Jean Perré,' Picandet replied.

At last I had found out how Alex had got away, and why he never went into detail about who had helped him. It wasn't the Resistance that saved his life, but someone in Vichy. Things aren't always clear; they can be grey. But always a careful salesman, Alex knew that grey didn't sell, so he burnished the story.

Picandet gave me a lift in his car out to Madame Gustave's house in Espinasse. At first I insisted he not go out of his way, but I soon realised why he made the offer: the house was down long windy paths, almost entirely hidden by surrounding forests, as far off the main road as it was possible to go. I felt like I was in a fairy tale being taken to a magic house in the woods, and when I saw the house, and Madame Gustave, I was sure of it. It was a pretty stone farm cottage in the middle of what can only be described as nowhere, with buttercup-dappled fields in front and thick woods behind. Madame Gustave herself was the tiniest adult I'd ever seen in my life, barely more than half my height, and spry and sprightly, living all on her own in the middle of the forest.

She had lived in this house her entire life, she said, taking us into the sitting room, where she had tea and biscuits waiting for us.

'So this would have been the house Alex stayed in?' I asked.

She looked at me, surprised I hadn't already realised: 'Oh yes! He was here for a long time. Tea?'

If Alex had been looking for a hiding place, he could hardly have found a better one, but had he really found this one? It seemed almost impossible. And just as I was thinking that if this had all been a wild-goose chase it had been a rather charming one, I saw something that made me splutter my tea out on her floor: there, laid out very carefully on Madame Gustave's table, were half a dozen photos taken

outside the house I was sitting in now. They were black and white, curled with age, and Alex was in every single one.

According to Madame Gustave, Alex arrived in Espinasse in the late autumn of 1943. General Perré made the arrangements. Quite how he had the time is a mystery, given that he was by this point the head of the Garde, Pétain's personal guard, meaning he was in charge of 6,000 officers, as well as the protection of the head of state. He had been given the job by René Bousquet, the man who organised the Vel d'Hiv. Once the Germans invaded France the French Army was almost entirely depleted, but Pétain was allowed to keep his Garde, meaning they were one of the last visible signs of French sovereignty. Perré's job was to be in charge of one of the last public symbols of French pride – an apt job for a man in Vichy who put patriotism above Nazism. The Garde was not exactly pro-German, but it was definitely anti-Resistance, as resisters were seen as upstarts against the rulers. And yet the head of the Garde was stashing Jews around the Auvergne countryside. Certainly Alex was taking a huge risk, but Perré was, too.

Alex was met at the train station, probably by a farmer's wife, who brought him to the local Maquis. Despite his injuries from having jumped off the train, he was obviously strong and in good shape, and so it was decided that Alex could pass as a farmhand. For the next five or so weeks, Alex was moved from farm to farm, as the more he moved in the first few weeks the less chance there was that he might be denounced and caught. But Alex was always terrible at keeping a low profile and from his first day in town he went around and introduced himself to everyone, telling them his name was Alex and he came from Cannes. He didn't even hide that he was Jewish, which made people suspect he had friends in high places protecting him. Then one day he did something that ensured everyone knew who he was: he got into a fight outside the village bakery and knocked out someone's two front teeth. If he had wanted everyone to know that no one could mess with Alex Maguy, then he succeeded, but he also drew a lot of attention to himself, and this story is, still, seventy years on, something of a legend in Saint-Gervais-d'Auvergne. So it was decided that he needed to be put somewhere a little more out of the way. As it happened, a friend of Alex's, called Imre, had also recently arrived in town, and the two wanted to stay together. Was there a farmhouse, a little off the beaten track, where they could both stay?

Jeanne Aymard, as Madame Gustave was known then,

first learned that Alex was coming to live with her when a friend at school told her: 'Hey, two men are staying at your house now!' The teacher hurriedly told them both to be quiet.

Alex and his friend Imre moved into the Aymards' attic; the Aymards had never taken in any lodgers before, resisters or otherwise, and they never took in any again. To this day Madame Gustave doesn't know why her parents took in Alex and Imre. In the attic they set up two small beds and a desk for them, and there is a little window with a view of the fields. The staircase to get up to the attic is behind a hidden wall in the kitchen and there is also a second staircase from the garage so Alex and Imre could run down one if they heard the police coming up the other. The attic today is still cosy and pretty, with slanted ceilings and only the sound of birds outside. As Alex looked around it for the first time he must have felt the same rush of relief as when he was lying on the train tracks after making his jump. Here, at last, he would be safe. Both he and his friend.

Imre's full name was Imre Partos and he was an aspiring fashion designer whom Alex had become close to in Cannes. They had met in Paris through Dior, and after the war Partos would work for several years with Dior, helping him create the designer's famous New Look collection of 1947 that would make the design house's name. But it was Alex who became his truly great friend. There were obvious surface similarities between them: they both loved fashion, both were eastern European Jews (Partos came from Budapest) and both were short – Imre was five foot three at a generous estimate. But

Imre was more classically handsome; in fact, he had the delicate, fine-boned looks of Jacques. He was also more relaxed than Alex, and more refined, too, and was occasionally horrified by his friend's coarse manners: he often apologised to the Aymards for his friend's 'pig-like character'.

Another difference was that Partos was openly gay, but when I asked Jeanne if there was ever any suggestion that he and Alex were in a relationship she looked so shocked that it was clear this was the first time she'd ever even considered it.

'No, never, never. Of course, I was only ten. But I never heard anything,' she said.

Whatever their relationship, the two men were extremely close: they were together the whole day, every day, sleeping together, eating together, working on the local farms together. One photo from that period shows them lying together in a field, dressed for what looks like autumn so probably quite soon after they moved into the Aymards'. They're finishing lunch and Imre is looking towards Alex and Alex is looking into the distance. They are both smiling, happy.

They rarely, if ever, spoke of home. Instead, Alex and Imre spent much of their time talking about fashion: who was good, who was a hack, who knew how to sew, who knew how to style. Alex invariably won these arguments. 'Alex was quite bossy, assertive. Definitely a man who got what he wanted,' Madame Gustave said, squashing any tiny doubts I might have still held about whether it was actually my great-uncle Alex who had stayed in her house. Many decades later, after Imre – or Emeric Partos, as he became known when he anglicised his name after the war – had become a world-famous designer with a celebrity clientele that included his friend and neighbour Katharine Hepburn, Alex was credited with getting him interested in fashion.

'[Partos] became an operative in the French underground. There, he met Alex Maguy, a couturier who also designed for the theater.[10] Mr Partos joined him as a coat designer and did an occasional stint costuming ballet,' Angela Taylor wrote in his obituary in the *New York Times*.[11] (This was not entirely correct: as Alex says in his memoir, the men had met years earlier in Paris.) And unusually for Alex, he stayed friends with Partos for the rest of his life. Among my grandmother's shoebox papers I found a letter from Alex dated 7 December 1975: 'My dear sister, I've just learned with great sadness of the death of my dear friend, Imre. What a wonderful guy he was. To think that we telephoned each other several times lately and the bad weather kept me from seeing him – ah, that's life. Let's talk of nicer things . . .'

That Alex was a fashion designer was the beginning and end of all the Aymards knew about their lodger. He lived with them for a year but he never put up any photos of his family, never talked about his life before the war, never even explained what he was doing there. He was always polite, even formal, but the word that really described him was private: he kept himself entirely to himself.

'He seemed "*très soupe au lait*" at first,' Madame Gustave said, using an old-fashioned French expression for rapidly changeable (the English equivalent would be 'he went from

0 to 60 mph'). 'But he was always very, very sweet with me, pinching my cheek and calling me "*ma petite Jeanne*". His habits were totally irregular, more so than Imre's. Sometimes I would find him in the woodland outside but you never knew where he had come from.'

He was probably coming from meeting other resisters who were hiding in the woods; remnants of secret cabins and lookouts are still scattered around the Auvergne, and Picandet showed me some very close to Madame Gustave's house.

I asked Madame Gustave if Alex did anything odd while he was staying there, and she laughed.

'Oh yes, he could be very odd! He once asked my mother for some butter and then rubbed it all over his body and went out to work without a shirt – we were worried the bugs would be after him!' she said, pointing to a photo of him in which he was indeed topless and shiny with grease. 'He said it helped him work better', she shrugged.

I noticed that he was often topless in the photos she showed me of him and Madame Gustave laughed again.

'He was always taking some item of clothing off – his shirt, his shoes, his socks. I never saw him with all his clothes on here. We just thought, Oh well, I guess that's what Bohemians are like!'

But as I looked at the photos of Alex, shirtless, pushing around a horse and cart and working in the field outside Madame Gustave's house, he didn't look like a bohemian artist: he looked like a peasant. After having run away from

Chrzanow so fast as a teenager, suddenly he found himself back living the kind of rural life he thought he'd left behind. And after decades of disparaging that world, referring sneeringly to 'Polish peasants', it's clear from the photos how much he loved living in Espinasse. In all the photos he's grinning delightedly, clutching his tools, ready to work.

'We had very happy times here – Alex liked being here a lot,' agreed Madame Gustave.

Coming to Espinasse had allowed Alex to love his past. No longer did he have to spit when he talked about it, associating the rural life with pogroms and stasis and death. He didn't have to build a bulwark of glamour around himself for protection, filling his world with fabulousness out of fear he would otherwise end up like his father. Even though the Second World War was still raging and Alex had just escaped from a train taking him to a concentration camp, when he was in Espinasse Alex felt more relaxed than he had in decades, possibly ever. Here, he could simply enjoy a life in which his breakfast came from the barnyard outside and not worry about pushing ever forward, away from where he'd come. He could just sit still in a field, enjoying a life his father and brother Jacques would have liked for themselves, had two world wars not swallowed them up.

So was Alex just sitting in a field here or was he actually in the Resistance?

'We never heard he was in the Resistance,' Madame Gustave insisted.

But Picandet had his theories.

'The British were very keen to hear about French people's morale, so it is likely Alex was writing reports on that and sending them to Britain.'

'Perhaps he was just communicating with the Sizaines?' I suggested. But what I really meant was, maybe he wasn't doing anything at all. Maybe he was just having a nice year in Espinasse with Imre. Not every Frenchman, after all, was a member of the Resistance, no matter what they said after the war.

But Picandet shook his head firmly and pulled out a piece of paper on the top of my pack of notes, which were photocopies from the various files I'd found on Alex scattered around France. This particular piece of paper was a certificate and on it was written the following:

'I the undersigned, the commanding officer of Zone 13, certify that Mr Alex Glass, an active member of the French Forces of the Interior, is allowed to move freely and for all reasons. He is entitled to any help he requires in order to do so.'

It was signed, stamped and dated 7 September 1944, meaning it was given to Alex when he was still at the Aymards'.

'This certificate proves without a doubt he was working in the Resistance. Other members of the Resistance in this area, Zone 13, didn't have such certificates, so Alex had powerful people behind him, and he was in contact with them while he was here,' Picandet said.

Alex left the Aymards in the winter of 1944 after more than a year in their attic. He first went to Cannes to get his mother, the Yiddish-speaking, kosher-keeping Polish Jew who, miraculously, had somehow survived the war. Her survival is a testament to Alex's friend, Madame Armande, who hid Chaya during the war, and to Alex who had the wisdom to place his mother with her. Paris was now liberated and Alex, along with Chaya, was among the group of Jews who had managed to survive the war and now returned to the capital city. It was a shockingly depleted group. During the war, of the 300,000 Jews who were in France in 1939, more than 80,000 had been sent to the concentration camps from France – mostly, but not entirely, immigrants. Only 3% returned alive.[12] Alex and Chaya arrived to find the wreckage of their family. Henri and Sonia were alive and waiting for them.

Alex could be a Zelig figure, slipping in and out of different social sets and leaving few ties behind him. But he stayed in touch with the Aymards for years – proof of how much he loved his time with them. Madame Aymard even worked as his housekeeper in Paris for some years and he invited Jeanne to visit him several times during her childhood and teenage years. 'But when I came, there was no more cheek pinching, no more "*ma petite Jeanne*". He was a different man in Paris – more formal, serious. Different,' she recalled. There were many versions of Alex, and he left one of them behind in Espinasse. He was now back to his Parisian self.

The Germans and collaborators kept better records than the resisters, who destroyed everything as they went along for their own safety, and Alex threw away his own records later. When you've been arrested three times and lost your brother and most of your extended family to state-sanctioned murder you tend to be cautious about what you reveal. In fact, Alex never fully trusted France again, even though he lived there for the rest of his life. When he became phenomenally wealthy in later life, he kept his money in more than two dozen bank accounts in as many different countries. France had turned against him once, how could he know it wouldn't again? So who could blame him, really, for keeping some things to himself? As I left Espinasse I thought how, even though I knew most of the story, I would never know for sure about his relationship with Perré, or even if Perré was the powerful person who saved his life. Some things will just have to stay in the shadows and be taken on faith. But when I got back home to London, something very unexpected was waiting for me.

My uncle Rich had found another copy of Alex's memoir, which was identical to the previous one but with one crucial difference: the pages that were missing in the copy were present in this one. They were crumpled up, like someone had thrown them away but then (someone else?) rescued them from the rubbish bin at the last minute. And they detailed exactly what happened immediately after Alex jumped from the train.

'Staying in Lyon was suicidal. I needed to find a place to hide. The thought that contacting General Perré in Vichy would be a good move seems quite mad today. But that's what I did because I had total confidence in Perré. He was a soldier and, although the personal bodyguard of Pétain, he could not betray a fellow soldier,' Alex wrote.

According to Alex, he simply phoned Perré's house and spoke first to Perré's wife who 'couldn't believe what had happened to me' which, if true, says a lot about the Perrés' self-deluding hypocrisy, given that what had happened to Alex was what Perré was ensuring would happen to the Jews in France. Alex writes that Perré sent one of his senior officers to pick up Alex – still dressed as a railway worker – in Lyon and bring him to Vichy 'in a car flying the flag of the military headquarters'.

Once Alex was at Perré's headquarters, Perré offered to provide him with a military disguise.

'I told him I preferred to remain in plain clothes and rejoin the Resistance,' Alex told the man whose specific job was cracking down on the Resistance. But Perré again agreed to help. He told Alex that his officers had contacts in the resistance in the Auvergne, so he would take him there so he could rejoin them. Alex describes how he and Perré would discuss how much danger they were in: Alex would be condemned to death if captured, but Perré was in an almost equally perilous position. He was, he said, being watched by the Gestapo, and they had been to his house to interview him multiple times. And yet despite this, Perré incredibly took the risk to visit Alex several times in Espinasse, and Alex would try to persuade him to flee to London with him. But Perré refused, partly because of his sense of duty to Pétain, and partly because he didn't want to be in the same city as de Gaulle, Alex was disappointed but he understood. He knew that Perré could not desert his post.

Alex and Perré had a friendship that went deeper than either ever acknowledged publicly, and although Perré's old rivalry with de Gaulle stopped him from escaping with Alex to London, it's clear from the risks Perré took how much he respected Alex, and loved him. As for what Alex was actually doing in Espinasse, all he says is that he was 'a noisy recruiter for the Resistance', and then the story ends again, and Alex's memoir slips briskly on to after the war. Some stories are still in the shadows.

After the war finished, Perré went on trial in November 1946, not for hiding Alex, but for collaborating with the Nazis. More than 300,000 people in France were investigated in the '*épuration légale*' – or legal purge – as part of the country's desperate attempt to maintain the myth that the majority of its citizens were part of the Resistance and only the bad apples were collaborators. The people caught up in this country-wide blood-letting were, in the main, certainly guilty, but also served as convenient scapegoats for a country mortified by its collective culpability. Probably the most notorious example of this was the vilification of French-women accused of 'horizontal collaboration' – sleeping with Nazis, in other words – who had their heads shaved and were marched through the streets, where they were jeered and attacked by people who may well have done a fair amount of collaborating of their own.

The trials of the high-ranking Vichy officials presented their own kind of weird hypocrisy, in that while some of the most high-profile figures were tried, many were not, including lots of Vichy civil servants, simply because General de Gaulle, who was now in charge, knew he needed them to help run the country. Others were simply too big to convict. It would take another half-century, when President Chirac was in the Élysée Palace in the 1990s, until France would truly look at its past and summon people for their long overdue trials for their crimes against humanity.

Perré, however, had the misfortune of being prominent enough to grab attention, but not so high-ranking that he could avoid a trial in the 1940s, like his boss Bousquet. Details of his trial are kept in an archive in Poitiers and the initial testimonies against him, from soldiers who knew him, are devastating: he was accused of sending children to concentration camps; committing war crimes against military families (sending them to the camps, in other words); punishing any officers who showed sympathy for resisters and viciously repressing the Resistance. But French historian Camille Chevallier, who helped me with my work in Poitiers, told me she was sceptical about some of the claims: 'My opinion as a historian is that the accusations about General Perré are exaggerated. This is often the case with these trials with the German enemy, so that the accused are punished quickly and severely so that the French can only remember the Resistance and erase all traces of collaboration. I think that the accusations are not false but they are probably exaggerated and expanded so that Jean Perré was condemned quickly. There was also a strong national desire for revenge settling of accounts between collaborator and Resistance.'

The testimonies in Perré's defence told a much more complex picture than the sweeping prosecutions. One man, Charles Levy, said in his testimony: 'All I know is that under the German occupation, my friend Émile Perrot went to [Perré] to get me an identity card in the name of Leroy instead of Levy, which allowed me to escape the racial persecutions. I am grateful to General Perré.' And then I read the testimony of Captain Dodane, made on 26 November 1946: General Perré, he said, 'continued to camouflage equipment and gave many non-commissioned officers false identity cards, food to allow them to foil the Gestapo. At the same time, he hosted and concealed Mr Alex Maguy, wanted by the Germans.' According to the court records I read, Alex did not give a witness statement at the trial, but he did attend it: on a small slip of paper in the archive file about Perré's trial is a list of nineteen names, including Perré's son and various military officials. Number four on the list is Alex Glass. Alex would have had to give his real name to get into court, although General Perré – having met Alex originally when he was his daughter's couturier – would have known him only as Alex Maguy, which is why he was referred to as such during the trial. And yet, according to Alex's memoir, he didn't just give testimony at the trial in Perré's defence. He – as he characteristically puts it in the chapter heading – saved Perré's life. He describes telling the tribunal about his escape from the train, and how afterwards, Perré put him in touch with the Maquis, thereby saving him. 'I made the jury cry, and they were not – believe me – little girls who cried easily,' Alex wrote.

Perré handwrote his own defence, which ran to sixteen pages. He didn't mention Alex in it, and Camille Chevallier said this was probably because 'out of friendship, he did not want to involve Alex in his trial, and also he knew it wouldn't help him anyway'. But he does mention that he knew that some of his men had connections with the local Maquis. He also says that he provided 'fake identity cards, food, etc. to enable [resisters] to carry out their task and foil the Gestapo'. He adds, somewhat improbably, that he was creating an armoured division to beat the '*boches*' (pejorative word for Germans). Throughout his defence, Perré stresses Bousquet's culpability, and Pétain's innocence, a Pétainiste to the end. But his guilt, as he knew, was a given, and on 28 November 1946 he was found guilty of '*national dégradation*', the most common conviction among the *épuration légale*, and almost

50,000 others were similarly condemned. He lost his pension, was banned from living in the area for a decade and was ordered to give up his worldly goods. For good measure, he was also sentenced to twenty years of hard labour.

In the immediate aftermath of the war, France was keen to make a show of punishing the traitors. But it was also desperate to move on and not stew over the past – forget it entirely, if possible. So in the end, Perré was punished very little. Like many other figures from Vichy who had been convicted under the legal purge, he saw his sentence commuted in the 1950s and then pretty much overturned. He died in 1971.[13]

As far as I know, Alex never mentioned Perré to anyone in his family. But occasional vague allegations of collaboration were lobbed at him, based on misunderstood whispered half-truths, and these continued long after he died. In 2014 he was named in a case against the Fred Jones Museum in Oklahoma, brought by a Frenchwoman called Leone Mayer, who claimed that a Pissarro painting on display in the American museum was rightfully hers as it had been confiscated from her father by the Nazis. During the trial Mayer mentioned other works owned by her late father, including a 1906 painting by Raoul Dufy, which had been sold in 1955 to Alex Maguy, who, the lawyer casually added and the stenographer faithfully recorded, 'had been active with the occupying German forces during WWII in Paris'.

It is entirely possible Alex handled art that had been seized from Jews during the war – a lot of art was looted. But the idea that Alex was deliberately part of some kind of anti-Jewish art scene, let alone 'active with occupying German forces', is ludicrous. But it's also understandable that some sensed a grey cloud of suspicion around him because to survive he lived in twilight, and it had long been that way. He admitted as much in his memoir when describing his too busy salon in Cannes. Maybe Alex simply understood, better than others, that in wartime nothing is simple.

Alex spent his life spinning webs, alternately obfuscating and exaggerating. This wasn't simply to hide the truth, but to give him security and establish footholds – which he believed he needed to survive. And hadn't the war proven he was right about that? After all, he'd survived only because he had connections. He always needed to make himself look more established than he was because he knew that, in the eyes of France, he would always be a Polish Jew.

Yet for all his obfuscations Alex wasn't a Tom Ripley – yes, he talked a lot of nonsense, but he also had the goods. He really did know this person, own that painting, escape from a train. He hadn't collaborated, but the person who saved him was a collaborator. The proof had always been in front of me: after all, against every odd, he'd survived. And like a good salesman, he took his best goods and put them in the shop window. The rest he kept in the closet.

THE AMERICAN RED CROSS

NASSAU COUNTY CHAPTER
MINEOLA, N. Y.
Telephone: GARDEN CITY 1160

Miss DOROTHY L. TAPSCOTT, *Executive Director*

*HOME SERVICE
DEPARTMENT*
1501 FRANKLIN AVENUE
MINEOLA, N. Y.

In reply, refer to:

(Mrs.) Herbert M. Karp
Case Work Aide

November 6, 1944

Mrs. William Frieman
506 Secatogue Avenue
Farmingdale, New York

Re: GLASS, Jacques
France

Dear Mrs. Frieman:

We are enclosing herewith a letter address to you which has been
received from the International Committee of the Red Cross through our
National Headquarters in Washington.

We regret the distressing news contained in the report.

Sincerely,

(Miss) Dorothy A. King
Home Service Director

Ethel Karp

(Mrs.) Herbert M. Karp
Case Work Aide

EK:DAP
enc.

II

THE SIBLINGS –
The Ordinary and the Extraordinary

Post-war life – France and America

IN SEPTEMBER 1948 Sara finally sailed back to Paris. She made and froze enough meals to last Bill for her month-long absence, brought her two young sons, Ronald, then nine, and Richard, five, and boarded the ship. Sara was so excited that when she walked on French ground for the first time in nine years she cried with happiness. But as she and her boys travelled by train from Le Havre to Paris, and she saw what the war had done to the country she loved so much, she cried for a very different reason. Sara had spent the war dreaming of the time when she would go home; the journey from the dock to the French capital showed her there was no home to go back to.

France was devastated after the war, physically and morally. Paris, once the grandest city in the world, was dilapidated and grey, its buildings in desperate need of repair that no one could afford, its people in worse need of food that no one had. In April 1945, almost a year after the city was liberated, Parisians were still living on about 1,300 calories a day.[1] When Sara took her boys to Henri and Sonia's house, Henri gave Ron an apple. Fresh fruit had only recently become available in Paris again after years of deprivation, but Ronald – raised on Long Island where fruit had never been rationed – didn't know that. So he proceeded to eat the apple the way his slightly germ-phobic father had taught him back home, by cutting all the peel off. Henri was horrified: 'Stop that!' he cried, and he fell to the floor, frantically collecting all the apple peel. In America, Sara had tried to soothe her homesickness by imagining her family in Paris, picturing them exactly as they'd been before the war. But watching her normally calm and fastidious brother scrabble about for food scraps, Sara saw all too clearly how much they'd been re-shaped by the war.

By 1944, Bill, Sara and their two little boys had been living in a hotel in midtown Manhattan for two years. In Farmingdale their house was next to four aeroplane factories – Grumman, Republic, Ranger and Fairchild – and the constant noise of fighter planes flying at very low altitudes over their house convinced Bill they'd be safer in the city. What finally settled the matter was that Bill's new business, which he started during the war, had become his most successful venture yet. Called Roxy Corporation, it made medals for the US Army. It was based in Manhattan, and because petrol and coal were hard to come by during the war, regular commutes from Long Island were just impractical. And so, in 1942, Bill, a then pregnant Sara and three-year-old Ronald moved to a small two-room suite in the Park Central Hotel on 56th Street and Seventh Avenue. Sara was thrilled: at last, she was living in New York City, and she happily took her toddler son for walks up and down Madison Avenue looking in all the fancy stores, just as she had dreamed she'd do when she had originally sailed over from France. Ronald also enjoyed living in the city, but for very different reasons from his mother. When he talks about that period now, what he remembers is how much he enjoyed roller skating on the hotel roof and how he would tease all the nice ladies who sat on benches up there smoking all day. It wasn't until many years later that he realised they were all prostitutes.

Being based in the city proved to be a great help to Sara at the end of the war when it came to finding out what had happened to her family. For three years, she'd had no contact with them, no idea whether any of them were even alive. She was frantic for news but even after D-Day it was months before full mail, telegraph and phone services were resumed. So word of mouth was the best source, and it was a lot easier in New York City than it was in Farmingdale to find people who knew what was happening in France. My father, then aged five, remembers 'a series of foreign visitors to our little two-room suite. There were intense conversations. And tears.'

According to Alex's memoir, one of those foreign visitors was Yvonne Vallée, the French actress and ex-wife of Maurice

Chevalier. Alex had become friendly with Chevalier before the war, and the two would remain close for the rest of their lives, even spending their final years as neighbours. (Chevalier was yet another member of Alex's social circle who lived in the twilight: he was accused of collaboration both during and after the war and always denied it.) Vallée divorced Chevalier in 1932, but Alex stayed sufficiently friendly with her to ask her to deliver a message to his sister while on a trip to the United States. Through Vallée, Alex reassured Sara that not only was he alive, but so were Henri, Sonia, Chaya, Mila and Lily. No one, he wrote, had heard from Jacques for a while.

In November 1944 Sara finally got the news that Alex, Henri and Sonia had expected. She received a letter from the Red Cross, signed by a Mrs Ethel Karp, confirming that Jacques had been killed in Auschwitz-Birkenau. Mrs Karp apologised for 'the distressing news contained in the report'. Sara had dearly loved her gentlest brother, the one who was most like her adored father and who she most resembled, physically. She tucked the letter into her shoebox of keepsakes, alongside the photos and drawing Jacques had sent her from Pithiviers, and his plaque from Cambrai. She never spoke about these mementos to her husband or even her beloved sons, but she kept them close to her for the rest of her life, carefully bringing them with her through multiple house moves, hiding them in the darkness at the back of her closet.

Compared with other families, the Glasses came through the war pretty well: they had lost Jacques, and almost all of their cousins, but most of the immediate family survived. Even Chaya was fine; when Alex brought her back to Paris she was still faithfully keeping kosher, still only talking in Polish and Yiddish.

But emotionally they were in as much of a mess as Paris itself. They were deeply traumatised by the betrayal of a country they thought they could trust and in deep grief for those they had lost – Jacques, mainly. But there was no way of talking about such things then, and who had the time anyway? Everyone had suffered through the war – talking about your suffering was indulgent and unhelpful, was the general attitude. Yet trauma resists repression.

Sara knew that her mother and two brothers had survived the war, but it would be another four years before she was able to sail to France to see them. So the Freimans moved back to their home in Farmingdale, and she busied herself by sending packages and letters to Sonia, Henri and Alex. Because it was against the law to send food to private citizens in France, she sent them via a young soldier, called Bob Spencer, the son of her Farmingdale neighbours who happened to be stationed in Paris near Henri and Sonia's home. Every time he received a parcel for them, he personally took it over to their house. Until the end of her life, Sonia talked reverently about Bob Spencer and how he had saved their lives, and it's very possible that he did, because Henri and Sonia were never in greater need of food than after the war: on D-Day, 6 June 1944, their daughter Danièle was born. Henri was forty-three and Sonia forty-one, almost unimaginably old at that

Henri, not long after the war.

time to be first-time parents. But they hadn't been able to conceive before and Danièle was like the physical manifestation of relief, or just a release: after so many years of anxiety, and four long years of living in a shadowy existence, Henri and Sonia were free at last. And as soon as they could relax, out came little Danièle, their only child.

Only children started to run in my family at that point. Henri had Danièle, Jacques had Lily and, in the 1950s, Roger and Renée Goldberg, the Glasses' cousins who almost certainly were involved in the Resistance movement, had one child, Anne-Laurence. Armand Ornstein, the little boy who was hidden in the woods after his parents were shot while crossing the river, had one child, Philippe. Even Alex, who never married, eventually had a child, an only daughter.* Given that the previous generation had multiple children – there were five Glass children originally (Mindel died as a child) and seven Ornsteins – this was a marked shift and the sharp change in the shape of the family tree is a visual representation of what fear does to the human spirit. 'They never really believed they were safe again, and if they weren't, they couldn't bear to put their children through what they had been through. One child was all they would risk,' was how Anne-Laurence Goldberg explained it to me. The sole Glass sibling who dared to have more than one child was Sara, the only one living in a country that had never tried to kill her.

* She later cut herself off from the family, and to respect her privacy I will neither name her nor tell anything of her story.

Sara's brothers were able to write to her, thanks to Bob Spencer who posted their letters via the US Army postal service, and the surviving letters show they were responding to their post-war life in characteristic form. For Alex, that meant a combination of exuberance and fury. Ecstatic at having improbably survived the war, he was more determined than ever to seize life. In January 1945, less than two years after he escaped from the train that was taking him to death, Alex sent a joyful postcard to his sister from the French ski slopes: 'The weather is magnificent, the sun is splendid, and the snow is great. I'm preparing my new collection for the summer season. One hundred kisses to you, Alex.'

Alex's ambition was even greater after the war. As soon as he got back to Paris, he seized his fashion business from Paquin, who had tormented Alex and the CGQJ by demanding Alex not be allowed to work down in the south. But Alex definitively won that argument: on 24 July 1945, as the punishments against collaborators were really starting to bite, Paquin killed himself. He left behind an apartment full of fancy trinkets bought with the money he made from running the seized businesses of Jewish designers, and little else.

Alex did not pause to gloat, and he doesn't even bother to mention Paquin's suicide in his memoir. Instead, he desperately scrabbled around to rebuild his salon by whatever means necessary. He regularly updated Sara on his progress.

'My dear little sister,' Alex wrote to her on 8 June 1945. 'I once again take advantage of Mr Bob Spencer to send you this letter. I hope you now have the press clippings that I sent you and that you like them. I'm also sending you some photographs, and I would be happy if you could have them published in American fashion magazines. I'm counting on you.'

After asking his sister, a housewife on Long Island, to get his photos into US *Vogue*, Alex had another request for her: 'I must ask you to seriously look into the matter of finding Émile Best. He did much evil in France during the occupation [and] he's hiding now in New York. He was a dealer in drawings and he was intending twelve bullets for me. I would be very happy for him to receive the fate that he was planning for me.'

It's hard to say if Alex truly intended my grandmother to stalk through New York with a Smith & Wesson, hunting a collaborationist who had escaped to the United States. But he was certainly serious when he turned his attention to Sonia, whom he loathed almost as much as he did the Nazis:

> I have told you not to include the food packages
> for Mila and Lily in Sonia's parcels. But you recently
> did so again, even though you know that Mila and
> Lily only receive what [Sonia] doesn't want. Please
> address the packages separately to Mila, this way we
> will know she gets them intact. I'm sorry to have
> to tell you this but you know the mentality of your
> sister-in-law of whom I am ashamed.

Alex's loathing of Sonia outweighed his hatred of Mila, even though Sonia had saved Henri during the war thanks to her black market contacts and excellent German, whereas Mila had sent Jacques back to the concentration camp. But Sonia was smart; this meant Alex couldn't merely dismiss her as an idiot, as he did with Mila. Instead, he had to hate her personally for being unworthy of his brother. That Alex's feelings about her remained so implacably unchanged, even after all they had been through during the war, proved – as Sonia's relatives also confirmed a few years earlier, complaining bitterly about one another while in the shadows of the Nazis – that not even war can alter familial relationships.

As for Henri and Sonia, few letters from them in the immediate post-war period have survived. Instead, what has lasted are the many, many photos Henri sent to his sister of his new baby daughter. At last, he had a new photographic muse. In one photo, Danièle, plump and round-eyed like a Renaissance cherub, sits on his knee while Henri, looking about a decade older than his forty-three years, gazes at her with almost dopey love. In another, Sonia, with characteristic frankness, looks straight at the camera while holding a tightly swaddled Danièle in a park in what must have been the winter after Paris was liberated. They had, against all odds, survived the war and, more than that, they had reproduced. As a statement of their survival, Danièle was the final word. As an expression of their love, she was the much-longed-for completion of their family.

For Sara, the end of the war had meant a reluctant move back to Long Island, but there was another change, too. For reasons I've never understood and no one alive now can explain, at some point towards the mid-1940s my grandmother's adopted French name unmoored itself and slipped back to its Polish roots. She started being referred to again as Sala, both in her correspondence and on official documents. This was probably because she, like Jacques, never officially changed her name, so it just got too complicated in America having two different names, one of which didn't match her documentation. The result was that, by the end of the war, she was Sala Freiman and when she was finally able to travel to France in 1948 with her sons, her name on the passenger list appears as 'Sala Freiman, h'wife'. The 'Sara Ryfka Glass, draftsman' who first went to America nine years earlier was long gone.

Alex met her and her two sons at the train station in Paris. Someone, probably Henri, took a photo of this meeting, and it shows Sala looking even more glamorous than usual, in a bell-sleeved fur coat made by Alex, and a hat that moulded itself around her perfectly coiffured hair and tied under her chin with an attached crocheted scarf. She had dressed her boys carefully for their arrival in Paris: both are in matching coats and hats, Ronald in a smart light grey pea coat and coordinated cap, Richard in a looser checked one and checked cap. What's striking is how much the boys look like Glasses: serious Ronald is like a young Henri, while Richard has Alex's pouchy cheeks and his mother's bright eyes. They

Alex welcoming Sala, Ronald and
Richard to Paris.

all look happy and excited, Alex most of all, clutching little Richard in his arms. But if Sala thought this meant he would help her, she would soon be disabused of that notion.

Before the war broke out, Sala wrote to Alex that she wanted to leave Bill and come back to Paris. Would he, she asked, support her and her then only son? The war temporarily stopped that conversation but, according to family lore passed down by Alex and Sonia, Alex made his answer very clear on this trip, and the answer was no. There was, he said, nothing for her here: France was destroyed and America was thriving. He was trying to build his business, plus he had to look after Chaya, and Henri had a new baby to look after. Sonia, for once, was in agreement with her brother-in-law: as soon as you had the second boy, she told Sala, 'c'est fini' – game over.

BUT THIS WAS not true. Alex, Henri and Sonia loved Sala very deeply, and they could have supported her and the boys. Alex always found a way to do something he wanted and, yes, Sonia had a new baby, but she had managed to hide Mila and Lily during the war – looking after Sala, Ronald and Richard in peacetime would hardly have tasked her abilities. Part of their resistance to her return stemmed from their very conservative background and the time in which they lived: they believed that the mother of two boys belonged with their father, and a wife's responsibility was to her husband. But even more than that, they didn't want her to come back because they thought she was safer where she was. Even aside from France's current political and financial turmoil, Alex, Henri and Sonia could still feel the past's hot breath on their necks. The war was over, but the memories of how their countrymen had tried, and nearly succeeded in killing them all were very fresh. None of them felt safe in France, and they never really would again, even after they all, eventually, became French citizens. By telling Sala to stay in New York with Bill, they were trying to protect her, just as they'd protected her by sending her to New York to marry him in 1937. It was their way of expressing love for her, but to her it must have felt like another cold rejection.

For years Sala had quietly nursed the dream that it was just the war that was keeping her from her home. But she now realised she would never live in France again, at least not while Bill was alive. Perhaps because of this, while on this trip she sent a photo to Bill of Ron and Rich in Paris, looking up at her from the street while she was apparently leaning out of a window. She wrote on it, in slightly wobbly English: 'This was taken [she crossed out the word "talking", having written that initially instead of "taken"] from the 6th floor from Alex's window, and these two little Frenchmen are your sons'. This could be read as either a fond message or a pointed one, a proud assertion of her children's French identity despite their American father. It was probably a mix of both. Her family would not help her if she left him, and she couldn't live without their help. So she resigned herself to wait until he died, and this was the grandmother I would forty years later meet as a child: one who was still waiting, in her seventies, for her real life to begin. And when she boarded the ship back to New York a month later with her sons, she and her brothers made what they could of their post-war lives.

FOR HENRI, this meant continuing to build Photosia with Marc Haenel while looking after Sonia and Danièle. The company was even busier after the war than it was before, and one of its first big jobs came in 1948 when the French government hired the company to microfilm the Marshall Plan, the US initiative to help Western Europe rebuild after the war. This commission gave Henri particular pride. Before that, he was asked to do another job: 'At the end of the war, the Ministry of Prisoners and War Deportees entrusted us with the task of microfilming the concentration camp archives in Germany and in Poland,' he wrote in Photosia's meticulous record book. Nowhere does he mention seeing – or looking for – Jacques's name in the archives.

Over the next decade and a half, Henri and Haenel built up an extraordinarily successful business, and their clients included some of the biggest companies in the world, including BP, Esso, IBM and Renault, as well as nearly every branch of the French government. By the end of the 1960s, Photosia was worth millions. To a very large degree this was thanks to Henri's technical ingenuity, but it was also because Henri and Haenel made the perfect team: Henri the quiet but brilliant engineer, Haenel the extrovert salesman. Henri was suddenly able to keep his wife and daughter in the kind of comfort he could never have imagined during the war when he and Sonia were half-starved and fearfully skulking in the dark.

Henri and Sonia almost never spoke about what they had been through, but they were marked by the experience like a block of clay is by a firm fingerprint. Henri became even more withdrawn, and he turned prematurely grey. Sonia seemed outwardly unchanged, as loud and forthright as ever. (When her nephew Ronald met her in Paris at the age of seven, he wrote to his father Bill: 'Aunt Sonia is like fire.') But rather than clinging proudly to their Judaism after their persecution, both she and Henri were more desirous than ever of blending in. Being Jewish was something to be endured, never flaunted. They were naturalised soon after the war, delighted to be accepted at last by the country that had tried to kill them, and they barely raised their daughter Jewish at all, never taking her to synagogue or giving her a bat mitzvah. They observed the Jewish holidays, but to those around them it seemed like this was done out of an inner compulsion that they couldn't control.

They did their best to protect the next generations from it. Danièle later had children of her own, Alexandre and Natasha de Betak, whom Henri and Sonia adored and often looked after. But they would shoo their grandchildren out of the house when they lit Friday night candles: 'You don't need to see this, go outside,' they would say, shutting the door behind them. If Alexandre or Natasha asked about Judaism, decades after the war ended, Sonia would put her fingers to her lips and say sharply, 'Better not.' 'Don't tell

Dinner with Henri and Sonia. Renée Goldberg is smiling at
the camera, her daughter, Anne-Laurence, on her lap.

people you're Jewish,' they instructed Alexandre – a sad echo
of their late Ornstein cousins, Maurice and Giselle, trying
to protect their little son Armand when they hid him in the
woods. They just wanted to be French, and for their daughter and grandchildren to be seen as purely French, because to
be French was to be safe. Even after being naturalised Henri
never entirely believed he was safe and for the rest of his life
he would do anything to avoid conflict or drawing attention
to himself.

So when Haenel came up with a plan in 1960, he knew
he'd be able to get Henri to agree.

'Do me a favour,' he said to Henri one day. 'My wife, she's
giving me a hard time. She says I really run the company and
you're just the engineer, and so the company should really be
mine. I know, I know, but you know women, right? So could
you just write a letter saying that you're signing the company

over to me? It won't mean anything and it will give me more peace at home. Be a friend.'

One of the ironies of Henri's life is that after the war he became increasingly like the one member of this family whom the Nazis had managed to murder. He adopted some of the tendencies of Jacques that had so infuriated the rest of his family when he was alive and, ultimately, helped to get him killed. It was as if he were paying some kind of homage to Jacques, keeping his closest brother alive by re-enacting him, or it might be simpler than that: Henri's nervousness was a reaction to how utterly traumatised he had been by the war. It had depleted muscles and pared him back to the bare Glass bones, becoming increasingly like his gentle father. So he didn't laugh in Haenel's face, as most people would have done. Instead he agreed to sign the letter. Sonia understood her husband and she also knew she had to protect him. So she said to Henri, 'Fine, tell him you'll sign the letter, but only if he signs another letter saying that the other letter is meaningless.'

Haenel agreed to this rather bizarre plan, but when he signed the second letter he crammed his signature into the bottom right corner of the letter, and made it so small it could hardly be seen by the naked eye.

Haenel died soon after signing the letters and in 1962 his wife, in a wholly predictable turn of events, sued Henri for control of Photosia, saying that the first letter he signed proved it was now hers. Henri was terrified: he dreaded going to court up against Madame Haenel's fancy lawyers, and he had visions of ending up bankrupt, like Jacques had done. Alex, who was by now starting to become very wealthy, immediately hired one of the best lawyers in Paris for his beloved brother. '*Tout ce que j'ai est à toi*,' he told him – 'All that I have is yours.'

But ultimately it was Henri's wife – as had so often been the case before – who came to his rescue.

Madame Haenel insisted Henri hand over the second letter as evidence for the trial, but Sonia stopped him.

'Haenel's signature is so small, and right in the corner, that wife of his could flick it off with her thumb and then you'd have nothing,' she said to her husband.

So Sonia came up with a plan: she put the letter in a thick, transparent plastic envelope, sealed it shut on all four sides, and handed it over to the court like that. Madame Haenel, realising her plan was being thwarted, was furious, and insisted the plastic envelope made the letter too hard to read and was therefore inadmissible. But the judge overruled her and Henri got to keep his 50 per cent of the business.

Henri won the case, but it was now impossible for him and Madame Haenel to run the company together. Fortunately, a large Dutch company, called Van der Grinten,[2] offered to buy it. Henri and Madame Haenel sold Photosia to them in 1966 for almost $12 million, or $50 million today.

Henri was suddenly an extremely wealthy man, one who, at the age of sixty-five, would never need to worry about money again. But the money hardly changed his and Sonia's lives at all: they continued to travel in economy class, and they didn't move to a big fancy house. To become a flashy show-off like his brother Alex would have gone completely against Henri's nature. But if he had always dreamed of wrapping his entire house in gold he wouldn't have done so because, even in the 1960s, he never felt he could relax; rather, he saw the money as a way to protect himself and his family should things go bad again, as they surely would. He put most of the cash in Swiss bank accounts – away from the French, in case the country turned on him again – and invested in property and art, as protection if currency rates dropped. He and Sonia bought a small weekend house in Neauphle-le-Château, which they loved and kept beautifully maintained. A new neighbour arrived in the late 1970s who was, however, less house-proud and he let his house and lawn deteriorate badly. Sonia complained, but to no avail – her neighbour was, she later recalled, very stubborn. Newspapers from that period also described her neighbour's 'unkempt' garden, because he was not just Henri and Sonia's neighbour in the countryside – he was the Ayatollah Khomeini, then in exile from Iran. He returned to Tehran in 1979, from where he launched the Iranian Revolution and founded the Islamic Republic of Iran. Many in the west at the time were worried about Khomeini's return, and with good reason: the effects of it are still felt today throughout the world. But as far as Sonia was concerned his departure meant that her neighbourhood improved, so she was one of the very few in France who wholeheartedly celebrated his departure. Once again, by a quirk of geography, Henri and Sonia had a front-row seat to some of the most formative events of twentieth-century politics.

Henri also allowed himself a small taste of the French style that he'd always admired. When he first got his windfall, he bought a small selection of smart suits, Charvet shirts, tailored pyjamas and custom-made shoes. He also bought an Hermès wallet and, the final treat, a Jaguar car. Henri drove that Jaguar for twenty years, only giving it up when he thought his age made him a risk on the road. He wore those clothes to the day he died, and his grandson Alexandre still wears some of them now. This was Henri's small expression of defiance: after so many years of deprivation, he at last had the money and freedom to enjoy himself, and he did. But it could also be seen as a show of submission: after all this time, Henri was still desperately keen to pass as a Frenchman, to be assimilated, to be accepted.

SALA, LIKE HENRI, also wanted to be seen as French. She never loved the country less for what it did to her family during the war because, somehow, she was able to separate what the country symbolised to her and what it had actually done. But Sala's deep desire to be seen as French had as much to do with America as it did with France.

Like Henri's, her post-war life was about raising her family. She made a life for herself in Farmingdale: she was polite enough to Bill's family and, in particular, helped to look after his mother, Rosy. She started painting again, and would spend the afternoons while the boys were at school working on canvasses in the living room, creating beautiful French girls in the Long Island suburbs, who were perhaps an expression of her frustrated desire for a daughter, her own idealised self-image or maybe simply a grasp at a connection to the past when she would look at such girls in the Paris museums with her older brother. She got to know her neighbours and, most of all, she threw herself into the boys' lives, always making sure they were beautifully dressed and that her home looked perfect. Dr Brenner, her cousin Rose's husband, moved nearby, and he became the doctor for the family. Years later, Alex Ornstein came to visit and Bill drove him, along with his son Ron, to Dr Brenner's house, where Alex's sister Rose should have been living with him. My father Ron remembers watching Alex and Dr Brenner falling into one another's arms in tears, two men who should have been lifelong brothers-in-law had the war not swept away the woman who connected them.

Sala and Bill bickered at times, and these fights were all underpinned by the central conflict in their relationship: she did not love him like he wanted her to. She started to take long naps during the day, gratefully losing the hours to unconsciousness.

'Why is your mother always sleeping?' Bill would demand of his sons, his snappishness a cover for his hurt. But there was no good answer.

Yet Sala did not succumb to the paralysis of depression. Like so many immigrants before and after her, she decided that even if she didn't understand this strange land in which she found herself, she would ensure that her children had a better life there than she ever could. She made sure they always felt not just loved but secure, as she had not when she lived in fear in Chrzanow. She spoke to them in French, raising them bilingual, and taught them about French art and food and culture, determined to expand their mental horizons beyond Farmingdale. But she also made sure they succeeded in America. She read to them often, in English and French, and even though she herself had barely been to school at all, she, along with Bill, drilled the importance of education into both of them. The result of all this intensive home schooling was that her elder son, Ronald, could read years before the rest of his classmates. But the teachers in Farmingdale's local school had neither the time nor willingness to deal with students of varying abilities, so repeatedly reprimanded him for getting ahead of the class, trying in vain to rein him back to the level of his classmates. When Ronald was seven, not long after he came back from that first trip to Paris, he was in an English class and wilting with boredom as he listened to his fellow pupils slowly stammer their way through the set text, which they took turns reading aloud. To pass the time, he silently read ahead in the book.

'Don't read ahead, Ronald!' the teacher barked. But Ronald was so bored he didn't listen.

'I said stop it!' the teacher said and gave him a whack over the head.

Bill, still the fighter from the Lower East Side, had taught his boys that if someone hit them they should always stand up for themselves and hit back. He hadn't told them what to do if the person doing the hitting was a teacher, but his instruction probably wouldn't have changed that much. So Ronald, proving he really was Bill's son and Alex's nephew, pulled his fist back, and punched his teacher in the stomach.

Corporal punishment in New York public schools wouldn't be banned until 1985, so Ronald's teacher had another forty years ahead of her in which she could wallop kids as much as she desired. But while teachers hitting kids was completely fine, kids hitting teachers was considered completely outrageous. After Ronald punched his teacher the school called Sala and informed her that her son was probably 'mentally retarded'. They would need a psychologist to test him and if the tests came back positive they would send him to a special school. Terrified, Sala awaited the psychologist's verdict. After a long hour of waiting outside his office, while he asked Ronald a seemingly endless series of questions, the psychologist emerged and sat beside her.

'Mrs Freiman, there is nothing wrong with your son, except that he has the highest IQ I've ever tested,' the psychologist told her.

Sala then began to formulate a plan to get her boys out of this small town that she knew would only stifle them.

Not long after the meeting with the psychologist, Ronald came home from school one day, went to his father and asked, 'Dad, what's a kike?' A group of bigger boys had shouted anti-Semitic abuse at him on his way home from school. It was at this point that my father, like Henri, started to see his Jewishness as akin to a club foot, something he had been burdened with through no fault of his own, and it was a feeling he would never entirely shake off.

That Ronald experienced anti-Semitic bullying in Farmingdale was not a surprise: when Bill first moved there the Ku Klux Klan was still thriving. Even in the 1940s, Jews in Farmingdale kept to themselves and were seen as separate from the rest of the town, and there was a sense of a soft segregation. 'There was a level of anti-Semitism, but nothing publicly demonstrated. Just the usual thing, certain organisations not open to Jews and black people then,' William Rappaport, who owned the pharmacy in Farmingdale then, told me. 'Jews followed their usual ways by not doing anything that would result in problems and kept a low profile.'

Bill and Sala were both much less religious than their parents and they reflected the increasing shift towards assimilation among Jews in mid-century America: they went to synagogue on the High Holy Days, but not for Shabbat; they sent their boys to Hebrew school but Sala's attempts to keep kosher when she arrived in America soon faded away. Bill in particular bucked against the restrictive religious binds in which he had been raised, but after the war, when the Jews of Farmingdale gathered up their courage and their money and decided to build a synagogue, despite the local bigots, it was Bill who spearheaded the fundraising for it. He even laid its cornerstone on which his name was engraved. So although he wasn't observant, being Jewish was a central part of his

Bill, working as an auxiliary policeman
during the war, with Ronald.

identity and while other Jews tried to keep their heads down and not stir up trouble, Bill was always more like Alex than Henri.

When he heard that some anti-Semites were causing trouble in town and even bothering his son, he didn't hesitate. During the war, he was too old to fight so he worked as an auxiliary (or volunteer) policeman, providing support to the depleted police force, and he had kept his badge and truncheon. Bill picked up his truncheon, marched straight out the door and, as he put it, beat the hell out of them. Bill returned home, satisfied with this outcome, but Sala knew she had to get her boys out of Farmingdale.

In 1952, while Bill was at work and her boys were at school, Sala got into her car and drove to Manhasset, a small Long Island town only 18 miles away on the map but another world away socially. There, she met a broker and the two of them spent the day looking at houses. Sala soon found one she liked, on a broad, tree-lined street called Old Mill Road, and she took out nearly all of her and Bill's savings and paid a non-reimbursable deposit on the house. That night, back in Farmingdale, she told Bill what she had done and he hit the roof, raging at how she had spent all their money on a house they didn't need. The next morning they all went to look at the house Sala had blown the family's savings on. It was big, three storeys and almost three times as big as their bungalow in Farmingdale. There was a garage, a pretty front garden and a bay window in the sitting room. Just down the road, walking distance from the house, was a shopping centre, with designer stores lined along a promenade where people sat at outdoor tables and drank coffee. There were no white supremacist groups here, no pokey little school staffed with underqualified teachers, no gangs of racist bullies in the street – and no extended Freiman family. All his life, Bill had wanted to break away from his family and move up in the world. At last, fifteen years into their marriage, Sala had helped him to do just that. He was ecstatic about the new house and the family moved in almost immediately. For the rest of his life, he proudly bragged to everyone who would listen about the time his pretty French wife went out one day and bought a fancy house.

The same year the family moved to Manhasset, Bill – at his thirteen-year-old son's urging – legally changed their name from Freiman to Freeman. It was an uncanny echo of the then twelve-year-old Jehuda Glahs convincing Reuben to westernise their name to Glass, forty years earlier, thousands of miles away. Jehuda/Henri and Ron were so similar they were always more like father and son than uncle and nephew, and they both would always regard their Jewishness as an encumbrance, a hurdle thrust upon them on the path to a smooth and successful life. Bill's extended family was horrified and kept Freiman, but Bill had no sentimentality about his surname, which had frequently been bastardised by census takers anyway, and he was happy to be seen as a typical American rather than an urchin from the Lower East Side who grew up speaking Yiddish. It was the definitive break from the past he had always longed for, and my family's assimilation, which began almost half a century earlier in Chrzanow, was now complete.

WHILE IN MANY ways privileged (in Henri's case, very privileged), the oldest and youngest of the Glass siblings led ordinary post-war lives. They raised their families, they bought property, they strove to improve their lot. They worked to make sure that their children had better lives than they'd had, and they succeeded in that, too. Theirs are stories of successful Jewish aspiration. They are also stories of assimilation: they held on to their Jewishness as a personal and private identity while sloughing off many of the outward shows of the religion. In his work for the French government and in her efforts to raise educated, highly ambitious American children, they also played their parts in shaping post-war France and America respectively, which is another key part of the twentieth-century Jewish story. Jews hadn't just survived the war, they would go on to play enormous roles in the countries in which they lived.[3] There were obvious variations between their lives: Henri was very happily married, Sala was less so; Henri and Sonia went from being working class to upper class; Sala and Bill moved more incrementally from working class to lower middle class; Sala and Bill's sons went to college, Henri and Sonia's daughter did not. But in the brushstrokes, their stories are very typical of mid-twentieth-century western Jewish lives. Successful, quiet and largely anonymous lives.

Alex, by contrast, led an extraordinary life.

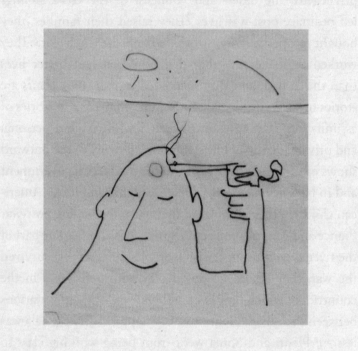

12

ALEX – Social Mobility

Paris, 1940s–1970s

IN APRIL 1961, Alex returned to Cannes, but whereas last time he went to the city in order to save his life, this time he went to change it forever. Almost vibrating with excitement, Alex walked up the driveway of the Villa La Californie and rang the doorbell, ready to meet his idol. He was shown into the house, which looked out over the Cannes bay where he had worked and lived with Seytour during the war. He then walked into the sitting room, where Pablo Picasso was waiting for him.

Only two decades earlier Alex had been arrested on that bay and sent to a concentration camp; now he was having an idyllic day with the greatest artist of the twentieth century. And this was possibly the real reason Alex stayed in France, despite his fury with it: only by living alongside ghosts from the past could the triumphs of the present taste even sweeter.

'I wasn't simply happy. I was at the summit of happiness. It was the most beautiful, the greatest day of my life,' Alex later remembered. The little boy who once had to steal meatballs was now friends with some of the most revered creative minds of the twentieth century, first Dior and now Picasso. Sender had brawled his way out of what was ostensibly a ghetto and was now among the gods.

Jewish social mobility has long been the subject of plays, racist jibes and even hip-hop lyrics: 'You ever wonder why Jewish people own all the property in America? This is how they did it,' Jay-Z rapped in his 2017 song 'The Story of OJ', in which he offers the timeless advice to his fans that they should buy property instead of drugs and lap dances. (And to think, some people argue that hip-hop has lost its connection to its young urban origins.) Donald Trump reportedly once expressed shock on seeing a black accountant: 'Black guys counting my money! I hate it. The only kind of people I want counting my money are short guys who wear yarmulkes every day . . . Laziness is a trait in blacks. It really is, I believe that. It's not anything they can control.'[1] Whereas an ability to count money, by implication, is a natural skill for Jews. If only Shylock had been available to do the accounting for Trump's casinos.

These stereotypes – in all their grosser permutations – have existed for centuries. And yet it is also the case that Jews in the West have experienced more social mobility than pretty much any other minority group in the late twentieth century. In his study on Jewish social mobility,[2] Paul

Burstein makes this memorable point of comparison: in the 1940s, Jewish representation in *Who's Who* was lower than the overall American and the British average; by the 1990s, Jews were represented proportionally over 4.5 times more than the American average and almost six times that of the British.

In America, Jews make up less than 2 per cent of the national population yet account for one-third of American Nobel laureates. Similarly, two out of every three European Jews were killed in the Holocaust, yet those who survived, and assimilated, were more likely to enjoy social mobility than any other minority. In Britain by the mid-1980s, for example, despite making up only 0.5 per cent of the population, Jews accounted for 5 per cent of the country's doctors and 9 per cent of its lawyers.[3] 'By the opening of the 21st century, it was no longer possible to find any significant area of British life from which Jews were excluded,' Howard M. Sachar writes in *A History of the Jews in the Modern World*. And given how few Jews there actually are in the United States and Europe, it is remarkable how well represented they are in public, intellectual and cultural life.

Yet there are few satisfying explanations as to why this is the case. As Burstein puts it, undoubtedly correctly, the reason there are hardly any good studies about Jewish social mobility is that Jews have resisted drawing attention to this trend, let alone explaining it, out of fear of provoking anti-Semitism. There are, after all, plenty of historic examples of Jewish success being used as an excuse for the targeting of Jews, and the Glass family experienced multiple incidents of that in their lifetimes. In the absence of proper analysis, the most popular theories range from the unhelpfully vague (they work hard, they care about education – as if other minority groups don't?), to relying on repulsive eugenics ideas and conspiracy theories.

The rise of anti-Semitism on the Right[4] and Left[5] in the twenty-first century has reignited gross comments about Jewish prominence and alleged power. But it would be bizarre, and maybe even flat-out detrimental, to ignore this part of the modern Jewish story when talking about Jews in the twentieth century, because pretending this truth doesn't exist merely leaves it free to be exploited by bigots and conspiracists. So when I started writing this book I knew I wanted to look at Jewish social mobility in the last century, and it didn't take me long to realise that the person in my family who best embodies this storyline, as well as the probable reasons behind it, was Alex.

The path that brought Alex to Picasso began when he returned to the fashion business after the war. Some might think that the gravity of what he'd endured during the war would have made fashion seem intolerably superficial and ridiculous in comparison. But this would be a misunderstanding of what fashion means, and has always meant, to France.

Today Paris comes at the end of the fashion week cycle – the order always running: New York, London, Milan, Paris – and, sure, there is usually some kind of acknowledgement in those other cities that fashion week was happening.

A minor politician might sit in the front row at some of the shows. The local mayor will make a speech welcoming the fashion journalists, dutifully trotting out statistics about how important – meaning lucrative – fashion is to the city. But these nods invariably feel merely dutiful – half-hearted and token. You can all but hear the faint grinding of teeth as these politicians demean themselves to consort with the low-brow world of fashion.

Fashion weeks aren't important to those cities. They are accessories rather than the main outfit, something that could easily be removed without anyone noticing the lack.

Paris is different. There, it feels like the whole city is invested in fashion week, as much as if a major football tournament or film festival was happening in the centre of town. Taxi drivers know where the main shows happen and waiters in cafés talk knowledgeably about whether the new designers at the big brands are living up to their hype. In Paris, fashion isn't just an add-on, it is an integral part of the city's identity; it has always been thus, and never more so than in the aftermath of the war, when Alex was reentering the industry.

In the run-up to the war, and during it, while women in Britain and America were being told to make do and mend, French women were instructed it was their patriotic duty to look fashionable: 'Fashion will remain Parisienne in its most intimate fibre. You will dress yourself simply but elegantly. Those who are at the front want you to be pretty,' read a fashion editorial in 1939.[6]

Even the Nazis understood the importance of fashion to Paris's identity. Early in the war, Hitler set out to make Berlin the fashion capital instead of Paris, so in July 1940 Nazis marched into the offices of Lucien Lelong, a designer and then president of the Chambre Syndicale de la Haute Couture, and demanded he hand over all the records of the French fashion business. Lelong understood this was an attempt to hijack not just the French fashion industry but France's culture and pride, so in November of that year he travelled to Berlin to insist that haute couture must stay in Paris. He argued that the designers and workers wouldn't be able to produce anything if they were torn from their homes and families in France and forcibly repatriated to Germany. Surprisingly, the Nazis agreed and Lelong saved not just French fashion, but also thousands of lives, as many of the seamstresses who worked in haute couture – as well as the occasional designer like Alex – were Jewish refugees.

After Paris was liberated, some of the British and American forces were outraged at the fashionability of the Frenchwomen they saw. But as historian Anne Sebba writes, staying fashionable was seen in France as a form of resistance: 'To look dowdy was a negation of patriotic duty, when by sporting extravagant costumes they could thumb their noses at the Germans. Fashion was, for the French, even after four years of occupation, anything but trivial.'[7]

Fashion was considered so untrivial that the resumption of the fashion industry was seen by the French as analogous to France reemerging from the ashes of wartime humiliation.

So in 1945 Lelong, along with Nina Ricci's son, Robert, came up with the Petit Théâtre de la Mode, an exhibition in which French designers dressed small dolls in their latest fashions. Despite the country being pretty much broke, the French Ministry of Reconstruction supported the show, because this was an important statement about the resurgence of French industry. The dolls were placed in sets designed by French artists, including Jean Cocteau, and the designers who took part included Balenciaga, Hermès, Lanvin, Grès, Schiaparelli, Rochas, and a designer described as 'Alex'.

This was almost certainly Alex Maguy. 'Alex's' doll, which is currently in the Maryhill Museum of Art in Washington, is wearing a loose black-and-white-checked coat with a green lining, which is very similar to Alex's designs before and after the war. More tellingly, Alex definitely contributed a design to a similar initiative four years later called the Merci Train, also organised by Lelong, and nearly all the designers involved in the Petit Théâtre de la Mode also took part in the Merci Train. On top of that, he would certainly have known Lelong (through Dior, who worked for him) and Robert Ricci (through his mother, Nina) beforehand. 'We can be almost completely sure he was also part of the Petit Théâtre,' academic Ludivine Broch, who has written on the Merci Train extensively, told me.

But why would he omit his surname? Broch pointed out to me that several designers who took part in the Petit Théâtre 'were going for the one-name brand', probably to make themselves sound a little more ritzy, more like Hermès or Chanel. But because 'Maguy' sounded so similar to the then popular Parisian designer Maggy Rouff – and it also wasn't actually his name – he opted to use 'Alex' instead. But it may also be because of a message that was being subtly pushed by the Petit Théâtre, and France itself, in the immediate post-war era. There was no reference to the Resistance in the Petit Théâtre, and it's notable that various designers who had openly worked for the Nazis, such as Rochas and Maggy Rouff,[8] were involved with it. The Petit Théâtre was staged in the middle of the *épuration légale*, in which France hurriedly condemned collaborators in an attempt to banish memories of the occupation to the past. So while there was certainly appetite in the country then to punish traitors, there was also a growing desire for the country to move on from this national shame. It was this mood that would ultimately lead to Perré's quiet readmittance into society. So it may very well be that Lelong felt that Alex's full name was too closely associated with his Resistance activities, or just his Jewishness, and this would serve as an undesired distraction – hence 'Alex'. In normal circumstances Alex would never have gone along with this, but he was absolutely frantic after the war to restart his fashion business, so it is entirely possible he would have agreed, for this one-off, to drop his surname. Alex was an extremely proud man, but if there was one quality he had in more abundance than pride, it was pragmatism.

The Petit Théâtre was hugely popular from the day it opened at the Louvre in 1945, ultimately attracting more than 100,000 visitors and raising more than 1 million francs

A crowd at one of Alex's fashion shows.

for the war effort.[9] It was so successful it then went on a world tour, travelling to Stockholm, Vienna, Leeds, New York and San Francisco, sending a reminder of France's superior couture culture to the world. After years of occupation and submission, France was defiantly reasserting its national pride.

Two years later, Drew Pearson, an American journalist and anti-communist campaigner, organised what would become known as the Friendship Train. This was literally a train, filled with $40 million – $500 million today – worth of donated food and similar supplies that the train collected from American citizens during the course of its much publicised journey from Los Angeles to New York. The train was then shipped to Europe – France and Italy primarily – and was written about by the American media as a charitable effort to help the poor and humiliated European countries, which of course it was. But Pearson had an alternative political motive for sending the Friendship Train, which was that he feared that France in particular was now vulnerable to communism. This gesture from America would, it was hoped, remind France of the benevolence of its capitalist friends. It was a kind gesture, but one with a definite political edge. France promptly responded in kind.

The Merci Train was sent to the United States in 1949 and consisted of forty-nine boxcars filled with donations from French individuals and companies as thank yous to the American people, and each boxcar went to a different American state.* The gratitude the French people felt was real, but what they chose to send the Americans shows something was going on here beyond mere thankfulness. Church bells, French art, First World War souvenirs were all offered, all of which were very nice, but possibly not that useful to, say, families in North Dakota. And as with the Petit Théâtre, there were certainly no references in the Merci Train to the occupation and the Resistance.[10] Instead it was a proud statement of France's cultural dominance and endurance, emphasising the country's glorious military past with mementoes from the First World War as opposed to the more recent one, and souvenirs from French industries, such as art, automobiles and fashion. France was undoubtedly grateful for the supplies America had sent, but it would not be treated as a grovelling peasant, thankful for crumbs. Ironically, France was a lot

* Washington DC and Hawaii shared one of the boxcars.

less bothered by the Friendship Train's ulterior motive – to save the country from communism – than it was by its more euphemistic purpose, which was to help a poor, struggling country. The Merci Train shows that even if France itself was still barely on its knees in 1949, the country had lost none of its pride.

To represent French fashion, Lelong repeated his Petit Théâtre initiative and commissioned what the Metropolitan Museum of Art in New York described as 'the most talented and well-known fashion designers of the time to create mini masterpieces'.[11] Alex was again one of those designers, and today his doll is in the Metropolitan Museum: she was wearing a beautiful full-length burnished blue dress with black piping around the neck and short sleeves, a cream blouse beneath, a black belt around the waist and black stripes at the bottom, and an elegant straw bonnet, with more black piping and long black ribbon.[†] Alex's inclusions in the Petit Théâtre and Merci Train were undoubtedly an honour, but they also show how France had been forced to change in the past half-decade, even if it couldn't acknowledge it openly. The former Polish refugee who arrived without a penny and unable to speak the language, whom France had tried to have killed only a few years earlier, was now seen as an integral part of the country's grandeur. Alex had been deeply hurt

---

[†] The dress worn by the doll in the museum is burnished orange, but it was originally blue. The blue dress had to be replaced due to wear and tear.

by France's refusal to naturalise him before the war; after the war, when he was considered an essential component to the country's sense of pride, he had his validation.

By the time Alex contributed to the Merci Train, he had fully resurrected his fashion house. This effort began in 1945 when he sold a painting by the Jewish artist Chaïm Soutine[12] – which he'd bought before the war and stashed away during it, probably with a friend – for 200,000 francs. From that sale he was able to rent a room on rue Jean Goujon, just behind the extremely posh Avenue Montaigne, which he turned into his new couture salon. In his memoir Alex claims that Imre Partos and Christian Dior helped him decorate his salon, which is certainly possible as Dior was building his own salon around the corner on the Avenue Montaigne, after spending the war designing for Lelong's label. Two years later Dior would launch his New Look collection, which would both establish his name as the greatest designer of his era and confirm at last that Paris had regained its position as the capital of haute couture.

Alex had the kind of salon he'd dreamed of since he was a teenager, and he filled the room with what he had managed to save of his small art collection, including paintings by his beloved friend Kisling. One thing he did not have, however, was material for making clothes.

It was hard for all designers to obtain fabrics in France after the war, and part of the reason Lelong originally commissioned the designers to make clothes for miniature mannequins was that they wouldn't need as much fabric as for actual models. Alex worked so hard – cobbling together whatever scraps of material he could find, asking friends abroad and almost certainly his sister to send over whatever fabrics they could, raising money, coming up with the designs, making them and finding the models – that the night before his show he collapsed with exhaustion. So Lelong, as eager as Alex for this show to be a success, stepped in and presented it for him.

Lelong and Alex shared a connection that went beyond an ambition for the French fashion industry: both were suspected of collaboration. Lelong saved the fashion industry from being relocated to Germany, but his success ultimately worked against him as it suggested to some that he was not to be trusted. Surely, they said, an innocent Frenchman could not work with the Germans as successfully as he did.[13] Alex, who himself was the subject of whispers because of his alliance with General Perré, became one of Lelong's more vocal defenders, insistently reassuring any sceptical designers of his innocence.

Alex knew some regarded him with suspicion, but this did not put him off dabbling in shadowy ambiguity. He himself believed, he writes in his memoir, that Lelong 'was guilty of much' during the war, although there has never been any evidence he was guilty of anything. Nonetheless, Alex also believed Lelong was worth defending because 'my real concern was to get my couture business relaunched'.

Lelong was not the only suspected collaborator Alex worked with. Serge Lifar was one of the greatest ballet dancers of the twentieth century and for three decades was the director of the Paris Opera Ballet, including during the war. After Paris was liberated he was tried and condemned as a collaborator and banned from the stage. Alex, however, took it upon himself to defend him and asked a journalist friend on *Nice-Matin* to write a piece in defence of Lifar.

His friend was astonished, asking Alex how he, of all people, could ask him to do such a thing.

'Don't think I am asking for the pleasure of it. I don't have a choice,' Alex replied.

Of course, Alex did have a choice, but Lifar had commissioned him to make costumes for his ballet, for the career-saving sum of 500,000 francs. At this point, the theatre was pretty much the only place where a designer could make money as few private citizens could afford couture, and Lifar's commission was a lifeline. Once again, Alex was looking out for himself, and he won: Lifar was able to stage his ballet and Alex finally got his company off the ground by making the costumes, with the assistance of his old friend Imre Partos.

When I first read these stories I was astonished, because the image of Alex working with known collaborators was definitely not the Alex his family knew. After all, at the same time Alex was defending Lelong he was instructing his little sister to hunt down Émile Best with a gun. Once in the 1960s, when my father was with Alex at his office, a German museum called him and asked, in careful French, if they could borrow a painting. My father watched Alex's face turning red as he listened. At last he spoke: 'As long as there is breath in my body, no painting of mine will ever be hung in your country!' he shouted back in German and slammed down the phone. In the 1980s, at a fancy cocktail party in Paris, Alex was introduced to someone he describes in his memoir as 'Austria's Consul General'.

'Come join us, Alex, you speak German so well,' a mutual friend said.

'Not German – Yiddish,' Alex replied loudly.

'A chilled silence fell over the elegant room,' Alex writes. 'I planted myself before the consul general: "You killed my father," I said. "He was a soldier in your army in 1914. He was gassed in Italy, on the Piava. He died from it. And now you have a Nazi president, Waldheim.[14] Have you no shame?"'

Even in the 1990s, when Alex was in his eighties and I would visit him in Paris, he would regularly hiss 'Collaborator!' at various galleries and businesses we walked past that, he swore, had sold out the Jews sixty years ago.

But by then, Alex had the luxury of being safe, established and secure. In the war period and its immediate aftermath, his life-saving pragmatism took precedence over his loyalty to a greater cause, and he worked with suspected and convicted 'collabos' when he needed their help, during the war (Perré) and immediately after (Lelong, who was probably innocent; Lifar, who definitely was not). Once he was reestablished, he would rather spit on such people than talk to them, but he didn't deny his past alliances, faithfully recording them in his memoir. He might not have been entirely open about some things, but he didn't lie about what he'd had to do to survive. He was passionately proud of being Jewish, but his ultimate cause was himself, and this is why he not only survived but would, very soon, become more successful than even he could have imagined.

The most popular credible theories for Jewish social mobility boil down to four arguments: there is a Jewish tradition of valuing education; Judaism itself encourages Jews to work hard because it is a religion that emphasises achievements in the current life as opposed to waiting for rewards in the afterlife; Jews tend to work, and succeed, in areas that have long been heavily Jewish, such as fashion, banking and the arts; and there is something specific to the way Jews are marginalised that encourages them to succeed. The first two theories aren't relevant in regards to Alex, because he barely went to school and was not observant.

The third one is more pertinent, given how many of Alex's art friends were Jewish, although it also raises the question why certain industries were and still are so popular with Jews. In his book about how Hollywood was founded by eastern European Jews, *An Empire of Their Own*,[15] Neal Gabler suggests that the movie business appealed to Jews because it allowed them to create an idealised view of America, even while American society denied them admission. American golf clubs might not allow Jews as members, but Jewish producers could make movies set in fancy country clubs. Connected to this was the practical consideration that movie-making was a job Jews could actually do, because 'there were none of the impediments imposed by loftier professions and more firmly entrenched businesses to keep Jews and other undesirables out'. Both of these points are equally relevant to Jewish immigrants in Europe who worked in the arts, like Alex: they were able to get into that industry, and, once in, they could celebrate the beauty of a country they loved even if it had, at best, ambivalent feelings towards them. Anyone who works in a business like fashion and fine art is someone who needs to be surrounded by beauty. It is not that surprising that eastern European Jewish immigrants, who had experienced so much ugliness in their lives, might crave a corrective.

The last theory, about the way Jews are marginalised, strikes me as being especially relevant to Alex. All minorities are, in different ways, marginalised, but Alex's specific experiences, ones that were common to countless Jews of his generation, unquestionably shaped his ambition. He was from the generation that lost ties – by choice or force – with traditional shtetl life, only then to be rejected by the country in which he'd been born. He then emigrated to another country, France, where he was reluctantly accepted, and then very much not. These events, in which he was repeatedly punished by the worlds in which he lived, encouraged Alex's strong individualism. It also, as Paul Burstein writes in his essay on Jewish success, created a marginality that made Jews like Alex 'sceptical of conventional ideas and stimulated creativity that led to intellectual eminence and, often, economic success.' I suspect this is partly why financial industries have also attracted so many Jews, as Donald Trump has eagerly pointed out. Jews over the centuries experienced enormous losses, over and over again, as their businesses and homes were taken from them simply because they were Jewish. Cash, something they could hold on to and hide, was a form of protection. Even Jews like myself who live in comparatively peaceful times grow up listening to stories of our parents' and grandparents' state-sanctioned bankruptcies, and so the idea of suddenly having nothing always feels very real. Money, like beauty, can feel like a protection against that, and certainly Henri and Alex felt like that. So did my father. He grew up seeing his parents often fretting and arguing over money, always feeling like they were on the verge of destitution. My father wanted a different life, and to provide a different kind of life for his family, so he went into banking, and he was then able to look after his parents and his children, which was the point. He hardly ever wears a yarmulke, and he definitely never counted Trump's money, but by going into banking he adhered to a Jewish tradition as much as Alex did by going into the arts. He, like Henri and Alex, worked extremely hard, not because Jews are naturally hard workers, but because they are raised to believe they have to work twice as hard to get ahead, because they will never be entirely accepted. I doubt if my father ever consciously thought like that, but his parents did and they imbued that work ethic in him, and Alex and Henri definitely believed that. It was only by working all the time, Alex thought, that he would get anywhere.

Alex realised early on that there was no point in following rules, because the rules were made to work against him. He had learned definitively during the war that he always had to help himself, and if that meant defending suspected collaborators who would be beneficial to his career, or screaming at them in the middle of a cocktail party, he would do so without hesitation or fear. He didn't care what anyone thought of him.

Alex's acceptance and then fierce rejection of collaborationists reflects how his war experiences shaped him. Like Henri, he believed that the world would turn against the Jews again, and this led to what Howard Sachar describes as the Jewish immigrant's 'drive for entrepreneurial success'.[16] But Alex's reaction to this sense of threat was the opposite to that of his older brother. Whereas Henri wanted to blend in and be unnoticed, Alex believed that the way to face this threat was not to hide but to stand out and fight, showing the world that the Jews, or at least this Jew, could not be pushed around.

This made Alex unusual, in terms of Jewish social mobility. Contrary to some ugly generalisations about Jewish success, there isn't something inherent in Jews that leads to success. If there were, then the most Jewish Jews would be the most successful, and clearly that is not the case: studies have repeatedly shown that Reform Jews earn more than Orthodox ones, and there aren't many high-profile ultra-Orthodox Jews in mainstream public life. Henri had been right from the start: assimilation leads to greater success for Jews. It contributed to Jews passing as Caucasians in a way they didn't before the twentieth century, and this in turn has helped their social mobility.

Alex was definitely not Orthodox, neither was he entirely assimilated. Unlike Henri, he never tried to be seen as French, because he learned from the war that true assimilation was a delusion – ultimately, he would always be seen as a Jew, and so he defined himself first and foremost as that instead of letting other people do it for him. His experiences – rather than any genetic tendencies – shaped his approach to the outside world and his ambition in it, and it just so happened that his unusual approach worked for him. He consciously hugged his Yiddish accent close and he loathed Germany, refusing to visit the country ever – that Sonia could speak fluent German, and continued to do so after the war, was yet another count against her in Alex's eyes.

As angry as he was at Germany, he was more furious at France for having betrayed him. Yet he never considered living somewhere else. Maybe he thought it would be too hard to start another business elsewhere, maybe he didn't want to leave Henri. I suspect there was a part of him that simply needed to triumph over France as a form of revenge on it. They couldn't throw him out during the war, and he would not be chased out afterwards. But this meant that for the rest of his life, he stayed in a country that he loved dearly but had hurt him worse than any single person. He loved France, and he never forgave it.

Wounded by the French, and long ago abandoned by Poland, Alex became a very vocal supporter of Israel (another common reaction among Jews of his generation, also borne from experience). He and Henri bought Chaya an apartment in Haifa, and they visited her there often. Photos show them grinning happily in a Jewish homeland none of them could have imagined when they all lived in Chrzanow. 'Israel is the realization of all my dreams, a dream come true after the worst atrocities which humanity has ever known. No one can doubt that Israel will become a leading country in developmental potential and the light of the Middle East,' he wrote. This prediction was a rare instance of Alex being overly optimistic, but such uncharacteristic sunny hopefulness is a testament to how shocked he was by what had happened to him and his family in France, and how much he hoped – had to hope – that the new Jewish state would protect them all forever. When, as a Jewish designer, he was invited to Israel shortly after the country was admitted to the United Nations in 1949, to show his collection in Tel Aviv and Jerusalem, he was so overcome that when writing about the trip thirty years later he lapsed into near hysteria, describing how much the invite meant to him as a Jewish couturier, and how much Israel meant to all Jews. Because of Israel, he wrote, all Jewish children will now have a 'beautiful, happy, rich' childhood, the opposite of the one endured by him.

While nowhere near as successful as his former illustrator Dior, Alex had a genuine talent for making beautiful clothes that lasted. As a child I loved to play with the coats he had made for my grandmother, which she still had in her closet thirty, forty, even fifty years after he made them. And given that he was an independent designer with no financial backers, he did impressively well. The sleek and sporty look for which he became known before the war turned out to be a canny choice, because even if all of France had fallen in love with Dior's feminine New Look, Alex's smart coats, sharply tailored dresses and streamlined suits were a popular look in America. Ava Gardner bought dresses from him; Marlene Dietrich bought a jacket. His friends from the Foreign Legion, including General Koenig and Lieutenant-Colonel Magrin-Vernerey, occasionally came to his presentations, and some of the most carefully preserved photos I found of Alex's salon show him proudly posing with his fellow legionnaires – all of whom look a little bemused by their couture surroundings. Sala tried to come to Paris as often as possible for his shows, and she kept several photos that show him accompanying his beautiful sister, wearing an elegant Alex Maguy dress and coat, to her seat in his salon. His friends from the art world came too. Kisling was by now living in the south of France, but when he was in Paris he would come to Alex's salon every day and certainly to the shows if he was in town. Alex always thought of 'Kiki' as a foster brother, the one who taught him how to be both Jewish and Parisian, Bohemian and serious. Most of all, Alex writes in his memoir, Kisling taught him to look at paintings, to seek out the life of happiness in art that had eluded him in childhood.

Kisling felt just as fond of Alex and wrote Sala reports of their times together.

Alex and Sala at a ball in Paris.

Chaya, Alex, a female friend and Kisling at one of
Alex's fashion shows in Paris.

'I have made an unexpected visit to our dear brother,
and you should see our Alex, how happy he is. His wit,
his humor, and his life are marvelous!' he wrote to Sala on
29 March 1947.

Alex's life was glamorous, but it was not exactly marvellous. My father remembers sitting backstage at Alex's shows
and watching him carefully style and dress his models, pinning this sleeve, lowering that hem. And then after the show,
he would watch his uncle obsequiously thank every fashion
editor and store buyer who had come to his show, bow his
head humbly as American and French customers told him
they liked the dress but it was in the wrong colour, they liked
the coat but it was too long.

'For you, madame, I will fix it,' Alex would murmur.

Afterwards, my father would see Alex almost prostrate with despair in his workroom, worrying that he hadn't sold enough clothes, infuriated that the designs he'd sweated over were casually dismissed by ignorant customers, terrified that he wouldn't be able to pay his seamstresses, that he wouldn't be able to eat.

Today, the big labels like Dior are awash with money (mostly from make-up and accessories rather than clothes), but in the main it is very, very hard to be a fashion designer. When I was a young journalist occasionally posted to New York and Paris, I would often interview well-known designers who quietly spent their days shivering in under-heated studios, barely keeping creditors from the door. In several cases, I'd interview a designer one day and find out he or she went out of business the next. For all the lipstick-shiny confidence fashion projects from the pages of magazines, the truth is not that many people have more than $3,000 to spend on a dress, and so designers are forced to give clothes to celebrities for free, in the hope of some publicity. They then have to write off the loss, hoping against all likelihood that their little gamble will pay off. As Alex's memoir makes clear, it has always been thus:

'The fame of a couturier is linked to the fame of the women he dresses. They were often more celebrities than normal clients and needed to be treated as such. They often "forgot" to pay. It's part of the business. So a couturier has a dual responsibility: First, make women more beautiful in the great tradition of Parisian fashion. Second, support a business. To reconcile these two responsibilities is unimaginably difficult,' he wrote.

Alex's clothes were regularly featured in fashion magazines, French and American, and he himself was photographed in the society pages of French papers with beautiful women, such as the French singer Lucienne Dhotelle (known as '*la môme* Moineau') and the American singer-songwriter Betty Comden at the races at Longchamp or the Parisian nightclubs. But despite the surface fabulousness of his life, his business was crippled by debts, and he would go for days without eating in order to pay his staff of 150.

In 1951, after 108 collections, Alex was invited by the French ambassador to Denmark to take part in a charity show for 'the most famous haute couturiers'. By this point, his business was nearly bankrupt, so Alex hesitated to accept. But he hadn't got this far by being shy, and he thought to himself: 'Remember when as a child you dreamed of French couture in your little, lost Galician village. Now, after a twenty-five-year career, they're inviting you. Prove by your presence that you're not finished.'

So Alex went, but initially felt humiliated when he saw how the other designers had been able to bring dozens of models with them, dressed in the most expensive brocades. He couldn't afford even a single model or outfit. But if the Nazis couldn't destroy Alex then certainly fashion wouldn't, so he decided to make a virtue out of his poverty. When it was his turn, he borrowed a model from a designer friend, got up on stage 'taking my courage into both hands', and with only a case of pins and about two metres of cotton, constructed an evening gown in front of the astonished audience in seven minutes. He got a standing ovation, and one Danish newspaper that covered the event described it as 'a sensation'.[17] A one-off dress he made with his own hands in front of the audience: it was a characteristically defiant gesture from Alex in defence of the art of couture, and an illustration of Alex's refusal to give up, ever, even when the odds seemed utterly hopeless.

Alex returned to Paris and carried on as a designer for a few more years, but it was clear that couture was becoming part of the past. In 1955, *Le Monde*'s fashion critic compared Alex's classical style with the more modernist looks that would define the 1960s when the journalist reviewed his show alongside that of Pierre Cardin: 'We are seeing two trends clash: some still want to reflect the female silhouette, others want to reshape it. We will soon learn who played it best,' wrote the critic of the two designers.[18]

There was no competition: although the journalist praised Alex's 'sylphan silhouettes' and 'the astonishing and much-applauded striped pieces', Pierre Cardin's 'shocking spectacle inspired by interplanetary journeys' was clearly the future.

At the same time Alex's fashion business was struggling, someone else's was taking off. His cousin Maurice's son, Armand Ornstein, was no longer the little boy hiding in the woods but an extremely handsome young man-about-town. Around this time, he teamed up with a young designer called Daniel Hechter, and Hechter's name would become as much of a byword for French 1960s fashion as Mary Quant and Biba were for British 1960s style, thanks to the extremely successful business he and Armand built together. Today, Hechter is widely credited with popularising prêt-à-porter and helping to kill off exactly the kind of fashion that Alex made. *Prêt-à-porter* literally means 'ready to wear', as in buying clothes directly off the rack, and this is how nearly everyone buys clothes today, whether they shop at Zara or Prada. Alex, however, was firmly in the older tradition of haute couture, which means each outfit is specially created for each customer, making it extremely beautiful, but expensive and ultimately impractical. By the 1950s haute couture was already on its way out, and today, even in the big fashion houses like Dior, it accounts for an infinitesimal percentage of the company's overall sales. Alex, as a small Parisian couturier, was one of the last of an already dying breed, and while his stubbornness about retaining his independence undoubtedly hastened his end, it would have come eventually. The fashion world was changing and would soon be unrecognisably different from the one in which he trained. Alex could be pragmatic about some things, but not his art, and in this area alone he would not compromise for the sake of survival.

Alex never explicitly blamed Armand for the death of his fashion business, or even talked with Armand about fashion. In fact, he would have been furious to hear anyone suggest they were even in the same business: Armand and Daniel Hechter's clothes were intended to last just a fashion season, whereas Alex's, as he would be the first to say, endured forever. But he certainly raged against the fashion revolution Armand and Hechter inspired:

'Once there were forty great couture houses in Paris. How many exist today? Four or five at most. Ready-to-wear finally killed personal elegance and individual charm. It made Paris ugly. Today, it's the brand a woman wears that is noticed, not the woman herself. One wears Sonia Rykiel or Chanel and circulates like an automobile and its nameplate. What an absence of taste. How sad,' he writes in his memoir.

Even though his business was, in part, killed by one member of the next generation of his family, Alex later managed to pass his legacy on to another younger relative: Alexandre de Betak, his great-nephew and Henri and Sonia's grandson. Almost every week through the 1970s and early 1980s, Henri brought Alexandre over to Alex's for lunch – Sonia, of course, was not invited, and nor were Alexandre's mother and sister, Danièle and Natasha – and Alex would lecture his great-nephew about art and elegance. (When I later heard about these lunches I thought of Gigi in the 1958 MGM film, adapted from Colette's novel, enduring regular lunches with her Aunt Alicia, who would teach her niece about all the important things in life, like how to admire jewellery and the right way to eat an ortolan.) Alexandre resented having to get dressed up in a suit for these lunches – why did he have to spend his day all hot and uncomfortable when his sister could wear what she liked and stay home and play? While Alex would talk to the bemused little boy about fashion and all the beautiful people he knew,

Alexandre would quietly wonder why, if his great-uncle knew so much about style, did he have lifts on all of his shoes? But something about these lunches stuck in Alexandre's mind, because this introduction to fashion would prove to be a formative one.

Before Alex shut his salon for good, he had one last gift to give a favoured customer: a young Chinese architect called Ieoh Ming Pei, better known now as I.M. Pei. Alex and Pei met in Paris in 1951 when the latter was on the Wheelwright Traveling Fellowship, and Pei and his wife, Eileen, had been told about Alex's salon by the American architect Philip Johnson. Alex never lost his knack for spotting who was worth schmoozing, and as his alliance with Perré proved to him, befriending powerful and prominent people could only be beneficial. Alex spotted early on that Pei was worth keeping in his life, and in the hope of achieving this, he wrote in his memoir, one of his last gestures as a designer was to send the Peis a small Modigliani sketch as a token of gratitude for their support. I emailed Pei's sons, Chien Chung and Li Chung, to verify this story and initially they thought it unlikely as they doubted if their parents had ever owned such a sketch. But a few days later they emailed back. They had found the Modigliani in the back of their father's closet. Pei might have never bothered to hang it, but, once again, Alex had told the truth.

But while Pei might not have been overly awed by Alex's present, he liked Alex: whenever Pei would spot him at parties he would call out, 'Shalom, Alex!' much to Alex's delight and everyone else's bemusement. In the early 1980s, when Pei was being widely vilified for his plans to build a small pyramid in front of the Louvre, Alex was one of the very few who supported Pei, and stood up and said so. He wrote letters to Pei and about Pei to newspapers, saying that what French art needed was Pei's pyramid. Pei later returned the favour by putting Alex, by now extremely wealthy, in touch with Moshe Mayer, a real estate developer who worked with Pei, about planning the Alex Maguy Foundation in Israel, which had it been built would have been the ultimate proof of Alex's social ascendency. The foundation never actually materialised, probably due to cost and Alex's health, but yet again Alex was proven right about the value of having successful friends.

Alex finally shut down his salon in the mid-1950s, ending that chapter of his life. The next chapter would bring him the immortality and enormous wealth he had always longed for, and expected.

ALEX'S CAREER IN art began, naturally, with his friends. He first sold off his last fashion pieces, settled his most urgent debts, and with what was left, opened a small gallery on the rue du Faubourg Saint-Honoré, just around the corner from Avenue Matignon, where he'd had a salon before the war. He named it Galerie de l'Élysée, emphasising its proximity – and insinuating a connection – to the Élysée Palace, the residence of the French president. Alex had always longed to be established in French society, and being neighbours with the president proved his establishment status. In characteristic fashion, he threw a glamorous opening night party for the gallery to which he invited all his old friends and colleagues, including Dior.

'I've come to wish you good luck, Alex. Have no regrets. Don't forget, I began with paintings and you will finish with paintings,' Dior said to him.

Another person from his fashion past who supported Alex in his move to the art world was the illustrator René Gruau. He helped Alex to decorate his gallery, and shortly afterwards he painted an extraordinarily evocative portrait of Sala on one of her trips to Paris. This painting originally hung in my grandmother's apartment and now hangs over my parents' fireplace in London, and it captures her elegance and wistfulness better than most photographs. Her elbow is leaning on a table and her chin rests on the back of her hand while she gazes behind her; he immortalised her as always looking back, towards the past. In its tenderness and precision, it was clearly painted by someone with enormous feeling for the subject and her family. In 1974, almost forty years after they first met, Alex hosted an exhibition of Gruau's work in his gallery which he called 'Alex Maguy Présente Son Ami Gruau'. For the chosen very few, Alex could be extremely loyal and sentimental. (Kisling also painted a portrait of Sala; Alex had told Bill at that fateful dinner in Chaya's flat in rue des Rosiers that famous artists loved to paint his sister and, decades later, thanks to Alex and his extraordinary career path, that lie eventually became true.)

Alex's idea with the Galerie de l'Élysée was to have shows that featured only seven paintings – seven was his lucky number, and it's also a significant number in Judaism, representing creation and fortune. Each of his shows would be centred on a theme, and his first show was called 'Paris, Parisians, and Parisiennes'; his second was 'The Landscapes and Faces of France'. When he was a designer he made adoring near-pastiches of French style, and as a curator he put on shows specifically celebrating French style. Little Sender was still enchanted with the fantasy of the country his father used to describe to him on Kostalista, despite everything it had done to him and his family.

Over the next decade, he built up a hugely successful gallery, showing works by, among others, his old friends Chagall, Pascin and Kisling (who sadly died soon after the gallery opened), as well as Bonnard, Renoir, Monet, Braque, Miró, Bacon and Boudin, and sculpture by Giacometti, Henry Moore and Gauguin. Alex had exceptionally good taste in art, the kind only someone with a deep love of his subject can have, as opposed to someone merely chasing after the hot new thing in the art world. The gallery quickly developed a reputation for having the finest pieces from the greatest modern artists, and Alex became a name again that was cited in the gossip magazines:

'Among the many notable celebrities at the party, we saw Jacqueline Auriol [a French aviator] in the company of Alex Maguy', read a typical caption from a French magazine, which Alex cut out and sent to my grandmother and which she faithfully saved. But there was still one goal he hadn't achieved yet: meeting Picasso.

Alex had been trying to attract Picasso's attention for decades. He genuinely revered him as a lover of art but he also liked him as a person: short, tough, sexual, a fighter, deeply moral but complicated, adored by men and women, one who didn't obey the rules and was rewarded for it; Picasso was an idealisation of Alex's own self-image. After the war, Alex had a tangential connection with Picasso through his friends Georges and Suzanne Ramié. Like Alex, the Ramiés had been involved in Resistance activity in the south of France, but now ran a pottery, called Madoura, on the Côte d'Azur. Fortuitously for Alex, this workshop became one of the most important centres of twentieth-century ceramics, because it was the exclusive producer of ceramics by Picasso. Alex tried in vain to utilise this connection. In 1949 he'd designed a dress covered with images from Picasso's paintings and wrote to the artist to tell him, under the pretence that he was asking for permission but really just making his presence known to his artistic hero. (If Picasso did reply to that request it has long since been lost, but Alex did make the dress.) Alex became friendly with a young woman, named Jacqueline Roque, who worked at Madoura Pottery. But Alex was not the only male friend of the Ramiés to have noticed Jacqueline: in 1953, at the age of 26, she caught the eye of Picasso, who was more than four decades older than her, and he embarked on a long campaign of seduction. Now Alex had yet another connection to the artist, and once he opened his gallery, he wrote to him more frequently, asking for his blessing to feature this or that painting, inviting him to his shows, even sending him birthday greetings. 'Dare I ask you to do me the honor of being my guest for the baptism of my little yacht?' he wrote on 13 April 1960, referring to the boat he'd recently bought and kept moored down in Cannes. (Picasso declined that invitation.) Undaunted by constant refusals, Alex tried again almost exactly a year later, saying that he had a proposal for Picasso that involved Alex's 'very, very close friends at the House of Dior'. A few days

Alex on his yacht in Cannes.

later the phone in his gallery rang: it was Jacqueline, inviting him to their house in Cannes, Villa La Californie. Barely
able to breathe with excitement, Alex said he would be there.
Once again, a personal connection worked in Alex's favour.
Eventually.

In April 1961, Picasso was eighty and a newlywed, having
married Jacqueline the previous month. Jacqueline was
devoted to her new husband, sorting through his correspondence, attending to the daily chores, fending off the
endless stream of visitors and collectors, dealing with the
lawyers, and generally arranging their lives.[19] After Picasso
died in 1973, the degree to which Jacqueline controlled
Picasso's life would become a somewhat controversial subject,
when she stopped his children from a previous relationship,

Paloma and Claude, from attending their father's funeral, and was later accused of stealing their inheritance. But Picasso was besotted by her, and at the very least grateful for her attentiveness: he made four hundred portraits of her, more than of any other single person, and for the last seventeen years of his life she was the only woman the former womaniser painted.

Almost certainly, Alex's friendship with Jacqueline helped to get him his long sought-for invitation to meet Picasso. But the artist guarded his time and privacy fiercely, and he was certainly not opening his doors to every art world hanger-on who Jacqueline had met at Madoura. So there had been something about Alex's letter that 'captured Picasso's attention', Jacqueline explained, and it turned out that had less to do with art and more to do with Alex. Picasso had lived in Paris during the occupation and was fascinated by Alex's story of fighting in the Foreign Legion alongside Spanish Republicans in exile, as Picasso was himself a Spaniard essentially in exile. (Franco was then still in power in Spain, and Picasso was seen as an enemy.) And so he summoned him to Cannes, and that is when Alex first met Picasso at Villa La Californie.

As much as Alex saw himself in Picasso, Picasso apparently saw himself in Alex. When he entered the sitting room Picasso stood up, walked towards Alex and – reaching up because, for once, Alex was the tallest man in the room – jabbed a finger into his chest: '*T'es juif, comme moi!*' Picasso barked.

Alex assumed at the time that Picasso was speaking meta-phorically, that he thought of himself as an outcast and a fighter, two qualities associated with Jewish Resistance fighters, and that Picasso, rightly, saw in Alex. The two men talked for about half an hour. It doesn't sound, however, like Alex talked that much. Instead he listened to Picasso and didn't explain what, exactly, it was that he wanted from him after all this time: 'I did not dare distract from our precious moments together to talk to you about something that is very dear to my heart,' he wrote to him after the visit. In fact, Alex wanted Picasso to design a scarf for a collection Dior was putting together that year; Dior had asked Alex's assistance in contacting Picasso, and Alex realised that, if he pulled this off, it would make him look like a big player in both the fashion and art worlds.

I couldn't find any evidence that this scarf project ever happened. But Alex got something else from Picasso even he hadn't dared to hope for: friendship. Picasso took a genuine shine to him and they entered into an extraordinarily regular correspondence. In the National Archives in Paris there are sixty-two letters from Alex to Picasso, far more than from almost any other business associate. They are all addressed to both Picasso – who Alex always refers to as '*grand maître*' – and Jacqueline, as was common with all of Picasso's corres-pondence, such was the degree of Jacqueline's involvement in her husband's business affairs. But they are also written with a fond familiarity unusual in both men. Among the various business discussions – Alex asking Picasso to authenticate

Alex with Picasso.

a painting, Alex inviting him to a party at his home – are chummy postcards from Alex's trips to the United States, as well as a joint postcard, sent from the south of France, signed by both Alex and Maurice Chevalier, in which they tell him they've been speaking of him fondly.

Picasso occasionally asked Alex to check on an exhibition of his work for him, especially in Spain, as the artist was still ostensibly exiled from his home country. In April 1962, Alex went to Barcelona, as Picasso had recently donated a huge number of works to the Aguilar Palace, and he wanted to know they were hung and received properly. Alex sent back a typically effusive telegram: 'Everyone from and around Barcelona is embracing your wonderful present. Even the sun shone on the party.' Some of Alex's artist friends were understandably jealous of how clearly starstruck he was by Picasso. Chagall, who had known Alex for almost forty years, would make pointed comments about his constant name dropping and ask, 'So tell me, how's your Spanish friend?' But Alex couldn't be teased out of bragging about Picasso.

Shortly after returning from Barcelona, Alex's loyalty paid off. He asked Picasso to look at the selection of paintings for his next show – only seven, as usual, including a work each by Chagall, Braque, Renoir, Monet, Degas, Dufy and Picasso – and he wanted Picasso's approval. Picasso didn't just look at the paintings: he took the unusual step of summoning Alex to his home in Mougins, where he almost never had visitors because he considered it a place of solitude and work. His attitude was so extreme that even those close to him looked at his life there as 'a form of self-imprisonment'.[20] For Alex, Picasso broke this self-imposed imprisonment.

It turned out that Picasso did more than approve of Alex's exhibition: he made a poster for it.

'This is for you,' Picasso said, presenting him with the drawing when he arrived.

It was a portrait of a face with curly hair and big eyes, on top of which Picasso wrote Alex's name, as well as the name and address of his gallery, and beneath which he wrote the name and dates of the exhibition. And then he signed and dated it: 15 April 1962.

'No one can know the joy I felt. It was more than a surprise, more than a gift – I looked at the lithograph as a reward,' Alex writes.

A reward for what, he doesn't say – surviving? Perseverance? Someone – Jacqueline, or more likely one of Picasso's assistants – captured the moment Picasso gave Alex the poster. Picasso is looking at the camera and Alex at Picasso, and he looks like a cat who knows he has caught the prize mouse. For the rest of his life, when he talked about the poster he would say, 'Picasso gave me my birth certificate.' Reaching the zenith of the art world, through his own determination, gave Alex his identity.

But even winning the prize couldn't stop Alex from burnishing this story a little more. In his memoir he claimed that Picasso drew the portrait the first time he met him, which was not true. He also insisted that the big-eyed, curly-haired figure in the poster was a portrait of him. In fact, it is most commonly identified by Picasso scholars as Jacqueline, which would make a lot more sense: Alex had small eyes and his hair had long since given up the fight, whereas Jacqueline was a wide-eyed, wavy-haired beauty. And considering how much Picasso painted her, it seems a lot more likely that she would be the subject rather than Alex. Even at what felt to him like the summit of his achievements, Alex couldn't resist giving himself a few extra inches of height.

But whoever was actually portrayed in the poster, getting it was an enormous coup for Alex. Picasso occasionally made posters for other small galleries, particularly ones

Picasso presenting Alex with the poster.

around Avignon and Arles. (He also, the year before, made one for a show in Haifa, further confirming his solidarity with the Jewish people.) But by 1962 such gestures were rare, further proving the exceptional nature of his relationship with Alex.

The two men met several times over the next decade. Photos of those meetings show Picasso talking excitedly and Alex bowing his head with uncharacteristic humility, listening to him. Picasso was always intrigued that Alex had come to art via fashion, and when Alex was one day fussing about what frames he should put on Picasso's work, the artist thought for a moment and said, 'You were a couturier, and you must dress them. It is absolutely right.'

Just as Alex knew it would, his alliance with Picasso gave him a new level of credibility in the art world. By the late 1960s, the French newspapers referred to him as the '*célèbre marchand de tableaux du Faubourg Saint-Honoré*' (the famous art dealer of the Faubourg Saint-Honoré) and invariably described him as Viennese, due to society journalists' inability to differentiate between the Austro-Hungarian Empire and Austria. He was photographed at parties, often alongside Georges Pompidou, the prime minister of France and a regular at Alex's gallery, as the Élysée Palace was just next door. In 1964, the foreign correspondent of *The New Yorker*, Janet Flanner, wrote a long and glowing review of one of his shows that featured, as always, only seven paintings: 'What a joy to see so few, and those so fine!' Flanner wrote,[21] praising in particular the 'superb' Cézanne painting, 'unfamiliar' work by Soutine, and 'immortal' Toulouse-Lautrec sketch. Her references to the paintings' buyers give a sense of how important, and global, Alex had become in the art world: a watercolour by André Derain had been bought by Brandeis University in Massachusetts, and the 'Proustian interior' by Bonnard was going to the National Gallery in Washington. Alex was so proud of this praise in an American publication, he wrote to his sister and instructed her to buy every copy of the magazine she could find and send them to him, which she immediately did.

Alex's celebrity buyers were as international as his museum customers. Edward G Robinson – born Emanuel Goldenberg in Romania – frequently visited the gallery, and he and Alex would converse happily in Yiddish. Similarly, Kirk Douglas (born Issur Danielovitch Demsky) who, like Sala's husband Bill, grew up speaking Yiddish in New York, bought two paintings. 'Actors get a better price from me,' Alex told him in Yiddish, to Douglas's delight. Aristotle Onassis, Peter Lawford, Yul Brynner, Jerry Lewis, Ingrid Bergman and Frank Sinatra all visited the gallery, and Alex's old friend Maurice Chevalier was a regular, although he never bought anything, leading Alex to gripe forever about Chevalier being cheap. Elizabeth Taylor, on the other hand, was very eager to buy from him. In Richard Burton's diary entry dated 11 January 1969, he describes going to Alex's gallery with her: 'He's a tiny man who claims to be a great friend of Picasso's,' Burton wrote.[22] Despite this somewhat sceptical initial impression, Burton got on well with Alex thanks to, Burton assumes, and probably rightly, 'my gift of the gab, even in French, and my fame!'. Taylor wanted to buy a Picasso portrait of a woman in blue 'which made her mouth water'. Burton preferred the Picasso painting of a harlequin on a horse for $40,000. 'I saw many other paintings and will obviously end up buying one,' he writes. 'But the most impressive was two paintings by van Gogh painted on both sides of the canvas – one of a man at a loom and one (the other side) of a man sitting in a chair near a fireplace. But they are beyond even my purse.'

Every New Year, Alex would send out cards to his favoured customers that were actually lithographs of his latest and favourite new painting. In an undated article from the mid-1960s, *Le Figaro* breathlessly wrote about Alex sending out lithographs of *The Pétanque Players* by Cézanne to, among others, Picasso, Onassis and President Nixon.[23] Each lithograph was worth about 15,000 francs (the equivalent of about $115,000 today), meaning Alex spent hundreds of thousands on his New Year cards. But, as the journalist added, 'That is not very extravagant, if we consider the strength of his bank account.'

By the late 1960s, Alex was an extremely wealthy man thanks to his art dealing, and his own personal collection of art was at least as impressive as his bank account. The Picasso portrait that made Elizabeth Taylor salivate was part of Alex's collection at home, and although he never sold his own paintings, 'Alex has promised to invite us to his home to see it,' Burton writes in his diary. Alex loved to tell journalists about all the famous people he refused to sell his paintings to, from Taylor to Pompidou (a Nicolas de Staël painting, according to *Le Figaro*). Once French politicians had tried to kill him, now he had the power to deny them what they wanted. A particularly satisfying instance of that was when André Bettencourt, the then future minister of foreign affairs, begged Alex in vain in the early 1970s to sell him the beautiful painting by Raoul Dufy, *Le Port du Havre*. Bettencourt had been decorated for his Resistance work, but in 1989 it emerged that during the war he had been a member of a French fascist group and written about Jews in the most anti-Semitic terms for the Nazi propaganda paper *La Terre Française*. Bettencourt exemplified the moral grey shades that were all too common in mid- to late-twentieth-century French politics, and he eventually, and somewhat begrudgingly, apologised. It would have pleased Alex enormously that a former fascist had begged him for something and he'd defiantly refused.

Alex's personal art collection was as fine as any museum's. He now lived on Avenue Foch, then and still now one of the chicest streets in Paris. His ground-floor apartment was filled with, at various times, works by Monet, Renoir, van Gogh, Braque, Cézanne, Manet, Degas and, of course, Picasso. When I would have lunch with Alex in his apartment in the 1990s, even I – a cynical, grouchy teenager – was impressed that in his bathroom, almost as an afterthought, was a Matisse personally inscribed to him. The little boy from the shtetl who had always wanted to live surrounded by beauty created a home for himself filled with the greatest treasures of the nineteenth and twentieth centuries.

When Israel won the Six-Day War in 1967, Alex donated his favourite Picasso painting, *Sitting Woman* (1949), to Israel, and the Israel Museum in Jerusalem still has the work. Just as he had given his most treasured paintings, a Kisling and a Pascin, to the Tel Aviv Museum before going off to war, so he gave his most beloved one to Israel to celebrate the country's military triumph almost thirty years later. Edmond de Rothschild had a reception at his home in Paris to commemorate Alex's donation, and the guest speaker was General Koenig, Alex's general from the Foreign Legion. General Koenig talked about seeing the Jewish legionnaires carrying the Zionist flag in 1941 in Bir Hakeim in Africa, 'and that immediately made me feel a kinship with them', he said. Alex was deeply moved by his general's words, which he took as proof of his 'attachment to the noble and just cause of Israel', and the two men stayed close until the general's death three years later.

Not everyone from Alex's military past felt such an attachment. Alex had always been proud to have been in England alongside the Free French and de Gaulle, but that changed in 1967. In the months leading up to the war, relations between Israel and the neighbouring countries of Egypt, Jordan and Syria became increasingly strained. De Gaulle, then the president of France, warned Israel not to launch preemptive strikes against Egypt, advice Israel promptly and rightly ignored. These strikes helped Israel to win the war, as the early attacks nearly wiped out the Egyptian air force, and save themselves. De Gaulle's advice had been bad, his motives questionable and he was so irritated that he had been ignored that he held a press conference at the Élysée Palace – five minutes away from Alex's gallery – in which he described the Jews as 'an elite people, domineering and sure of themselves . . . [with] ardent and conquering ambition'. *Le Monde* mocked de Gaulle's speech with a cartoon that appeared on the paper's front page, showing a skeleton behind barbed wire in a concentration camp, a Star of David on his striped pyjamas, which – only twenty-five years earlier – Jews had to wear on their clothes in Paris. 'An elite people, domineering and sure of themselves' was written underneath.[24] Others were even more cutting, such as Michel Debré, France's former prime minister, the grandson of a rabbi and once a deeply loyal supporter of de Gaulle, who said the president's comment showed 'an infantile-psychological-senile' attitude.[25] De Gaulle's statement probably had a lot more to do with the hurt ego of a seventy-seven-year-old politician than any proof of long-dormant anti-Semitism within him. But Alex didn't care. To him, de Gaulle's remarks sounded like the kind of attitude he had fought against, alongside the general, the attitude that had led to his brother's death and nearly his own. It was yet another betrayal by France, and he was hurt and, more than that, furious. So he picked up the phone and called his friend and neighbour Prime Minister Pompidou to inform him he was sending back his Croix de Guerre and Bronze Star, which he'd been awarded after the Narvik campaign. Pompidou begged him to calm down and reconsider, but Alex wasn't having any of it. He boxed up his medals, addressed them to the prime minister and president of France, and had his assistant run them next door to the palace. No matter how good Alex's life became, he never stopped thinking of himself as the Jewish outsider and he never stopped believing France saw him that way too.

Picasso's reaction to the Six-Day War was, for Alex, even more surprising than de Gaulle's. The artist was so moved by Alex's gift of his painting to Israel that he confided in him that the first thing he ever said to Alex – '*T'es Juif, comme moi!*' – was meant not metaphorically but literally: 'You should know that my mother was a Marrano,' Picasso told him, according to Alex. (A Marrano was a Spanish Jew who converted to Christianity, often by force.)

'So Picasso was one of us. And, I can add, he told me this with much pride and nobility,' Alex writes in his memoir.

As far as I know, there is no evidence that this was true of Picasso's mother, or that Picasso made this claim to anyone else. Certainly no Picasso scholars I spoke to had heard it. But Alex was adamant Picasso had told him this and, if Picasso did believe it, it would explain Picasso's well-established and longstanding loyalty to Jewish people, exemplified on an individual level by his friendship with Alex.

De Gaulle and Picasso were probably the two men Alex respected most in the world, and both stood up against fascism during the war. Their opposite reactions to the Six-Day War show how two people, even those ostensibly on the same side, could find themselves so divided when it came to the subject of Jews and, in particular, Israel. This split arguably developed in the way we still know it because of the Six-Day War, in itself a defining part of the Jewish story in the late twentieth century and still today. Israel's victory aggravated Palestinian frustration and, in turn, nationalism. Palestinians now knew that other Arab countries couldn't and wouldn't help them regain territories now held by Israel, such as Gaza, the West Bank, the Sinai peninsula and the Golan Heights, and this led to an escalation of the

Israeli-Palestinian conflict, which is still all too ongoing. Israel's response to this conflict has shaped its own identity and has led the country down a militaristic, far-right path that is far from the dream Alex and many other Jews harboured for it. Alex was right to take a stand against de Gaulle's cruel comments about Jews in regard to Israel's actions in the Six-Day War; how Israel reacted after the war led many others to say similar things and worse.

WHEN I FIRST FOUND the shoebox at the back of my grandmother's closet, there was only one object that made immediate sense to me. I didn't know who the bespectacled man in the photos was, or what that metal plate saying '*GLASS, Prisonnier Cambrai*' referred to, or why the Red Cross was writing to Sala in 1944 – but I knew exactly how my quiet, self-effacing grandmother acquired a Picasso drawing. That's because it came from the one member of the Glass family who was always happy to talk about his achievements and who achieved the kind of things that were written about in history books. What I couldn't understand was why she had it or why she had hidden it in her closet.

Alex introduced Sala to Picasso while she was on a trip to France in the late 1960s, and she was even more excited to meet the artist than Alex was the first time he went to Villa Californie. There is only one photo of her with Picasso and, although he is looking elsewhere while shaking her hand, perhaps for someone a little more interesting than a housewife, she is positively shining with happiness. If meeting

Sala and Picasso.

Picasso was a kind of self-validating success for Alex, for Sala it was proof that there existed a life out there where dreams really did come true, and that life was in Paris. She never said anything, but her trips back to France, which she took every other year or so, must have been almost impossibly painful for her: yes, going to America had possibly saved her life, but she surely looked at Henri and Alex and wondered maybe if she'd stayed whether she, too, would be living glamorous lives like her brothers, instead of being a suburban American housewife. They had been able to take active control over their lives and climbed up the social ladder in ways she'd longed to do too. But her role in life, as a woman from a traditional Jewish background, was to stay in the background, behind her husband.

Chaya's death in 1964 quietly devastated Sala: despite her and her mother's differences, they loved one another very deeply, and being on a different continent when her mother finally passed away in a retirement home in France that Henri and Alex had found for her when she got too old to live on her own in Israel, must have made Sala feel even lonelier. She paid for a death notice in the *New York Times,* even though no one else in America knew who Chaya was.[26] But that didn't matter to Sala, she wanted to make a public statement of her grief and for her mother's death to not pass unnoticed. Shortly after this, Sala went through one of her periodic 'blue' phases, and when Alex heard about this, he asked Picasso for a little sketch that he could send her. Picasso obliged, and he even signed it, which he often omitted to do with sketches, much to the frustration of dealers and collectors.

Until the end of her life, Alex sent Sala pictures, and she loved to brag to visitors about the priceless art her famous brother in Paris gave her. After she died we took down her pictures and out of their frames, and while some of them were worth something – some prints by Soutine, some by Vlaminck – others were worthless posters from art exhibitions. For years I assumed that my grandmother had been deceived by her brother with these posters, but after finding the Picasso in her closet, reading her letters to Alex and Henri and spending so long in Alex's head by reading his memoir, I realised I was too harsh in my judgement, of both Alex and my grandmother. Sala was not self-deluding. She, alone among the Glass siblings, had been happy to go along with Alex's exaggerations, fudges and self-mythologies, because she understood her brother. She knew that he loved his family, and that his ability to show it had its limits, so when Alex revealed something real, it had to be cherished and protected. That's why when he sent her a sketch by Picasso, she didn't hang it up for all to see: she kept it in her closet, where only she knew about it for the rest of her life. Here was real evidence of how extraordinary their lives were, that they had started in a shtetl in Poland, and now he was sending to her home in America a drawing by one of the greatest artists of all time, just for her. It was their secret and her secret, and like so many other things, she kept it that way until she died.

Hadley, Sala and Bill, in about 1980.

13

THE END OF THE GLASS
SIBLINGS

Paris and Miami, 1980s and 1990s

As they entered their fourth decade of marriage, Bill and Sala developed a kind of mutual dependence that could, from certain angles, be seen as love. Sala in particular felt a real marital loyalty to him that ultimately meant she was never at ease, wherever she was: when she was with him, she was dreaming of her family in Paris; when she was in Paris, she fretted about whether Bill had enough to eat at home. She was in a constant battle between her desires and her obligations.

A mutual respect had grown between them: they understood each other and in many ways appreciated one another's qualities as a spouse and parent. And yet, friends would say the two of them could argue over the oxygen in the air, and this was barely an exaggeration: one of their most frequent arguments was over the thermostat in their apartment. It was never too hot for Bill, whereas Sala liked it cool and fresh, and as fast as he would turn the radiator dial up she would turn it down, horrified at how cloyingly claustrophobic he made her home. But in 1973 it looked like he had definitively won the temperature argument when he announced they were moving to Miami, Florida. The family had often gone there on holidays and the reasons Bill loved Miami (the golf, the heat) were the same reasons Sala hated it (the lack of culture, the heat). But she went along with the move. She knew how much he wanted to go and when he was like this there was no arguing against him. It would, after all, be better for his health than the bitter East Coast winters, and maybe there was a part of her that thought, given Bill was now in his seventies, she might not be there for too long.

Once she was there, Miami turned out to have its advantages. She loved their apartment, with the ready-made community inside the building of other older Jewish couples with whom she could play cards and go shopping, and she especially enjoyed the local Jewish delis where she could buy lox and challah. While Bill played golf all day, she made a life for herself, introducing herself to everyone in the building and teaching them backgammon on the beach. When Bill stayed at home in the evenings, she went to the ballet, the theatre and every exhibition of French art. They led busy if separate lives. (She also valiantly maintained her side of the battle of the air temperature, insistently turning the air conditioner up as high as it would go in every room of their apartment, while he would turn it off behind her, barking

Hadley and Bill, in about 1986.

in frustration.) She made a young friend, named Stephanie, who was the same age as her sons, and the two of them liked to go on shopping trips together, during which Sala would try on miniskirts that Stephanie would never have dared to try on herself, and she always looked wonderful. When Stephanie told her one day that she was leaving her husband, despite the disapproval of their friends, Sala looked at the ground and said quietly, 'You have great courage.'

Best of all, their younger son Rich soon also moved to Miami to work as a lawyer. Just as each of the Glass siblings reacted so differently to what they went through during the war, so Sala's sons reacted in their own individual ways to their parents. Sala and Bill poured the love they couldn't give one another into their boys, but whereas Ronald found this at times overbearing and eventually moved overseas, Rich stayed close. Even as a popular bachelor about town, he saw his parents almost every day, and when he went to work during the day as a lawyer, Sala would often come to his apartment to restock his refrigerator. She loved doing this as much as he appreciated that she did it. (The Freeman boys, like the Glass siblings, are an eloquent argument in favour of nature over nurture when it comes to explaining a person's character. Despite having an identical upbringing, Ronald and Rich are in many ways as different as Alex and Jacques.)

What Sala really liked about Miami was the view from her living room. Their apartment was on the seventh floor, and faced the beach. Sala could stand at the window for hours, looking out at the Atlantic Ocean she had crossed so many years ago, gazing back towards her beloved France and home. But a few years after they moved in, a developer built an identical apartment building across the street, between her and the sea, and she watched the progress of the work creeping up closer and closer to her window. One day they were at level pegging, her and the builders. Then the new building was finished, blocking her view of the ocean, and she looked out of the window no more.

Over in Paris, once Danièle's son Alexandre de Betak was too old to be dragged to lunches with Alex Maguy, Henri and Alex saw each other less and less. Sonia and Alex, despite living just a few miles away from one another for most of their lives, never saw one another at all. It was up to Sala, far away in Miami, to hold the disparate pieces of her family together. ('Such *esprit de famille*,' Sonia would grumble when Sala came to Paris and insisted on seeing everyone.) But by the early 1980s even Sala was struggling to hold the family together. She wrote to Henri and Sonia on 15 September 1982:

> Ron wants to buy us an apartment in the building opposite ours, because that building hides our view, so it's logical. Unfortunately, where Ron sees only the positives his father sees only the negatives and says it would be hard to sell ours, with interest rates so high. But, I really want it.
>
> I just heard some terrible news. Terrorists in Lebanon. Princess Grace. What a tragedy. So sad. And how is our Alex Maguy behaving? He ignores me completely. Not a word since May or June. What a disgrace. Still, I miss you all very much.

Sala lost the argument about the apartment, but she won something more important, which was a promise from both her brothers and her sister-in-law that they would all take a holiday together, for the first time in their lives. This became the trip to Deauville, which my parents and sister went on too, and was the first time I met Alex, Henri and Sonia.

Not long after that holiday, the Glasses began to fall apart physically. Henri first, when he was diagnosed with cancer. He was deep into his eighties by now and his health deteriorated quickly. Sonia didn't want him to know what he was

Henri and Sonia in Paris, 1980s.

suffering from, so no one was allowed to mention his illness in front of him, even as Henri was visibly fading away in front of them, and he clearly knew he was dying. Finally, in 1989, Jehuda Glahs, the most studious boy in the Chrzanow shtetl, died. But he was a student to the end: on his bedside table when he died was a 'teach yourself English' book, so that he could talk to my sister and me on our next visit.

The loss of her oldest brother was heartbreaking for Sala, and Alex made it immeasurably worse. When he turned up at Henri's funeral, he pushed past Sala, Ronald, Danièle and the rest of his family and shouted at Sonia.

'You killed my brother!' he yelled, pointing a furious finger at her, shaking off all his family members trying to pull him away. 'I'd have taken him to America where I know the best doctors, but you insisted on staying here and you killed him! He's dead because of you. I will never forgive you!'

Alex had been hating Sonia for so long by this point, he probably no longer even remembered why. He never thought she was worthy of Henri, that was obvious, but the hate went deeper than that. Almost fifty years after Jacques's death, Alex was still blaming his sisters-in-law for taking his brothers away from him. In his mind, if these awful Polish women had just left his family alone, his brothers would have lived for ever.

Danièle's son, Alexandre de Betak, then just twenty-one, jumped up between his grieving grandmother and raging great-uncle. He had always liked Alex, and Alex had liked him, treating him as a surrogate son. But now, Alexandre glared at him. 'Get out of here and never talk to my grand-mother again. You are not a part of our family any more,' Alexandre said.

Alex only saw Sonia, Danièle and her children, Alexandre and Natasha, once more after that: at my bat mitzvah. All of them travelled to London, where I was living by then, but they studiously ignored one another all day. When the photographer asked everyone to come together for a family

Top row: Ann's partner Morty, Ronald Freeman, Alexandre de Betak. Middle row: Richard Freeman, Ann Horowitz, Danièle de Betak, Natasha de Betak, Sonia, Helen Freeman. Bottom row: Hadley Freeman, Nell Freeman.

Hadley and Alex Maguy.

photo, Alex refused to pose with Sonia, so he is the absence in the middle of the family portrait in the garden. Instead, he posed for a photo on his own with me in the living room.

Sala had always assumed she would move back to Paris when Bill died, and, thwarting her to the end, he managed to stay in the ruddiest of health up until his ninetieth birthday. But just as the once strappingly athletic Bill began to weaken with age, and the life Sala had dreamed about for decades was a mere breath away, it was, once again, snatched away from her.

Sala had said to several relatives and friends over the years that her greatest fear was being physically immobile but mentally alert. This happened to a rabbi she knew, who was struck down by cerebral haemorrhage, and although Sala often visited him often in hospital, his fate terrified her: 'God forbid that should happen to me,' she said to Rich. She had been trapped by circumstances for so long, the idea of being constrained even further, and all too aware of the constraints on her, must have been terrifyingly real and horrific. And with bitter inevitability, that is exactly what happened to her.

Where Bill had always been hardy, Sala was delicate, careless with her health and always happier feeding others than herself. She hated anyone fussing over her and regarded any efforts to remedy her ailments as unnecessary and embarrassing. So it was no surprise to her family that she often neglected to take the medicine her doctor prescribed for her high blood pressure. What none of us realised was that this then put her at risk of a stroke, and after a few minor ones she was finally felled by a major one. In one blow, it stilled her body and her tongue. All she could do for the rest of her life was wave her right arm and anxiously repeat the babyish sound 'la'. But her eyes were all too alert, and they wept in frustration.

The last time I saw my grandmother – both of my grandparents, for that matter – was in 1991, not long after my bat mitzvah. My parents took my sister and me to their Miami apartment, which I'd always remembered as elegant, decorated carefully by my grandmother and filled with her art posters. This time I walked into a modern geriatric nightmare. My once seemingly indomitable grandfather was laid out on the sofa, the muscles he'd once been so proud of all wasted away. Now it was the hard knots of his joints that bulged out, visible even through his blanket. My grandmother was even more unrecognisable, her normally perfect lipstick and hair now crooked and askew. She couldn't have looked more unnervingly wrong if she'd been naked. The apartment, which she had always kept meticulously tidy, was cluttered with medical detritus: bottles, charts, packs of tubing, piles of plastic sheeting and two wheelchairs, one for each of them. There also seemed to be about a dozen nurses rushing around, but in truth there were only two, each trying in vain to get their patients to take their pills. And while the rest of us – my parents, my sister, my uncle Rich and I – were dazed by the chaos, my grandparents carried on as usual, which is to say they were quarrelling. Sala sat in an armchair and made do with the little at her disposal, shouting, 'La la la la,' while pointing furiously at Bill with her one mobile arm. Bill, on the sofa, waved his hand impatiently back at her: 'Be quiet, Sala!' he said.

'Look, your grandmother is pointing at your grandfather – she's saying she loves him!' my grandmother's nurse said to my sister and me with a reassuring smile. My sister Nell and I were only, respectively, eleven and thirteen, but we knew: Sala was not telling Bill she loved him. She was saying she blamed him.

Sala had never exactly hidden her unhappiness, but she'd been so good at keeping it in check, ensuring the roil of emotions stayed just beneath her skin. It was terrifying to see all that now unleashed, all the anger, anxiety and frustration that had built up over her lifetime, and not even her sons could calm her down. The only person who could soothe her was Betty, my grandparents' housekeeper who had been with them since they moved to Miami.

'Come on, Sala. Come on,' said Betty, sitting on the armchair, holding her close. And Sala collapsed against her, her eyes closed, like a daughter cleaving to her much longed-for mother.

Bill died the next year, of many things but really just of old age. The fearsome fighter from the Lower East Side had fought until his tenth decade and, in many ways, won. Once his mother could barely afford to give him more than a meal a day, but by the time he died he had more than $1 million in the bank, thanks entirely to his skill at investing and indefatigable work ethic. Life had probably not worked out exactly as he wanted, but he never let it get him down. He had left behind the drag of his origins, made money, had a beautiful wife and successful sons. In his eyes he was a winner, and he was right.

I didn't go to his funeral, because by that point I was in hospital for anorexia. My grandmother might have understood that affliction better than anyone in our family, given that her own relationship with food could be described at best as complicated. But I never spoke to her about it, because she couldn't speak then. My father, of course, went to Bill's funeral, and he and Rich brought Sala, in her wheelchair. She cried throughout the service.

'Look how sad she is that her husband died,' other people whispered in awe. But she wasn't sad that Bill had died. She was sad that the day she had waited for had finally come, and it didn't matter any more. All those fantasies of living in Paris, travelling to London, to Israel – all gone.

Two years later, she had a massive stroke and was rushed to hospital, where doctors stuck so many tubes in her she looked more like a science experiment than the woman she was, adhering to the American medical establishment's belief that maintaining life is more important than considering what quality that life will have. Rich was at the hospital one afternoon with Betty, my grandparents' housekeeper, and the doctors said she was crashing and they would need to revive her again. He was about to sign the papers when Betty put her hand on his.

'Let her go, Richard,' she said.

Rich loved his mother more than anything on earth, but he also knew Betty was right. So he went to Sala's bed and held her close. He whispered that we all knew how much she had sacrificed for all of us, that she had given up her life so that we could all live. That we loved her, and he kissed her goodbye, from all of us. For the first time in God knows how long, Rich saw her make a small smile. And then she was free.

Few get good endings, and Sala definitely did not get the one she deserved. She had wanted to die in Europe, the continent of her birth and where her heart still was. Instead, she had a hideous protracted death in an American hospital, far from the place she still thought of as home, fifty years after leaving it behind. As children, my sister and I used to whisper to one another at night about how we wouldn't exist if it hadn't been for Hitler, and my father told me he used to think about that too. Because if it hadn't been for the war, Sala would never have married Bill and the rest of us wouldn't even be cells or ether. For a while this added another dimension to my already well-hewn sense of Jewish guilt: I lived only because of the pain and loss of others, and the pain of one person in particular – Sala. However, she would not have ever seen it that way. To her, our existence was what gave her loss, and her life, meaning. Her sons and grandchildren were not compensation for what she left behind; we were the explanation for it. She asked for nothing as a reward for her sacrifice, because she never asked for anything. She stayed on the side of the room, against the walls, in the shadows, loving us, erasing herself and her needs. But the one thing that she wanted, and expected, was to live back in Europe one day, with us, with Alex, on her own. And ultimately, even that was denied to her, because after giving up her dreams to come to America, her death there was her actual nightmare. Pretty little Sala Glahs, whose father used to buy her frilly dresses from the market, who wanted nothing more than to feel well enough to play with her brothers outside on Kostalista, deserved a better end.

SONIA, on the other hand, managed to have one of the best deaths of all time.

After Henri died, Sonia proved that, despite being in an extremely close and happy marriage for more than half a century, she was more than capable of leading a contented

Sonia with friends.

independent life. She busied herself every day spending time with friends, walking her beloved dogs and, most of all, playing bridge. She occasionally went on bridge cruises – boat trips where she and other like-minded bridge fans played cards all day; she sent back photos of herself flanked by the young and handsome male crew. Sonia had loved Henri dearly, but she was – as everyone knew she would be – fine without him.

Then one day in 1995, she went to her regular bridge game in Paris and brought her daughter Danièle with her. She took her seat at a card table and suddenly had a thought: 'Table seven! That's my lucky number,' she said, turning to her daughter. Then she turned back, keeled over and was instantly dead. Sonia was never one for dragging things out unnecessarily.

Helen, Nell, Ronald and Hadley Freeman with Alex
in Cannes in 1992.

Seven was also Alex's lucky number, but he did not
get quite as lucky a death. He was the last Glass standing,
although by the end he was so frail he could barely stand at
all. Not even those who fought against pogroms and Nazis
can beat old age. The last time my father saw him was in
1999, when Alex summoned him to Paris to visit him. My
father found him sitting in front of his apartment building
on the Avenue Foch, so depleted with age he was like a bal-
loon with half the air taken out. In order for Alex to stand
up and then walk around his beloved private garden, my
father had to support his whole weight, and that amounted
to hardly anything.

Alex died in October 1999. French death announcements in the newspapers are often written in florid and formal language, but Alex's was oddly apt. In *Le Figaro*, on 3 November 1999, a small article appeared, announcing the end of Alex Maguy Glass's 'tormented and ostentatious existence', summing up his beginning and his end. He'd told my father that he wanted to be buried by the Chrzanow Burial Society in Montparnasse Cemetery, alongside other Chrzanovians who had, through the twists of history and geopolitics, died in Paris. In Paris, he was friends with many of the greatest stars of the mid-century. But at heart, he was still little Sender, being cheeky to his family as they walked to synagogue together in Chrzanow, and in the end he wanted to be with the people who reminded him of his father.

Alex de Betak and Hadley, in Los Angeles
at a fashion event Alex produced.

14

THE NEXT GENERATIONS –
An Epilogue

Paris, the twenty-first century

THE GLASSES spanned the twentieth century, from Henri's birth in 1901 to Alex's death in 1999. They lived through probably the most dramatic shifts ever endured by the world's Jews, from the Holocaust to American immigration to the founding of Israel to assimilation, and their lives reflected it all. On an individual level, they took chances that are unimaginable to their children and grandchildren today, because we live in comfort that they created for us. But once they all died, whatever thin strands that connected us fell away entirely: Danièle and her children seemed to drift away from us – or us from them – and I certainly didn't know anyone connected to the Ornstein cousins. Part of this was undoubtedly laziness – my father can be especially bad at keeping in touch with extended family members – but it felt also like a reaction to the Glasses themselves.

There have been many studies about inherited trauma, looking at whether children of, for example, prisoners of war die earlier than children of soldiers who evade capture.[1] One study claiming that Holocaust survivors pass on trauma to their children and grandchildren through epigenetics[2] received a huge amount of excited coverage when it was published in 2016. But it was also criticised for, among other things, its tiny sample size,[3] and the shakiness of the science[4] (trans-generational epigenetic inheritance is well-established in plants, but decidedly less so in humans). I haven't studied science since I was sixteen, so my scepticism about the relevance of genetically inherited trauma to my family's story is based on something far more basic than epigenetics: knowing what my family is like.

The second generation – Ronald, Rich and Danièle – grew up with an instinctive understanding that their parents did not want to talk about the past, and it wasn't genetic inheritance that gave them this knowledge. They learned it from how hastily their mothers turned off the TV when Holocaust documentaries came on, how sharply their fathers said, 'Why do you ask these questions?' Many Holocaust survivors celebrated their survival by clutching their Jewish identity even closer, but the Glasses were different. Henri, Sonia and Sala assimilated, and so did their children, because that is what their parents encouraged them to do. Even Alex, who left many of his paintings to Israel and proudly kept his Yiddish accent, was hardly religious. The only time I ever saw him in a synagogue was at my bat mitzvah. Within their lifetimes, they threw off the ties of Orthodoxy and raised children who couldn't even read Hebrew. This was as much to do with pragmatism as it was to do with trauma: they wanted their children to be safe, and they knew from their own experiences that meant not being overtly Jewish. The past to them was ugly and painful – they were too close to it to see that it was also triumphant – and therefore to be pushed to the back of the closet, like a shoebox of yellowing photos. But what binds a family together if not the past? Blood is not thick enough, especially if the extended family is scattered on entirely different continents. Shared history is the stuff that sticks.

As the Glasses themselves knew, suppressing the past does not mean you don't think about it. This is the weird irony about Jewish assimilation, and also the joke about it: all these Jews living totally western lives, eating ham and doing Christmas, yet always talking about the Holocaust. Well, it's a lot harder to dismiss history than religious doctrine, because one is real and one is not. I cannot remember a time when I was not aware that the only reason I am alive is that my grandmother had to give up everything to escape the Nazis, and I felt in some vague way crushed by it. There is a neat divide in my family between those who are quietly haunted by the stories in this book (my father Ronald, Danièle's daughter Natasha, me) and those who are less so (my uncle Rich, Danièle's son Alexandre, my sister Nell). Yet we all reacted to our family's past the same way, which was to let the family drift apart. This was never the intention of the Glasses, who loved each other, but we took our cues from them: if reminders of the past should be pushed away, didn't that include our own family?

But as perhaps Jews know better than most, you can never entirely escape your past.

In the late 1990s, my parents became friends with a Jewish American woman who lived in Paris, named Flora Lewis, then in her seventies. Flora was an extremely impressive woman, a long-time foreign correspondent for the *New York Times*, and the first woman to be given her own column by that paper. But early triumphs are no protection against the cruelties of old age and when my parents met Flora she was facing eviction from her beloved flat in Saint-Germain-des-Prés, because her building had been bought and she could not afford to buy her apartment from the new owner. So my father offered to buy it and Flora would stay on as his tenant. This arrangement lasted until Flora's death in 2002, at which point my family moved in.

It wasn't until we walked in that we realised that the flat backs onto the École des Beaux-Arts, the school where my grandmother studied textile design before she went to America.

Shortly before we took possession of the apartment, I got my first job. I'd known since I was a teenager that I wanted to be a journalist, but while I was at university a strange and more specific idea took hold.

'I think it would be fun to write about fashion,' I said to my mother one morning when I was about twenty, as I read a style article in the *Guardian*.

'Mmm really, sweetie?' she replied uncertainly. But if my mother was surprised by my sudden interest in fashion then I was even more so. Up until then, the only appeal clothes had for me was how much I could hide my body within them, and my wardrobe largely consisted of long black skirts and shapeless long-sleeved tops, all bought from Camden and Kensington Markets. But as I slowly began to slough off the anorexia that had dominated my teenage years and blanketed my entire worldview, I realised there was some kernel in me, that I could neither explain nor even entirely understand, that was genuinely interested in fashion. Like Sala, like Alex, I too wanted to see beauty.

After university, I got a job on the *Guardian*'s fashion desk and helped to cover the shows in Paris, always staying in our family apartment. Every time I walked out of the apartment to go to a fashion show, I was walking in my grandmother's footsteps, going to the same shows – Dior, Rochas, Lanvin – that she loved to read about in the magazines Henri and Alex sent to her in America from Paris.

Then one day, at the Dior show in the Tuileries, I felt a hand on my shoulder.

'Aren't you my cousin?'

It was Alexandre de Betak, now known as Alex, and he was working as a fashion show producer. He had seen my name on the list of invited press, which is how he recognised me. He gave me a hug, but I felt a little shy, self-conscious about all the big-name fashion editors watching us, wondering why the cool show producer was talking to this lowly fashion writer. He didn't seem to notice, and he took down my phone number. I watched him run around the show, making sure all the editors were happy in their seats, the lighting was right, the flowers were perfect, the sound levels were correct, the models were ready to walk on. It was like stepping into the anecdotes my father used to tell about watching Alex Maguy getting his fashion shows ready. Today Alex de Betak is one of the biggest independent show producers in the world, with clients that include Calvin Klein, Yves Saint Laurent, Nike and H&M. But probably his closest and most loyal client is Dior, just as Alex Maguy's closest friend in the fashion world was Christian Dior. Neither Alex de Betak nor the Dior company knew of that connection until I started researching this book.

Not long after meeting Alex, I got an email at work: 'I know we haven't met but I think we're cousins. Could we meet?'

It was from someone called Philippe Ornstein, the son of Armand, the former little boy hidden in the woods who had grown up to help found Daniel Hechter. Philippe was then working in London at the fashion company Mulberry and he had seen my name on a list of fashion writers, which prompted him to get in touch. As soon as we met it felt like he had always been a part of my life. For hours we sat in a random bar in Soho and there was no time for awkward pauses because we were too busy talking and laughing; it was like the best first date of my life, but it was even better because I already knew he would be in my life for ever, because he was family.

The third generation found one another through fashion, or the *schmatte* trade as our grandparents would have called it when they were working for next to nothing as furriers, leather tanners, textile designers and dressmakers in the Marais. Alex de Betak was introduced to fashion by Alex Maguy, just as Philippe was by his father and I was by my grandmother. We are living proof that the past holds on to you in ways that go beyond science, and although the Glass siblings had long since died by the time their grandchildren met, we instinctively carried on their traditions.

The more frequently I came to Paris for the shows, the closer I became to my French family and the more of them I met. As we came together, we shared what little we knew of the past and I could see all of us getting a keener interest in it, and a sharper awareness of our roots, especially as I started to know more of my Ornstein cousins, descendants of those who had escaped to Israel. Alex de Betak and I see one another especially often and we still say how much Sala would have loved to have come to the shows with us, just as she once did with Alex Maguy.

Sala had dreamed of moving back to Paris, of being with her family, having lunches with them in cafés, revelling in the glamour of the French fashion world, walking among the boutiques in Saint-Germain. She never got to do that – but I do. Because she gave up everything, I get to live her dream. I think of her every time I walk out of my parents' flat and down the rue Bonaparte in Saint-Germain, past the gates of her old school, to the café to have my breakfast before going

to a fashion show. And I think of all of them every time my train from London pulls into the Gare du Nord, how they arrived in Paris by train almost a hundred years ago, knowing almost no one and owning less. How far they went in their lives, how politics and fate and familial dynamics tore them apart, and how we came back together in the end.

Just outside Jerusalem there is a tree for Jacques. Alex and Henri planted it in his memory around the time their mother moved there. They planted it because they remembered how much he loved to hide in the woods as a boy, and how for him – and all of them – trees were a source of comfort, giving them a place to hide as children from the poverty and the pogroms. Closer to my home, and his, Jacques's name is inscribed on the wall of names outside the Shoah Memorial in Paris: 'Jacob Glass', it reads, changing the name of the boy born Jakob Glahs, who became the man called Jacques Glass, one final time. He is listed there alongside the 76,000 other Jews, including 11,000 children who were deported from France. 'Take the time to look at a beautiful painting. Don't be afraid, just enter the painting, let it embrace you, like music. Life is worth the trouble of fighting death,' are the last lines of Alex's memoir, and I try always to take the time to look at Jacques's wall. It is in the Marais, just a few minutes' walk from where Jacques lived with Alex, and where Chaya lived with Sala, steps away from where Jacques boarded a minibus and was shipped off to Pithiviers. It's a lovely, peaceful part of the city now, and I walk through it often. I stop in to see Jacques's name, maybe make a small nod, and then I'll walk out, following Henri, Jacques, Alex and Sala's footsteps for a little while. Then I diverge, walking my own way as I cross the river, and go home.

ACKNOWLEDGEMENTS

I DEDICATED THIS BOOK to my father, Ron, because he is really its co-author. For two decades he has travelled with me around the world on research trips, acting as a tour guide in Long Island, a translator in France, a historian in Narvik and a travel companion in Poland. He put his faith in me when I showed little evidence of deserving it to tell the most intimate stories of his childhood, enduring years of nosey questions about some of the people he loved most in his life. I hope I have justified the trust he placed in me; he has always far exceeded any common definition of fatherly support.

I am also very grateful to my uncle Rich, who was extraordinarily generous with his memories and photos. A huge thank you, too, to his wife, my aunt Lynn, and their daughter, Gabrielle, for not just enduring my trips to Florida to pester Rich with more questions, but also for arranging interviews for me with Bill and Sala's friends in Miami, providing me with new perspectives of my grandparents.

By writing about my family in the past I got to know

my family in the present. This is especially true of Danièle, Alexandre and Natasha de Betak. Before, I hardly knew them at all; now I consider them among my closest relatives. They provided me with insights into the Glass family's life in France, and especially Henri and Sonia's lives. They have been unflagging supporters of this book, even at times when I felt decidedly flagged.

Anne-Laurence Goldberg is another relative I am lucky enough to have become close to through the writing of this book. She is an indefatigably cheerful travel companion – the best kind of travel companion – and her wonderful collection of letters and photos is a treasure trove of historical documents.

Armand Ornstein has been putting up with my questions about his past for so long it's a testament to him that he still agrees to meet me for dinner. I am very grateful to him for his constant support, and for putting me in touch with his sister Shoshanna and her daughter Idit Bloch, both of whom helped me to make sense of a shadowy past.

On the American side, Ann Horowitz has known me since I was born and she shared with me her thoughts and memories about the Freiman family. She put me in touch with Herb Freiman, and our time together in Long Island didn't just help me put that part of my family in context, but was a delightful experience I'll never forget. My sadly belated thanks, too, to Herb's sister, Eleanor, who spoke to me about the family shortly before she died. Charlie Reich, the grandson of Olga, great-nephew of Mila, was another lovely discovery I made through the writing of this book, and I am grateful to him for his kindness and insights.

Aside from my family, there is no one who has contributed more to this book than the brilliant academic, Daniel Lee. I met Daniel at a conference about the Resistance in London, and I don't know what good deed I did in a previous life to deserve this stroke of luck, but there is no question that this book would not have been written without him. He travelled with me all around France, gave up his holidays to research my family in dusty archives, put their story into historical context for me and pretty much made all the best discoveries that have gone into this book. More than that, he became a true friend, even though I consistently failed to live by his dictum: 'Historians don't stop for lunch'.

Jona Cummings, aka the Jew Whisperer, who coaxes memoirs out of neurotic Jews, helped me enormously with my research and, at least as importantly, gave me the confidence that I actually had a book here when I tortured myself with self-doubt. My friend and colleague Jonathan Freedland introduced me to Jona, and for that, and much more, I thank Jonathan.

I was inspired to write this book after writing an essay about my grandmother for US *Vogue*, at the encouragement of my editor there, Eve MacSweeney. I thank her and Anna Wintour for editing and publishing it.

The people in this book had a great number of friends, and I am very grateful to those who spoke to me for this project, some of whom have since passed away: William and Marcia Rappaport, Sue Guiney, Betty Laster, Dorothy Berger, Stephanie Freed, Nicole Rivoire, Ilie Wachs, Catherine Amidon and Jeanne Gustave. Chien Chung Pei and Li Chung Pei were very generous with their time in helping me to establish Alex Maguy's friendship with their father, I.M. Pei. My thanks to Emma Cobb for her help in contacting them.

I made use of many researchers and translators around the world and shamelessly pillaged the minds of academics far more brilliant than me. These include Simon Kitson, Matthew Cobb, Martin and Aga Kahn, Ludivine Broch, Agata Jujeczka, Camille Chevalier, Jane Winfield, Hugo Sharp and Beate Rozek. Thanks to Oriole Cullen for her insights into the life of Christian Dior, and for Laura Mitchell at the Victoria & Albert Museum in London for putting me in touch with her. I also owe a debt to Callie Adams at the Christian Dior press office in London. Isabelle Rouge-Ducos, Violette Andres and Emelie Bouvard at the Picasso Museum in Paris talked to me about Picasso's life and kindly arranged for me to look through his correspondence with Alex Maguy. Robert Picandet at the Resistance Museum in Saint-Gervais-d'Auvergne (Puy-de-Dôme) opened up a window into a part of Alex's life he had always kept shut to the rest of us. The Tenement Museum in New York helped me to understand the Lower East Side when Bill lived there, and the museum's director of curatorial affairs, David Favoloro, patiently explained to me what the Freiman family's day-to-day life was like. Alex Maws and Martin Winstone from the Holocaust Educational Trust talked to me about the evolving attitudes of different countries towards the Holocaust, and Alex especially has been a source of support and encouragement. Alisa Friedman, Noa Rosenberg, Yafa Goldfinger and Sophia Berry-Liftshitz at the Tel Aviv Museum, and Michal Marmary and Dr Adina Kamien-Kazhdan at the Israel Museum in Jerusalem kindly tracked down for me the paintings that Alex donated in his lifetime. Joshua Rothman at the *New Yorker* dug out an archival article about Alex for me, despite having more than enough to do in his full-time job. Richard Nelsson and Luc Torres at the *Guardian* were similarly patient with my bizarre requests (a review of a fashion show from seventy years ago in Denmark? No problem!). For archival research, I relied on the Mémorial de la Shoah, L'École des Beaux-Arts, Les Archives Nationales in Fontainebleau and Pierrefitte, les Archives de la Ville, La Fondation Pour la Mémoire de la Déportation, all in Paris, as well as Les Archives Départementales des Alpes-Maritimes in Nice, Yad Vashem in Jerusalem and the British Library in London. I am indebted to the archivists at CERCIL in Orléans, especially Nathalie Grenon, for providing me with details of Jacques's time in Pithiviers.

The following people provided invaluable support, advice and friendship during the writing of this book: Helen Freeman, Nell Freeman-Romilly, the Macrae family, Carol Miller, Jonathan Freedland, George Morton-Jack, Jess Cartner-Morley, Alex Needham, Oliver Wainwright, Jon Henley, Marina Hyde, Roland Woodward, Lauren Collins,

Ruthie Rogers, Hugh Hamrick, Adam Phillips and Arthur Ferdinand Freeman. My agent, Georgia Garrett at RCW, and my editors, Louise Haines and Sarah Thickett at 4th Estate in London and Emily Graff at Simon & Schuster in New York, never lost faith with this project, or with me. I am extremely lucky to have such wonderful women on my team.

My editors, past and present, at the *Guardian* have long learned to tolerate my wild-goose projects and pet obsessions. I am especially grateful to Katherine Viner, Melissa Denes, Kira Cochrane, Malik Meer, Ian Katz and Catherine Shoard for their enduring forbearance.

My partner Andy Bull was almost certainly the only sportswriter at the US Open in 2019 doing line edits on a chapter about Auschwitz. More than anyone, Andy made me believe this book was possible, and he provided not just emotional encouragement but practical support, too, not least looking after our children while I ran off again to spend my days with the dead. He edited every draft line by line and solved all my seemingly unsolvable structural problems. His love – and willingness to shoulder the domestic duties – made this book possible.

And finally, I thank my children: Felix and Max, who always know exactly when to come into my study and tell me it's time to stop working, and Betty, who was my in utero companion during much of the writing of this book and, with perfect timing, arrived the week after I finally finished it. This is the story of your past. You will write the future.

END NOTES

Introduction

1 Richard Allen Greene, 'A Shadow Over Europe', CNN.com, November 2018.
2 Elian Peltier, 'Sharp Rise in Anti-Semitic Acts in France Stokes Old Fears', *New York Times*, 12 February 2019.
3 'Anti-Semitic Incidents Remained at Near Historic Levels in 2018; Attacks Against Jews More Than Doubled', ADL press release, New York, 2019.
4 Maggie Astor, 'Holocaust is Fading From Memory, Survey Finds', *New York Times*, 12 April 2018.
5 Greene, 'A Shadow Over Europe'.

1. The Glahs Family

1 'Chrzanow: The Life and Destruction of a Jewish Shtetl', Chrzanower Young Men's Association, 1989 jewishgen.org/yizkor/chrazanow/chr100.html.
2 Lukasz Dulowski, 'The Jewish City of the Dead', *Przelom* newspaper, 28 March 2001.
3 Ibid.
4 Dr Itzchak Schwarzbart, 'Chrzanow: The Life and Destruction of a Jewish Shtetl', trans. Jonathan Boyarin, JewishGen.org. 1989.

5 Ibid.

6 It's very possible there were at least two more Ornstein cousins, but I couldn't verify their births.

7 Schwarzbart, 'Chrzanow'.

8 Reuben is the son of Jacob in the Old Testament and so is traditionally translated as 'son of Jacob'.

9 Reb Moyshe Bochner, 'A Tear for my Father', JewishGen.org.

10 Schwarzbart, 'Chrzanow'.

11 Harrison Fluss and Landon Frim, 'Aliens, Antisemitism and Academia', *Jacobin* magazine, March 2017.

12 On 5 October 2018 President Trump tweeted that the women protesting against Brett Kavanaugh's nomination to the Supreme Court were 'paid for by Soros and others'.

13 '[Soros] wants to transform Hungary into an immigrant country', from 'Hungary says EU's "irresponsible" migrant policy poses threat to Jews', Reuters, 16 April 2018.

14 'Farage Criticised for Using Anti-Semitic Themes to Criticise Soros', Peter Walker, *The Guardian*, 12 May 2019.

15 Peter Walker, 'Nigel Farage Under Fire Over "Anti-Semitic Tropes" on Far-Right US Talkshow', *Guardian*, 6 May 2019.

16 Agnieszka Cahn, 'A Critical Analysis of Adam Doboszynski's March on Myslenice in 1936', 2011.

17 Between 1921 and 1925, Jews made up 26.9 per cent of the German Polytechnic in Prague and 3.1 per cent of the Czech Technical University, both of which Jehuda attended.

18 Paul Hanebrink, *A Specter Haunting Europe*, Harvard University Press, 2018.

19 Yizkor Book Project, Jewishgen.org.

20 Schwarzbart, 'Chrzanow'.

21 Yizkor Book Project, Jewishgen.org.

22 Ibid.

23 Schwarzbart, 'Chrzanow'.

24 Five months after this bill was passed, after international outcry about this law, Duda downgraded it from a criminal offence to a civil one. So it's still wrong to suggest Poland was complicit with the Nazis, but you probably won't go to jail for saying so.

25 Alex Duval Smith, 'Polish Move to Strip Holocaust Expert of Award Sparks Protest', *Observer*, 14 February 2016.

26 Associated Press, 'Holocaust Scholar Questioned on Claim that Poles Killed more Jews than Germans in the War', *Guardian*, 14 April 2016.

27 Edna Friedberg, 'The Truth About Poland's Role in the Holocaust', *Atlantic*, 6 February 2018.

28 Editorial, 'The European Union Must Stand Up to Polish Nationalism', *New York Times*, 28 February 2018.

29 Tom Porter, 'Polish Official Claims Jews Were Passive in the Face of Nazi Violence', *Newsweek*, 10 February 2018.

30 Christian Davies, 'Poland's Holocaust Law Triggers Tide of Abuse Against Auschwitz Museum', *Guardian*, 7 May 2018.

31 James Masters, 'Polish Prosecutor: "Auschwitz" Football Chants Are Not Anti-Semitic', cnn.com.

2. The Glass Siblings

1 Nancy L. Green, *The Pletzl of Paris: Jewish Immigrant Workers in the Belle Epoque*, Holmes & Meier, New York and London, 1986.

2 Of the rest, 112,000 went to Canada, 150,000 to Argentina, 210,000 to England and 2.65 million to the United States (Ioan Mackenzie James, *Driven to Innovate: A Century of Jewish Mathematicians and Physicists*, Peter Lang, 2009).

3 Jacques Adler, *The Jews of Paris and the Final Solution*, Oxford University Press, 1989.

4 David H. Weinberg, *A Community on Trial: The Jews of Paris in the 1930s*, University of Chicago Press, 1977.

5 Vicki Caron, *Uneasy Asylum: France and the Jewish Refugee Crisis, 1933–1942*, Stanford University Press, 2002. The Aliens Act 1905 was written specifically to curtail eastern European Jewish immigrants allowed into the United Kingdom. It was amended in 1914 and 1920, imposing even more stringent restrictions which were only partly lifted in the 1930s. Similarly, the 1924 Immigration Act was conceived for the same purpose in America.

6 Weinberg, *A Community on Trial*.

7 Green, *Pletzl of Paris*.

8 M.K. Dzrewanowski, *Poland in the Twentieth Century*, Columbia University Press, 1977.

9 The first country in the world to liberate Jews was, ironically enough, Poland, 500 years earlier.

10 Green, *Pletzl of Paris*.

11 Vicki Caron, *The Path to Vichy: Anti-Semitism in France in the 1930s*, Center for Advanced Holocaust Studies, 2005.

12 Ibid.

13 Quoted in Paula E. Hyman, *The Jews of Modern France*, University of California Press, 1998.

14 Green, *Pletzl of Paris*.

15 William Wiser, *The Twilight Years: Paris in the 1930s*, Carroll and Graf, 2000.

3. Henri

1 Vicki Caron, *Uneasy Asylum: France and the Jewish Refugee Crisis, 1933–1942*, Stanford University Press, 2002.

2 Ibid.

3 David H. Weinberg, *A Community on Trial: The Jews of Paris in the 1930s*, University of Chicago Press, 1977.

4 Paula E. Hyman, *The Jews of Modern France*, University of California Press, 1998.

5 Jacques Adler, *The Jews of Paris and the Final Solution*, Oxford University Press, 1989.

6 Weinberg, *A Community on Trial*.

7 Ibid.

8 Adler, *Jews of Paris*.

9 One of the weirder background noises going on as I wrote this book was the seemingly never-ending obsession of former British politician and now somewhat dimmed left-wing firebrand, Ken Livingstone, and his certainty that Hitler 'supported Zionism' when he came to power in 1933. According to Livingstone, because Hitler supported getting the Jews out of Europe, this

meant he supported Zionism, as if Jews going to Israel of their own accord is analogous to Jews being persecuted and expelled, with all their worldly goods confiscated. Livingstone's obvious mistake was to conflate self-determination and freedom of movement with ethnic cleansing. Livingstone finally quit the Labour Party in May 2018, two years after he developed what I would call Hitler Tourette's and became incapable of talking about anything but Hitler's alleged Zionism.

10 Hyman, *Jews of Modern France*.

11 Ari Yashar, 'Shocking Figures Cite 85% Assimilation in Europe', israelnationnews.com.

12 In 1939, 9.5 million Jews lived in Europe. In 1945 the Nazis had shrunk this number down to 3.8 million. Today, it stands at about 2 million (Pew Research).

13 A foreign Jewish woman studying at the Sorbonne in this period wasn't as unusual as it might sound. In the early 1930s the Sorbonne had 14,500 students, 41 per cent of whom were women and 30 per cent of whom were foreign.

4. Jacques

1 AP, *Times of Israel*, 10 February 2018.

2 For example, in 'Is *Schindler's List* Fatally Flawed?' (*Jewish Chronicle*, 27 March 2013), Nathan Abrams argues that the film 'serves to embed a narrative of Jewish weakness and passivity, in which Jews were nearly always portrayed as undeserving victims. From this point of view, then, *Schindler's List* is not about the Holocaust or the Jews at all, but a biopic of Schindler and his conversion from ambivalent antihero to righteous gentile.' Arguing that a film that is called *Schindler's List* is too much about Oskar Schindler feels like a criticism in search of a point. The Jews *were* undeserving victims and given that they were trapped in Poland in the 1930s and 1940s, powerless and facing unimaginable brutality, arguing that they looked too 'weak' or 'passive' for the critic's liking, flirts weirdly close to victim blaming. As anyone who has read any books about the Krakow

Ghetto knows (and the first half of Roman Polanski's autobiography, *Roman by Polanski*, is not a bad place to start), the Jews were weak, because they were weakened by starvation and they were unarmed but up against the Nazis' military power. The truth is, Schindler did save their lives, they would have been killed without him, and not only is there nothing shameful about that but it is ahistorical to argue otherwise.

3   In 1976 an Air France flight 139 was hijacked mid-journey between Tel Aviv and Paris by members of the Popular Front for the Liberation of Palestine and the German Revolutionary Cells, and diverted to Uganda. Michel acted as the translator and mediator between the hostages and captors. He persuaded the main hijacker, Wilfred Bose, to start releasing hostages, including Michel's own son, Olivier, then twelve. When Michel himself was eventually released he was able to give Mossad details of the hijackers' compound and their daily habits, all of which was invaluable to the rescue mission. Michel wrote about this in his autobiography and Saul David writes about it in more detail in his book, *Operation Thunderbolt* (Black Bay Books, 1982).

4   Michel Cojot-Goldberg, *Namesake*, Yale University Press, 1982.

5   Vicki Caron, *Uneasy Asylum: France and the Jewish Refugee Crisis, 1933–1942*, Stanford University Press, 2002.

6   David Weinberg, *A Community on Trial: The Jews of Paris in the 1930s*, University of Chicago Press, 1977.

7   Marlise Simons, 'Chirac Affirms France's Guilt in Fate of Jews', *New York Times*, 17 July 1995.

8   Albert Sarraut was Prime Minister of France for, first, one month, October–November 1933, then again for the slightly longer term of five months, from January 1936 to June 1936.

9   Caron, *Uneasy Asylum*.

10 In 1940, Sarraut would vote in favour of Marshal Pétain's government drawing up a new constitution, thus helping to establish Vichy France.

11 Caron, *Uneasy Asylum*.

12 Weinberg, *Community on Trial*.

13 yadvashem.org

14 Combattantvolontairejuif.org.
15 Sergeant-Major Frederick Read, *A War Fought Behind the Wire: A Soldier's Tale of Life in the British Army, 1925–1947*.
16 Robert Satloff, *Among the Righteous*, PublicAffairs, 2007.
17 Jean Edward Smith, *The Liberation of Paris*, Simon & Schuster, 2019.
18 Michael R. Marrus and Robert O. Paxton, *Vichy France and the Jews*, Stanford University Press, 1995.
19 Ibid.
20 Ibid.
21 Sharon Waxman, '1940 Jewish Census Reopens French Sore', *Chicago Tribune*, 30 December 1991.

5. Alex

1 Marie-France Pochna, *Christian Dior: The Biography*, Overlook Press, 2008.
2 *Dior by Dior: The Autobiography of Christian Dior*, V&A Publications, 2007.
3 Drusilla Beyfus, 'René Gruau: A New Look at the Influential Dior Illustrator', *Daily Telegraph*, 23 October 2010.
4 Although both Dior and Gruau worked for Alex in Paris, according to Natasha Fraser Cavassoni's book, *Monsieur Dior Once Upon a Time*, they didn't actually meet one another until all three of them fled south during the war.
5 David H. Weinberg, *A Community on Trial: The Jews of Paris in the 1930s*, University of Chicago Press, 1977.
6 Richard D. Sonn, 'Jews, Expatriate Artists, and Political Radicalism in Interwar France', University of Arkansas, 2009.
7 Douglas Porch, *The French Foreign Legion: A Complete History of the Legendary Fighting Force*, HarperCollins, 1991.
8 Robert Gildea, *Fighters in the Shadows: A New History of the French Resistance*, Faber & Faber, 2015.
9 André-Paul Comor, *L'Épopée de la 13ième Demi-Brigade de la Légion Étrangère 1940–1945*, Nouvelle Editions Latines, 1998.
10 Commendation signed by Charles de Gaulle, 6 April 1945.

11 Oddmund Joakimsen, *Narvik 1940: Nazi Germany's First Setback During World War Two*, Nordland Red Cross War Museum.
12 Ibid.
13 Ibid.
14 Gildea, *Fighters in the Shadows*.

6. Sara

1 http://www.worldfuturefund.org/wffmaster/Reading/Hitler%20 Speeches/Hitler%20Speech%201937.01.30.html
2 Vicki Caron, *Uneasy Asylum: France and the Jewish Refugee Crisis, 1933–1942*, Stanford University Press, 2002.
3 Because I couldn't track down their descendants I have not used their real names.

7. Bill

1 Annie Polland and Daniel Soyer, *Emerging Metropolis: New York Jews in the Age of Immigration, 1840–1920*, New York University Press, 2015.
2 Ande Manners, *Poor Cousins*, Fawcett, 1973.
3 Ibid.
4 Polland and Soyer, *Emerging Metropolis*.
5 Rose Cohen, *Out of the Shadow: A Russian Jewish Girlhood on the Lower East Side*, Cornell University Press, 1995.
6 Polland and Soyer. *Emerging Metropolis*.
7 The Triangle Shirtwaist factory fire of 1911.
8 *New York Times*, 6 January 1900.
9 *Mail and Express*, 17 October 1900.
10 Arthur Minturn Chase, 'Children of the Street', *Outlook* magazine, 27 July 1912.
11 Deborah Dash Moore, *At Home in America: Second Generation New York Jews*, Columbia University Press, 1981.
12 Madison Grant, *The Passing of the Great Race; or The Racial Basis of European History*, 1916.

13 FBI, Hate Crime Statistics, https://ucr.fbi.gov/hate-crime/2016.

14 Suman Raghunatham, 'Trump's Xenophobic Vision of America is Inciting Racist Violence', *Nation*, 27 January 2018.

15 Pankaj Mishra, 'Watch This Man', *London Review of Books*, 3 November 2011.

16 Polland and Soyer, *Emerging Metropolis*.

17 A term from the Jim Crow laws, which classified anyone with black ancestry as black.

18 Jedediah Purdy, 'Environmentalism's Racist History', *New Yorker*, 13 August 2015.

19 Alex Ross, 'How American Racism Influenced Hitler', *New Yorker*, 30 April 2018. Ross also writes about how 'America's knack for maintaining an air of robust innocence in the wake of mass death [during slavery] struck Hitler as an example to be emulated.'

20 Polland and Soyer, *Emerging Metropolis*.

21 Even as late as 1957, my father's university, Lehigh in Pennsylvania, had a strict 10 per cent Jewish student quota.

22 Howard M. Sachar, *A History of the Jews in the Modern World*, Vintage, 2005.

23 It was thanks to certain individuals that the rot was, if not entirely reversed, then at least slowed. One especially notable individual was Franklin D. Roosevelt, who became President in 1933 and had no tolerance for old bigotries. To head up his New Deal programme, FDR installed two sons of Jewish immigrants, Louis D. Brandeis and Felix Frankfurter, who themselves then helped to find other Jews who worked to implement the New Deal. Roosevelt believed that no person of talent should be overlooked, and especially not in the early 1930s, when the country was so desperately in need of help. Around 4,000 Jews worked in the US government in the 1930s, 'an unprecedented number for any Western government' (Sachar, *History of the Jews*) and for his re-election campaign in 1936 FDR got 86 per cent of the Jewish vote.

8. Henri and Sonia

1 Jacques Adler, *The Jews of Paris and the Final Solution*, Oxford University Press, 1989.
2 Ibid.
3 Jean Guéhenno, *Diary of the Dark Years 1940–1944: Collaboration, Resistance and Daily Life in Occupied Paris*, Oxford University Press, 2014.
4 Ibid.
5 Marie-Madeleine Fourcade, *Noah's Ark: The Secret Underground*, Zebra Books, 1974.
6 Ibid.
7 Bousquet enjoyed a heady career after the war. Initially he was, like most Vichy officials, convicted of '*Indignité national*', and sentenced. But – also like most Vichy officials – that sentence was soon reduced as France hurriedly tried to move on as quickly as possible and pretend no Frenchmen had committed any actual crimes. Bousquet went on to make a name for himself in journalism and he became especially close to François Mitterrand. But the then President of France was forced to end that friendship when some rather inconvenient allegations about Bousquet's past came to light. Thanks to Serge Klarsfeld's tenacity, the myth that Bousquet was merely an innocent official in Vichy was shattered in the 1980s when evidence was produced that he personally had been in charge of deporting Jewish children to their deaths. Before Bousquet stood trial, he was shot and killed in front of his home in 1993 by Christian Didier, who proudly took credit for the murder. Didier was sentenced to ten years in prison for the killing, but his real crime was scuppering what would have been the first trial of a French citizen for crimes against humanity. Bousquet's trial would have been an extraordinary beginning to France reckoning with its Vichy past. Serge Klarsfeld, 'Nous n'attendons rien de ce procès', *l'Humanité*, 6 November 1995.
8 http://maitron-fusilles-40-44.univ-paris1.fr/spip.php?article166449.
9 Fourcade, *Noah's Ark*.

10 Ibid.
11 Shannon L. Fogg, 'Denunciations, Community Outsiders, and Material Shortages in Vichy France', University of Missouri Press, 2003.
12 André Halimi writes more about this in *La Délation sous l'Occupation*, Editions Alain Moreau, 1983.
13 Henry Samuel, 'Petty Disputes Led to Nazi Denunciation in WWII France', *Daily Telegraph*, 2 December 2008.
14 Ibid.
15 Serge Klarsfeld, *Memorial to the Jews Deported from France, 1942–1944*, B. Klarsfeld Foundation, 1983.

9. Jacques

1 The Nazis never asked the French to arrest Jewish children along with their parents. That was done entirely at Vichy's volition, partly to fill the deportation quotas imposed by the Germans, and partly to spare France what I guess could be described as the administrative burden of thousands of Jewish orphans. Michael R. Marrus and Robert O. Paxton, *Vichy France and the Jews*, Basic Books, 1981.
2 Premières rafles et camps d'internement en zone occupée en 1941, www.cercleshoah.org.
3 *L'Echo de Pithiviers*, 24 May 1941.
4 Incidentally, as I was writing that paragraph about Nibelle I did what no writer should do, which is check Twitter mid-writing. As it happened, someone had sent me an anti-Semitic tweet that included a reference to the Rothschilds. (A Soros reference was chucked in, too, ensuring this version of anti-Semitism was fully up-to-date.) Anti-Semites maintain traditions at least as faithfully as Orthodox Jews.
5 Sean Hand and Steven T. Katz (eds.), *Post-Holocaust France and the Jews 1945–1955*, New York University Press, 2015.
6 Yadvashem.org.
7 CERCIL (The Study and Research Centre on the Internment Camps in the Loiret).

8 There is an interesting contrast between France's attitude towards its concentration camps and that of Poland. Auschwitz-Birkenau are, famously, carefully preserved, whereas Pithiviers, Drancy and Beaune-la-Rolande have long since vanished. The only concentration camp in France that was really preserved was the Natzweiler-Struthof concentration camp, and that's because it was run by the Germans and was in Alsace. But whereas France has increasingly acknowledged its culpability, Poland, as I discussed in Chapter 1, is now doing the opposite. 'It's only since the 1990s that camps in France started being commemorated,' Martin Winstone from the Holocaust Educational Trust told me. 'That comes from the state on some level, but it's also a generational shift. People begin to question their parents' and grandparents' historical myths.'

9 Again, it was entirely Vichy's idea to arrest and deport Jewish children – the Nazis never demanded this.

10 https://history.state.gov/historicaldocuments/frus1942v01/d393.

11 Jean Edward Smith, *The Liberation of Paris*, Simon & Schuster, 2019.

10. Alex

1 Marie-France Pochna, *Christian Dior: The Biography*, The Overlook Press, New York, 2008.

2 Gitta Sereny, *The German Trauma: Experiences and Reflections 1938–1999*.

3 Anne Sebba, 'How Haute Couture Rescued War-Torn Paris,' *Daily Telegraph*, 29 June 2016.

4 In 2011, Hugo Boss issued a formal statement expressing 'profound regret' for its wartime activities (*Jewish Chronicle*, 22 Sept 2011). Admitting regret takes a long time sometimes.

5 Anne Sebba, *Les Parisiennes: How the Women of Paris Lived, Loved and Died in the 1940s*, Weidenfeld & Nicolson, 2016.

6 Michael Marrus and Robert O. Paxton, *Vichy France and the Jews*, Stanford University Press, 1981.

7 Serge Klarsfeld, *Les Transferts de Juifs de la Region de Nice Vers le Camp de Drancy en Vue de Leur Deportation* 31 Aout 1942–30 Juillet 1944. (Paris: *Fils et Filles des Deportées Juifs de France*, 1993.)

8 Ibid.

9 Ibid. Klarsfeld has first-hand knowledge of the brutality of the raids. When he was eight, his family home was raided in Nice, just a week after Alex was arrested. Serge, along with his sister and mother, managed to hide. His father, Arno, sacrificed himself to save them and was sent to Drancy.

10 As far as I can tell from his memoir, Alex did not start designing for the theatre until after the war.

11 Angela Taylor, 'Emeric Partos, 70, Fur Designer Noted for Innovative Flair, Dead', *New York Times*, 3 December 1975.

12 Jean Edward Smith, *The Liberation of Paris*, Simon & Schuster, 2019.

13 https://www.saint-cyr.org/medias/editor/files/1912-1914-97e-promotion-de-montmirail.pdf

11. The Siblings

1 Antony Beevor and Artemis Cooper, *Paris After the Liberation*, Penguin, 2007.

2 Van Der Grinten later changed its name to Oce and was sold to Canon.

3 Jews make up less than 1.4 per cent of the American population, and yet in polls Americans continually overestimate this to 20 per cent, 'because of our disproportionate visibility, influence and accomplishments' (Alan Dershowitz, *The Jewish Question for the 21st Century: Can We Survive Our Success?*, Little, Brown, 1997).

12. Alex

1 John O'Donnell and James Rutherford, *Trumped! The Inside Story of the Real Donald Trump – His Cunning Rise and Spectacular Fall*, Simon & Schuster, New York, 1991.

2 Paul Burstein, 'Jewish Educational and Economic Success in the United States: A Search for Explanations', *Sociological Perspectives* 50, no. 2, Summer 2007.

3 Sachar, *History of the Jews in the Modern World.*

4 In August 2017 a white supremacist group marched through Charlottesville, Virginia, the protesters chanting, 'Jews will not replace us!' (Sheryl Gay Stolberg and Brian M. Rosenthal, 'Man Charged After White Nationalist Rally in Charlottesville Ends in Deadly Violence', *New York Times*, August 12 2017.)

5 In April 2019 it emerged that the former Labour leader Jeremy Corbyn had, in 2011, written a foreword to J. A. Hobson's 1902 book *Imperialism: A Study,* in which he specifically praised Hobson's 'correct and prescient' theories about 'the commercial interests that fuel the role of the popular press with tales of imperial might'. These theories of Hobson's were that the financial system is controlled by 'men of a single and peculiar race, who have behind them many centuries of financial experience . . . [and] are in a unique position to control the policy of nations'. Hobson adds that the direct influence of these financial houses 'is supported by the control which they exercise over the body of public opinion through the press'. Just in case it's not clear who this 'single and peculiar race' is, Hobson asks, in the same paragraph, 'Does anyone seriously suppose that a great war could be undertaken by any European state, or a great State loan subscribed, if the house of Rothschild and its connections set their face against it?' Corbyn replied that any suggestion he was praising anti-Semitic theories was a 'mischievous representation of my foreword' made by 'Labour's political opponents'. (Justin Cohen, *The Times of Israel*, 3 May 2019.)

6 'Le Jardin des Modes', September 1939, via Sebba, *Les Parisiennes.*

7 Ibid.

8 Sebba, 'How Haute Couture Rescued War-Torn Paris.'

9 Sebba, *Les Parisiennes.*

10 Ludivine Broch, 'The Merci Train: Remembering the World Wars in 52,000 Objects', 2017, https: blogs.kent.ac.uk.

11 Metmuseum.org.

12 Like Alex, Soutine was an eastern European refugee in Paris, having emigrated from what is now Belarus in his twenties. But he was less lucky than Alex: during the war he tried to go into hiding but had to emerge when he desperately needed surgery for an ulcer. The surgery failed to save him and he died in 1943, something Alex does not mention in his memoir, probably because so many people in his circle died during the war that it became almost a given for him.

13 Lelong's close involvement in the Petit Théâtre and Merci Train is further proof of how both of those initiatives deliberately ignored the scandals of the recent past and, to a certain degree, served to imbue political credibility on those, like Lelong and Rochas, who were regarded with suspicion.

14 Kurt Waldheim, president of Austria 1986–1992. He repeatedly lied about his Nazi past, but during his campaign for the Austrian presidency it emerged that he had been involved with Nazi youth groups as a teenager, and then during the war had been affiliated with German military groups that deported thousands of Jews. Both despite and because of this, he was elected president. 'Kurt Waldheim, Former UN Chief, is Dead at 88', Jonathan Kandell, *New York Times*, June 15 2007.

15 Neal Gabler, *An Empire of their Own: How the Jews Invented Hollywood*, Anchor Books, 1989.

16 Sachar (*History of the Jews in the Modern World*) also writes that this drive 'stabilized' by the late twentieth century, and the children and grandchildren of Jewish immigrants now had the 'leisure to seek new outlets in the liberal professions'. This is certainly reflected in my family: while both my father and uncle worked in banking and the law, I was lucky enough to have the financial security to pursue my dream of being a writer and journalist.

17 *Aarhaus Amtstidende*, 14 April 1951.

18 'Les Premières Journées', *Le Monde*, 3 February 1955.

19 John Richardson, *The Sorcerer's Apprentice*, University of Chicago Press, 2001.

20 Pierre Daix, *Picasso: Life and Art*, Thames & Hudson, 1994

21 Janet Flanner, Letter from Paris, *New Yorker,* June 17, 1964.
22 Richard Burton, *The Richard Burton Diaries*, Yale University Press, 2013.
23 'La Semaine d'Edgar Schneider: C'est son Cézanne-ouvre-toi!' *Le Figaro,* undated article.
24 Lemonde.fr.
25 Jonathan Fenby, *The General: Charles de Gaulle and the France He Saved*, Simon & Schuster, New York, 2010.
26 Deaths, *New York Times,* July 20, 1964.

14. Epilogue

1 Proceedings of the National Academy of Sciences, National Bureau of Economic Research, 2018.
2 Rachel Yehuda (leader), 'Holocaust Exposure Induced Intergenerational Effects on FKBP5 Methylation', *Biological Psychiatry Journal*, 1 September 2016.
3 Olda Khazan, 'Inherited Trauma Shapes Your Health', *Atlantic*, October 2016.
4 Ewan Birney, 'Why I'm Sceptical about the Idea of Genetically Inherited Trauma', *Guardian*, 11 September 2016.